ADVANCED & PERFORMANCE DRIVING

REG LOCAL

Copyright © 2015
REG LOCAL
ADVANCED &
PERFORMANCE
DRIVING
All rights reserved.

No part of this publication may be reproduced, distributed, or transmitted in any form or by any means, including photocopying, recording, or other electronic or mechanical methods, without the prior written permission of the publisher, except in the case of brief quotations embodied in critical reviews and certain other non-commercial uses permitted by copyright law.

REG LOCAL

Printed Worldwide
Second Edition 2020
Second Printing 2020
First Printing 2015
First Edition 2015

ISBN: 978-1508535409

10 9 8 7 6 5 4 3 2 1

Visit my website
www.reglocal.com
Follow me on Twitter!
@RegLocal
My Youtube Channel
Reg Local

For Mum.

Sorry you didn't get the chance to read it.

And Dad.

Glad you did!

And for Mrs Local.

The best passenger I could ever wish for.

Table of Contents

Introduction 1
Notes On The Second Edition 5
1. What, Exactly, Is Advanced Driving? 6
2. Police Driver Training 14
3. The Police Standard Car Course 17
4. The Police Advanced Course 24
5. The Pursuit Course 30
6. The Security Escort Course 32
7. The Car Instructors Course 35
8. Time Constraints (And How To Deal With Other People's Mistakes) 39
9. Forgive Yourself 43
10. Anticipation 48
11. Planning 52
12. The Zone Of Relative Safety 55
13. Car Balance 59
14. Steering 66
15. Gear Changing 70
16. Automatic Gearboxes 81
17. Single Clutch Semi-Automatic Gearboxes 96
18. Dual Clutch Semi-Automatic Gearboxes 102
19. Electric Cars 107
20. Overtaking 115
21. Cornering Part 1 – Assessing The Bend Using The Limit Point 127
22. Cornering Part 2 – Assessing The Bend Without Using The Limit Point 135
23. Cornering Part 3 - Picking The Right Line 143

24. Cornering Part 4 - Controlling The Car Through The Corner 156
25. Cornering Part 5 - Linking Corners 160
26. How To Stop Things Getting Worse (Skid Control) 184
27. A Question Of Speed 194
28. Driving Commentary 201
29. Motorway Driving Part 1 211
30. Motorway Driving Part 2 226
31. Motorway Driving Part 3 241
32. Motorway Driving Part 4 253
33. We Make The Standards And We Make The Rules… 260
34. Critical Self-Analysis (Or How To Reboot Your Own Operating System) 265
35. Familiarity Breeds Complacency 273
36. Acceleration Nonsense 276
37. Braking Bad 282
38. It's Right For The Night… 297
39. I've Been Feeling Horny Lately 307
40. A Classic Debate 312
41. In The City There's A Thousand Things I Wanna Say To You 318
42. Roundabouts 327
43. Drive For Fun, For Free! 337
44. Do You Walk The Dog, Or Does It Walk You? 345
45. Driving Is Awful These Days, Isn't It? Or Is It? 349
46. A Police Car And A Screamin' Siren... 352
47. Weather The Weather 362
48. Left Foot Braking 375
Post Script – I Went Over To The Dark Side 383
About The Author 390

INTRODUCTION

I had my first experience behind the wheel of a car in 1975. The M55 motorway between Preston and Blackpool had just opened and we decided to give it a try.

I was driving a late 1960s Daimler Sovereign – a big old wafting bus with the air of an old gentlemen's club about it. I didn't drive it particularly fast – 55-60mph at the most, but I'll never forget the view out over that long, elegant bonnet to the brand new stretch of (almost traffic free) motorway stretching out ahead of me. I probably gripped the delicate large, thin steering wheel a little too tightly and I remember the car wandering slightly in its lane and needing constant, small corrections to keep it on the straight and narrow. But this time, it was *me* who was making those corrections, and when I moved the wheel, I could feel the car reacting and going where I wanted it to go.

I was driving!

I was also 5 years old.

My Grandad had been a police officer for 30 years and retired from the post of Detective Chief Inspector in the mid-1960s to take on a series of pubs in Blackpool. He was a stout chap with a no-nonsense approach to life and he didn't suffer fools, but I was his only grandson and he would let me get away with pretty much anything.

Which is how, aged 5, I came to be driving a huge luxury car along a brand new motorway by standing on the driver's seat between his legs, and holding the steering wheel.

I'm told that he really did let me steer the car too – for some 10 miles or so I weaved that old Daimler along lane 1 with very little help from Grandad as my Grandma sat cringing in the passenger seat and my dad sat terrified in the back.

I suppose my Grandad committed some quite serious driving offences that day, and I'm in no way condoning his actions, but I'm certain that it was this day on the M55 which lit the blue touch paper of my enthusiasm for cars, and particularly for *driving*.

I was 12 or 13 the first time I took *proper* control of a car for the first time. On a family day out to Southport, my Dad announced that anyone could drive on the beach at Southport. Did I want a go?

Did I? I don't think he'd finished the question before I was stood next to the driver's door – I may have actually physically dragged him from the car!

I had the usual struggles suffered by most new drivers – clutch use was a complete mystery and we spent a good hour kangarooing around the beach and scaring my dad half to death, but again, I was hooked and I then had a long wait ahead until I turned 17.

At 17 years and 6 weeks old, I passed my driving test. That's a very tight timescale by modern standards, but wasn't unheard of in the mid-1980s. In my mind, of course, possession of a full car licence actually meant that I was a driving hero up there with Senna and

Vatanen, but in reality I was very poorly prepared for life on the roads.

A couple of accidents and several cars later, at the tender age of 21 and 4 days, I joined the police. I had no ambitions to be a police driving instructor when I first joined. In those days, the force policy was that you would work a foot beat for at least 2 years until you went anywhere near the driving seat of a police car of any description. If the sergeant caught you even moving one of the cars a few feet in the garage you'd be in big trouble, so any ambitions to drive police cars had to be put on hold.

Over a period of approximately 10 years, I worked my way through standard and advanced driving courses, through a few years as a traffic officer and then achieved my ambition of qualifying as a police driving instructor, I've taught Police Officers at standard and advanced levels, as well as teaching pursuit tactics and protection driving.

I left the police in 2009 and I now work in local government.

In addition to my police career, I've always had an interest in motorsport, and I've followed rallying and circuit racing at various levels – I even worked as a race mechanic for a Formula 3000 team in the late 1980s.

I never actually intended to write a book. Some years ago I decided to write a series of forum posts & articles on performance road driving on the Pistonheads website. I should, firstly, emphasise the word **ROAD** in that sentence, as this is my particular area of expertise - I don't pretend to be an expert in circuit, gravel or off-road driving, although some techniques and skills are transferrable between disciplines.

I've now decided to edit the original posts & articles into a book, so they're all in one place and easy to dip into whenever you like without having to search an internet forum.

I don't intend to come across as smart-arsed and holier-than-thou, and neither do I wish to come across as though I'm in any way showing off.

There are no straight lifts from Roadcraft, as there are some significant differences between operational police driving and general performance road driving.

The main thing to bear in mind is that this book is intended to be read by anyone. You do not need to have any advanced driving qualifications, or to be a member of any advanced driving organisations to benefit from the contents. It can be read on its own, or in conjunction with other driving manuals. It is suitable for brand new licence holders and for anyone who has undertaken – or is undertaking a course of further instruction.

There are tips for new drivers, tips for experienced drivers and tips for instructors and observers. Something for everyone in other words!

Enjoy.

Notes on the Second Edition

The first edition of this book was originally published in Kindle format in January 2015, followed a few months later by the paperback version.

5 years later, I've had the chance to revisit the book & give it a refresh & an update with 4 new chapters and a postscript covering - well, I'll let you read that for yourself!

For those of you who have already read the first edition, the new chapters are as follows:

- Chapter 16 - Automatic Gearboxes
- Chapter 18 - Dual Clutch Semi-Automatic Gearboxes
- Chapter 19 - Electric Cars
- Chapter 48 - Left Foot Braking
- Postscript - I Went Over to the Dark Side

1

What, Exactly, is Advanced Driving?

What is advanced driving?

There should be a straightforward answer to what seems to be such a simple question. I should be able to easily define "advanced driving" in a couple of sentences, using a few key words and phrases. The trouble is, the more I think about it, the more difficult I find it is to actually define.

It might be easy to define an advanced driver as someone who is, in some way, "better" than the average driver. But what exactly is the "average driver"? And how do you determine if your driving is "better" or "worse" than the average driver?

Maybe there should be some kind of qualification which defines an advanced driver – you know – some kind of additional training followed by a test. Yes – that's a good idea.

But if you have a play with google, you'll find that there is the Institute of Advanced Motorists, the Cardington special test, the RoSPA advanced test, the DIAmond advanced motorist test and any number of additional private companies and individuals offering training from fleet driving up to high performance track skills.

And then there are the different police courses – standard, advanced, pursuit, close protection & instructor's courses. Where do they fit in to the advanced driving palette?

All these qualifications can be a measure of someone's ability, but their ability at what? What actually is the difference between an ordinary driver and an advanced driver?

I think I need to answer the question by examining a few different principles which I believe go towards defining "advanced driving". To begin though, I've lifted a paragraph directly from the old blue Roadcraft. Paragraph 6 to be exact:

"Quiet efficiency is the hallmark of an expert. Although alert he gives the impression of being completely relaxed. He drives in a calm, controlled style without fuss or flourish, progressing smoothly and unobtrusively. He will always be in the right place on the road, travelling at the right speed with the right gear engaged and he achieves this desirable state by concentrating all the time, planning ahead and driving systematically."

Now, apart from the subtly overt 1970's sexism, this is quite a nice little paragraph. It's quite dated, of course, but the basic principles are correct.

Now on to Reg's principles of advanced driving. Let's start with a few positive mental attributes:

1. An open mind and an ongoing willingness to learn.

This is the first attribute I would expect a more advanced driver to possess. There are a lot of drivers out there who aren't really that interested in driving. They see motoring simply as a mode of transport and they view driving as a chore to be carried out in much the same way as gardening, washing-up, painting the dog or hanging the kettle out to dry. Their driving "learning curve" flattened out the day after they passed their driving test and their driving style is a combination of skills which were taught by their instructor or developed over time – mostly for convenience.

In my view an advanced driver is never complete. They should always feel that, no matter what they have accomplished or how much experience they have gained, there is always something new to learn. They should treat each and every drive - no matter how mundane - as a learning experience.

2. A realistic assessment of their own abilities.

Let me put that another way – a good driver should never think they are better than they actually are.

There is nothing more dangerous than a driver who thinks their skill level is higher than it really is. This is particularly true in the police where newly qualified advanced drivers have a noticeably higher chance of having an accident in the first 12 months after passing their advanced course. There is a tendency for these drivers to think "I'm advanced – I'm invincible", right up to the point where they discover that they're not.

This discovery is generally followed by a swear word or two, and then road-sky-road-sky-ditch.

So an advanced driver should be aware of their own skill level, (and should, in my view, err on the side of caution by always underestimating it) and should never exceed it.

3. A calm and composed attitude with *just* the right amount of assertiveness.

This is a fairly obvious one, but should at least be mentioned. I've included assertiveness too as I don't believe a good driver necessarily has to be a completely defensive one. There should be a desire, when the time is right, to want to make good progress and that requires a positive, assertive attitude paired with the right amount of cautiousness.

That composed attitude also comforts passengers, who, generally, unconsciously pick up on drivers' emotions.

To put it another way, think Huggy Bear rather than Starsky & Hutch.

But without the platform shoes.

4. An ability to remove emotion from driving.

A good driver doesn't personalise situations and has the ability to forgive others and themselves. This is a very simple principle, but is one of the most difficult abilities to acquire & some of the most technically competent drivers can never achieve it completely.

I'm happy to admit I struggle myself sometimes.

5. An active (but not overactive) imagination.

Driving plans are based on what you can see, but just as importantly, what you *can't* see. It's important that you can imagine the likely hazards that are out of view, without being too cautious and imagining unlikely scenarios.

6. Sustained concentration.

An ability to concentrate is essential for any driver, but the very best are able to maintain a high level of concentration throughout any drive in any circumstances. They shouldn't get bored or distracted.

7. Planning.

Every action a driver takes should be planned in advance. Driving plans should constantly evolve and should include alternative plans in case the situation changes. In other words, plans can't be rigid and you must always have a plan b and usually a plan c to fall back on.

Planning also includes the ability of a driver to maintain excellent observation skills, combined with the ability to interpret what they are seeing correctly and understand what is happening.

Now, let's list some of the more practical skills I'd consider to be available to an advanced driver.

8. Smoothness with the controls.

There are huge benefits to adopting a smooth driving style. I make numerous references throughout the book wherever smoothness is a benefit, but maintaining vehicle balance, maintaining control of a vehicle on the limit and prolonging the life of your vehicle and its components are just three examples.

9. Accuracy.

By which I mean an ability to accurately place the car exactly where it should be at the appropriate point on the road. Accuracy also includes an ability to identify the correct time and place to brake, change gear, steer, accelerate etc. When I'm instructing, I teach accuracy at lower speeds until it becomes second nature – then the speeds can increase.

10. Mechanical sympathy.

A good driver doesn't necessarily need a comprehensive mechanical knowledge, but a little knowledge of how the oily bits work is useful. What they should have, however, is an ability to use a vehicle in a way which keeps wear and tear to a minimum. Smoothness is a key aspect of course, but other points like having a little sympathy with a cold engine & gearbox and avoiding riding the clutch are important.

11. Feel.

We should be using all our senses when driving, including our sense of touch. Fingers on the steering wheel should detect road surface changes and grip levels. Feet on pedals should detect clutch biting points and the reactions of the brakes. Backside and torso should detect the balance and attitude of a car – particularly when cornering.

That's my list for now – there are others, but for simplicity I'll keep it to 11 for the time being.

One thing I'd also like you to consider are the things I *haven't* included in the list – in particular, things which many people would consider qualities of an advanced driver.

Fast reactions, for instance. Reaction times have very little relevance in advanced road driving and the ability to plan ahead should remove almost all necessity for fast reactions.

Confidence is another. Confidence can so easily lead to overconfidence which can, in turn, easily lead to backwards-forwards-backwards-forwards-lamppost-hospital.

I've also left out any references to sliding, drifting and other skidding-around fun activities. These are skills that a good driver can learn and enjoy, but I'm not of the opinion that they have anything to do with advanced driving in its correct context, which is that of safe, smooth, quick and controlled road driving.

So, to summarise, here's Reg's 11 principles of advanced driving:

1. An open mind and an ongoing willingness to learn,
2. A realistic assessment of their own abilities,
3. A calm and composed attitude with *just* the right amount of Assertiveness,
4. An ability to remove emotion from driving,
5. An active (but not overactive) imagination,
6. Sustained concentration,
7. Planning,
8. Smoothness with the controls,
9. Accuracy,
10. Mechanical sympathy and;
11. Feel.

With all these points in mind, however, you should never forget that driving can still be an enjoyable experience. If you lose yourself too much in what is or isn't necessary, then you're in danger of letting the perceived rules and regulations of "advanced" driving spoil your enjoyment of what is still an enjoyable and fulfilling activity.

There are many other aspects which make an "advanced" driver of course, and I had to be very selective to reduce the list down to just 11 (10 would have been better, but I couldn't lose any more!).

One of the attributes I didn't include in the list is an ability to adjust your driving style to both the type of vehicle you're driving and the type of journey you are driving on.

There are loads of different journey types of course, but the one we shouldn't forget is the one we take just for pleasure. If we're out for a drive on our favourite roads just for the sake of it, an overtake couldn't really be classed as necessary, could it? Does that mean we shouldn't take a perfectly safe overtake when it is presented to us? No, of course it doesn't.

There is nothing wrong with enjoying driving our cars just for the sake of it, and that's probably where "advanced driving" is letting itself down. It seems to be promoted as safe and serious and sensible, when it can also be enjoyable, challenging and spirited - exactly the things which attract keen drivers and car enthusiasts.

The subject needs lightening up a bit - not without losing any of the key principles of course - but with a view to attracting more people, especially enthusiasts, to the idea that becoming a better driver is just as satisfying and enjoyable as getting a better car or improving your current one.

I suppose that's what I've tried to do with this book - to inject a little humour and enthusiasm & keep things interesting and relevant.

2

POLICE DRIVER TRAINING

Police driver training – particularly police advanced driver training – is generally held up as the highest level of road driving training available in the UK (and probably in the world).

But why? Where has this perception come from? Other "advanced" and "expert" driver training courses are available – what separates police training from these other courses of instruction?

Now, before I go any further, I need to be careful – my driver training experience is limited to police training and a short time when I was qualified as an ADI, so in effect I've got experience at the two extreme ends of the driver training spectrum, but no experience of the different levels in between those two extremes. So, instead of making the comparisons myself, I thought I would give a detailed breakdown of how police training is structured and the elements covered by the different police driving courses. I'll also share some of my own memories and experiences of the different courses I undertook during my police career.

From there, it's up to you to make the judgement about how good or otherwise police driver training is.

Before I go any further, there are some things to bear in mind. Firstly, my experiences were with one individual police force. Each police force teaches the same basic principles, but there are differences across the country in how courses are structured, and some minor differences in some of the details taught by individual police driving schools.

Secondly, I've been out of the police for several years now, but I do still work regularly with the police and I've not been made aware of any drastic changes in the way driver training is delivered.

And finally, in case you haven't guessed, I'm a car driver. I never went over to the dark, sinister two-wheeled side, so I'll keep my references to car courses only.

So what driving courses are available to police officers? More than you think, actually. I'll be examining basic, standard and advanced courses, together with pursuit training, security escort courses and the hardest of all – the instructors course.

Before I do though, it's worth looking at why police officers need additional driver training. After all, we're talking about people who are already qualified to drive – they have passed a driving test haven't they? And they hold a drivers licence – why should they need any additional training? A car is a car isn't it?

It's a fair (if uneducated) point and one I've heard from a number of senior officers in the past. Anyone with a driving licence can go and buy a high performance car can't they? Why would anyone need weeks of additional training to drive a diesel Vauxhall Astra? Or a BMW 3-series?

That blinkered view, however, completely fails to take into account the unique demands and pressures of operational police driving. Those demands and pressures aren't even shared with other emergency services drivers, who may have to respond to emergencies, but will never have to stop a drunk driver, pursue a fleeing vehicle, or follow another vehicle at speed in an unmarked car without drawing any attention.

In addition, police drivers are mostly highly visible and expected to set a good example to other road users, they are on the roads 24/7 in all road and weather conditions, they need to be able to respond safely and quickly to emergencies.

Most of the instruction given to students on standard and advanced courses is designed to improve their "normal" driving skills – their ability to look down the road, identify hazards, plan for them and negotiate them safely with the minimum of fuss. Students are taught a "system" of car control which, after much practice, gives them an acceptable "fall-back" standard which they will automatically revert to when they're suddenly under the increased pressure of attending a violent incident or a serious road accident.

So I'll go through the list of police driving courses in the order that police officers would normally attend them. Starting with the standard driving course…

3

THE POLICE STANDARD CAR COURSE

Back in the early 1990s, I had to spend 2-and-a-bit years walking the beat and sitting in the passenger seat of police cars until I eventually had my application for a driving course approved.

The concept of police officers "Walking the beat" has a nice, traditional, comforting and reassuring feel about it doesn't it? The reality is considerably different, and in my case involved trudging around miserable slum estates, dodging dog poo and avoiding irritating children whilst unsuccessfully trying to serve summonses and execute warrants on people who had long moved house or would simply not answer the door.

Night shifts were a blessed relief from this monotony, because the powers-that-be would allow us to double-up in cars and I could experience "mobile patrol". Occasionally, the probationers would be allocated to the night traffic car, which for a young PC with a love of cars and driving, was a real treat and sowed the seeds for the direction my police career would take.

It's very different these days. The demands on police resources and the dramatic cut in police numbers means that probationary police officers are given a "basic assessment" very early in their careers. This allows them to drive police cars for transport purposes only, but without using any legal exemptions – they are not allowed to stop other vehicles or respond to emergencies etc.

Once they have a little bit of experience, officers will be given a place on a standard car course.

A standard course is the starting point for any police officer who needs to drive "low performance" police cars. This course was my first introduction to the police "system of car control" and the police driving manual "Roadcraft".

A standard car course is three weeks long. Students are expected to already hold a full UK car licence and to have a little experience post-test (no prescribed period, but 12 months is a good starting point.

The first day-and-a-half of the course take place in the classroom and offices of the driving school. Students produce their driving licences, details are recorded, their eyesight is checked and they're given a tour of the driving school premises, garages, car park and vehicles. They then receive a series of lectures covering the system of car control, applying the system to hazards, cornering and use of the cars controls.

These lectures take the students up to lunchtime on day 2 and after lunch it's time to go out and play with the traffic!

Instructors are allocated three students per course and barring a few exceptions, the three students stay with the same instructor for the whole course. The first step for the instructor is to allow each student to drive for 20-odd minutes on a variety of roads and assess their driving. Following these assessments, the instructor will then give a demonstration drive and show the students what will be expected of them by the end of the course.

From this point, the hard work – for the students *and* the instructors – begins. Students get two 1-hour drives per day, one in the morning and one in the afternoon. The instructor will begin with the basics of systematic driving, separating braking and gear-changing, encouraging the students to extend their observations and make driving plans. The students in the back aren't having a rest either – they will learn from the mistakes of their colleagues and are expected to pay full attention as if they were driving themselves.

This doesn't always happen of course, and each instructor will have different techniques to deal with nodding rear-seat passengers. Mine was to tip the wink to the other two students, give a silent countdown 3-2-1 and for the three of us to then scream in abject terror for a few seconds.

They didn't tend to nod off again!

Sometime early in week 2, the students should be starting to get the hang of systematic driving, at which point commentary is introduced and everything goes to pot!

Students are expected to give a couple of minutes of commentary on their final test drive. A poor commentary won't fail them if their driving is ok, but a good commentary can lift an average drive. As week 2 continues, the pressure starts to build and the instructor needs to start making an assessment as to whether the students will be ready for test in week 3.

Every drive begins with a short "starting drill" - a sort of "pre-flight check" to ensure the car is good to go and that they have not forgotten something daft like their seatbelt or turning the engine on. Each drive also ends with a "stopping drill" for exactly the same reasons. These are the times when students are most nervous and these drills are a routine which settles their initial nerves and removes most of the likelihood that silly mistakes will be made, like driving off with the boot open or forgetting to set the mirrors.

Mid-week-2, the students will receive a day of skid correction training. Years ago, this would involve a traditional skid-pan with a low-grip surface and old cars with bald tyres. These days, it will involve a specialist skid-simulation car or a car on a skid frame at an old airfield. Students are taught how to recognise the different types of skids and how to correct them. They're taught the older techniques, such as cadence braking and recovering from split-surface braking skids, but they're also given a demonstration of the benefits of traction control, anti-lock brakes, stability control etc. and how to make the most of these systems.

It goes without saying, of course, that avoiding skids in the first place is always the best technique, and this is one of the many points pressed home during the on-road training.

Speeds during the first half of a standard course tend to stay within the posted speed limits, but there is an exemption from speed limits for police training purposes and later in the course, where it's judged to be safe, the instructors will encourage students to make progress on national speed limit roads – usually with a "20mph over" rule. There will be some overtaking, practising of following position, higher speed cornering etc. These elements are all dependent, however, on the abilities of each individual student. If a student is struggling to steer correctly or apply system consistently, then the slightly more advanced stuff will be avoided so that full attention can be given to correcting their faults.

At the end of week 2, instructors will swap crews for an afternoon and assess each other's students. They need to be up to an acceptable standard (close to test standard) before going into week 3, as this is when the course moves on to the part of the course every student (without exception!) has been looking forward to - response driving.

Week three begins back in the classroom. Students are shown videos and given an outline of the principles of response driving and their legal exemptions before then going out with their instructor for a demonstration drive. It's usually this point in the course where the systematic approach really clicks with the students as staying on the brakes whilst waiting for the correct reactions from other road users *before* taking a gear really works well with response driving.

The students then spend the next couple of days in liveried police cars practising their normal systematic driving, interspersed with regular simulated response drives – 5 or 10 minutes long – usually in busier areas or where there are build-ups of traffic. I don't care who you are or how experienced a driver you are – the first time you switch on the blue lights and siren, and traffic starts reacting – is *very* exciting! For some people, it's the primary reason they joined the police!

As well as learning response driving, the instructors will also teach the students how to safely stop other vehicles. And keep themselves safe when getting out of the police car and speaking to the driver. For example, it's never a good idea to walk in between the police car and the stopped vehicle, as there is a danger that the other driver will deliberately ram the police officer and trap them between vehicles.

On the last day of week 3, if the instructor thinks they are ready, the students will be tested. They will need to pass two written tests – one on Roadcraft and one on the Highway Code, together with two driving tests – one on the road and one manoeuvring test on the schools car park.

The road test will be approximately 30 minutes long and is the most important of the final tests. The students will be tested by the school sergeant or an experienced instructor on a mix of different roads and speed limit areas. They will be expected to drive safely, systematically, smoothly and progressively where appropriate, showing a good ability to recognise and plan for hazards and good overall awareness of their environment.

The manoeuvring test involves driving in and out of several different parking spaces, forwards and backwards, in a limited space within a reasonable timeframe. It starts and ends with a parallel park and is designed to replicate the manoeuvres required to get a police car out of a tightly-packed police station yard in an emergency without hitting anything.

If a student passes all these elements (and their instructor has given them a pass for response driving), then they're awarded a standard car permit and will be allowed to drive low-performance liveried police cars as part of their duties as operational police officers.

If they fail any of these elements, a plan is put in place to address their weak areas and get them through a re-test of the failed element as soon as possible.

4

THE POLICE ADVANCED COURSE

The advanced course is seen very much as the "gold standard" of driver training in the UK and internationally. For police officers, the advanced course is required if they are moving to a specialist role which involves driving high performance police cars.

There used to be two levels of pass available to advanced students – class 1 and class 2. Being a "class 1 advanced driver" meant you'd achieved particularly good scores in your final tests. Less than 30% of advanced students achieved a class 1 pass, so it was quite an achievement.

In recent years, however, it was felt that a second-class pass wasn't really good enough. Officers were going to their specialist units with a driving standard which probably wasn't really good enough for their new roles, and the system was overhauled. In most (if not all) forces these days, the only qualification available to police students is "advanced". Standards haven't been reduced – these days, a class 2 performance at test would simply be a "fail" and anyone who achieves a pass can consider themselves as first class advanced drivers.

Classes 1 and 2 have only been retained for non-police students, so some armed forces students will still be given second-class passes.

Roles requiring an advanced "ticket" include roads policing, armed response, accident investigation, dog handlers, surveillance officers,

FIU officers (Special Branch), Counter-Terrorism and a range of other specialist investigation units.

In addition, advanced car courses are available to certain members of the armed forces (EOD, specialist units of the military police, special forces etc.) and selected members of the security services.

But let's not be too precious about the advanced course – I'd rather break down some of the myths and misconceptions about the course and the standards required to pass. It is only another level of driving, after all, and anyone with motivation, commitment and the right attitude can pass the course if they're willing to put the work and effort in.

Police students attending an advanced course will already have previously attended and passed a standard car course and will usually have at least a couple of years' experience in operational police driving. Armed forces students and those from other outside agencies, on the other hand, will not usually have had any previous police driving instruction, yet these students are just as likely to pass as police students. This should, at least, demonstrate that an advanced pass is achievable by anyone willing to put the work in.

An advanced car course is, in essence, very similar to a standard car course. The principles of safe, smooth, systematic driving underpin the whole course and the style of driving taught is exactly the same for standard and advanced courses. The key differences are that an advanced course is 4 weeks long rather than 3, students drive higher-performance cars, and much greater use is made of legal exemptions, which allows students to drive at much higher speeds where it is safe and appropriate.

Another thing to bear in mind is that it is not necessary to be a driving enthusiast, or even to have any interest in cars whatsoever to pass the course. If you're reading this, you're likely to have at least a reasonable level of interest in cars and driving, but the advanced course is not designed for people who love driving, or people who compete in motorsport, or people who are already driving gods.

The point I'm trying to make is that the advanced course – at least the first half of the advanced course – isn't really *that* advanced. In fact, many people find that it's a little back-to-basics at first. But there is a very good reason for this.

Once the speeds start to increase, it's important to know that students have a good "baseline" driving standard which they will fall back on when they're starting to feel the pressure. And feel the pressure they definitely will!

The course starts in exactly the same way as a standard course – licence checks, eyesight test, tour of the facilities and a couple of days in the classroom learning the theory which they will soon be putting into practice.

Once they're on the road, students will initially be assessed and then given a demonstration drive by the instructor to show them what standard will be expected from them by the end of the course.

Weeks 1 and 2 then progress in almost exactly the same way as a standard course – Instructors concentrate on getting the students accurate at first – placing the car where it should be at any given time – and on looking in the right places and, of course, driving systematically.

Advanced students are given the same skid input as standard students – but with an added element. On advanced courses, a couple of old de-commissioned police cars are taken along, together with some spare wheels and tyres. Students are then given the opportunity to carry out some exercises in on-limit handling – in and around cones at speed, threshold braking etc. When it comes to recognising how far is required to be able to "stop in the distance you can see to be clear", this experience is extremely helpful.

Towards the end of week 2, the speeds start to increase & students start to make more use of their speed exemption on national speed limit roads. They are taught how to assess bends using the limit point and other methods, how to balance the car through corners at speed and how to link corners to make smooth, quick progress.

Students will be taught overtaking – starting with practicing the following position and then moving on to making full use of the cars performance to overtake other vehicles safely and efficiently.

Week 3 is the fast week. Speeds increase, and by the end of the week, students are taken beyond the levels expected on test – the idea being that the instructor will turn things "up to 11" by the end of week 3, so that students can then cope more easily at the 8.5 to 9 required on test.

Be in no doubt – speeds on advanced car courses can be very high, but the instructors are trained to an extremely high level and will only allow students to go as fast as it is safe and appropriate. Risks are minimised as much as possible and instruction will always be appropriate for each individual student and their own level of ability.

ADVANCED & PERFORMANCE DRIVING

There is no response element on an advanced course, as police students have already passed this element in their standard course, and most outside students will not be required to drive in response to emergencies. The only exceptions to this are students from EOD (bomb disposal), who would normally get an additional half-day response instruction.

By week 4, the students should be pretty much ready for test. Week 4 allows the instructor to polish off any remaining rough edges and prepare the students for test – mentally, as well as practically.

Test days are generally on the Thursday and Friday of week 4. On the Thursday, students will be required to carry out two separate driving tests on a variety of roads – one in a manual car and one in an automatic. One of the drives will include a motorway section and when not on test, the remaining students will be ferried between start/finish points by their instructors.

The students will be assessed on their ability to drive safely, systematically, smoothly and progressively. They will be expected to make significant progress where it is safe and appropriate and to continually look for opportunities to overtake. Where those opportunities present themselves, they will be expected to take them with as little hesitation as possible. Commentary is mandatory on both drives – 10 minutes of commentary plus starting and stopping drills is normally expected.

The advice I gave my students was to keep the examiner interested. You don't want to bore them, and you definitely don't want to scare them. You can excite them a little occasionally, but in general, just try to keep them interested.

The examiners will start with a score of 100% for every driver. As the drive continues, they will deduct marks for driving faults and errors. To obtain an advanced level pass, the students need to score at least 85% for both drives. 85% is a good pass. 86% is an outstanding pass and 87% is an extremely high standard, only obtained by one or two students a year. 88% is just about achievable and no-one has ever scored more than 90% (at least at my force driving school).

In addition, the students will receive a score from their instructor based on their performance through the whole course. The instructor does not disclose their scores to the examiners until after the final drives. Once they have returned to the driving school, the three scores for each student are added up and divided by three. They must achieve an average of at least 85% to pass the course.

It doesn't end there of course – the students then have to achieve 85% in their written Roadcraft and Highway Code exams on the Friday, and they must pass the manoeuvring course on the car park. The course is the same as that used by standard students, but for an advanced course, the car is larger and the time allowed is much shorter.

Pass all these elements and you'll receive a much-coveted advanced ticket. It's a very nice addition to your CV and you will learn skills which will stay with you for the rest of your life. It also qualifies you to apply for a few further courses which I'll look at next.

5

THE PURSUIT COURSE

A pursuit course – sometimes called a TPAC (Tactical Pursuit and Containment) course – is a course specifically for operational roads policing, motorway and – in some forces – armed response officers.

A pursuit course is designed to teach students a series of tactics designed to stop a fleeing vehicle safely and with a minimum of risk to the public, the officers involved and the fleeing driver. The tactics were developed by Sussex police in the late 1990s following a series of high-profile fatalities during police pursuits.

Students are expected to have already passed an advanced driving course, and to have some operational experience driving higher-performance police cars before they are nominated for a pursuit course.

The course is one week long and as with all driving courses, starts in the classroom where the students are taught the theory behind the tactics they will be learning.

The next couple of days take place at an old airfield, where students are taught how to safely use a "stinger", how to give a clear and concise pursuit commentary when following a fleeing vehicle, how to employ rolling road-blocks, and how to physically block and gradually bring the "subject" vehicle to a safe stop.

The last couple of days of the course take place on the public roads. An instructor, driving an unmarked car, is pursued seven or eight times during each day on a variety of roads. The students practice different roles, from the initial pursuit phase, through to the tactical phase where the vehicle is brought to a controlled stop.

There is no final test on a pursuit course – students are constantly assessed by their instructors and will achieve a pass if all the instructors agree that they have reached the necessary standards.

I don't think it would be appropriate to go into the tactics taught on these courses in too much detail for obvious reasons, but I will say that driving the "subject" car on a pursuit course is probably one of the best jobs I've ever had!

The other observation is that, when employed correctly, the tactics taught on these courses are extremely effective. As an instructor, I knew the tactics inside out and I knew exactly what was going to happen and when, but despite my knowledge, I almost always felt as though I had no choice other than to stop when the students got things right. If I felt like *I* had to stop, then a genuine fleeing driver would have no chance and these tactics are regularly used in genuine pursuits with great success.

6

THE SECURITY ESCORT COURSE

Some police officers are required to carry out escort driving duties when a VIP is visiting. I should say at this point, that by VIP, I don't mean this year's X factor winner or someone who was evicted from the Big Brother house three years ago.

The definition of VIP has been somewhat diluted in recent years, but in policing terms, we're talking about a high-profile individual such as a senior member of the Royal Family or a Cabinet Minister carrying out their official duties.

These individuals are particularly vulnerable when they are carrying out duties which have been publicised in advance – anyone with criminal intent can easily find their itineraries and probably make a good guess as to their possible routes to and from the venue. Their vulnerability is at its highest whilst they're being transported in a vehicle, so the police have developed a series of tactics designed to transport these individuals by road as safely as possible.

As well as VIPs, the same tactics are often used when transporting particularly dangerous or high risk prisoners between prisons, police stations and courts.

Students on a security escort course will be expected to already hold an advanced driving permit and to have some experience in driving higher performance police cars operationally.

The course is two weeks long. After the obligatory classroom input, students spend the first week practicing a series of "escape and evasion" techniques on an old airfield, including handbrake turns, "J" turns (turning a car around at speed in reverse in a limited space), "Y" turns (a very fast reverse into and out of a side-road) and how to physically ram through a roadblock when there is no other option available.

Another good week at work!

Week 2 brings something of a change in pace. Students are taught the principles of driving in a close 3-vehicle convoy and the tactics required to protect the principle, who would normally be travelling in the middle car in the convoy.

The pace of the convoy should not be too fast – the protected individuals should travel in a calm, composed manner, but the skill is in keeping a very small gap between vehicles, almost as though the three-vehicle convoy is one, large vehicle. In addition, various tactics are employed on the approach to junctions and other pinch-points to avoid other road users getting too close to the principle's vehicle.

Later in week 2, the students get to practice their convoy driving whilst accompanied by a team of escort-trained police motorcyclists. The cars aim to maintain a steady speed, behind the lead motorcyclist who will set the pace, whilst the bikes race ahead to block each junction so that the convoy does not need to stop. This is where police motorcyclists really earn their wages – stopping traffic for the convoy, and then overtaking the convoy to get to the next junction in a constant game of leapfrog for the whole journey.

Students are tested on the final day by way of a simulated VIP visit which will call at a number of stops throughout the day. Students change places so that they are tested in each different position (the passenger's job is to maintain communication amongst the convoy – so there are no "rest" stages during the final test). They are expected to achieve a pass in each of the six stages of the final test in order to pass the course.

7

THE CAR INSTRUCTORS COURSE

You've passed your standard course and had a few years driving panda cars before moving to a specialised role and passing your advanced course. What's next?

Other than bike courses, there's only one other qualification left, and it sits above all others – the car instructor's qualification. Going by numbers alone, probably only about 1 in 1000 police officers will ever hold an instructor's qualification. That's not because it's an extremely difficult course to pass (it *is* very difficult to pass, but we'll come to that later), but because there is only one job within the police which requires an instructor's ticket. Can you guess what that job is?

Of course you can – underwater search.

Only kidding! If you want to undertake a car instructor's course, you'll only get a place if you're going to work at the driving school as an instructor. There's probably no more than one instructor for every thousand police officers, which is where the 1 in 1000 figure comes from. Now, being a car instructor is quite a plumb job in the police, so vacancies don't come up very often, and when they do there is a lot of competition for them, so you've quite a job on your hands just being selected for the course.

I had to undertake a 45-minute advanced-level driving test with two examiners using commentary from start-to-finish. I also had to take a couple of written tests and sit an interview. I was up against 6 or 7 other candidates for 1 vacancy, and although it all seemed to go by in a bit of a blur, I must have performed reasonably well, as I was successful and given a place on the next instructor's course.

The course is 6 weeks long and I can quite honestly say that it was the hardest, most demanding 6 weeks of my life. My fellow students were three colleagues from the RUC (now PSNI) and two police officers from other forces.

There is an expectation that your knowledge is second-to-none, so students are expected to pass two written exams at the end of week 1 with marks of 100%. Anything less than 100% will mean the end of the course and a return to your division.

Part of the course centres on classroom and presentation skills, something which most police students – including me - are deeply uncomfortable with at first, but which have served me well throughout the rest of my career, even after leaving the police.

If I had to describe an instructors course in one word it would be "pressure". Pressure is applied from the morning of day 1 and maintained until you leave at the end of week 6. There are three main elements – you should be able to give an extremely high level demonstration drive (with full commentary), you should be able to demonstrate your ability to instruct standard-level students of varying abilities, and you should also be able to demonstrate your ability to instruct advanced-level students in higher-speed driving.

You are tested on these abilities once a week and if you're not up to standard, or if you're not improving at the required rate, you'll be booted from the course. One fellow student lasted until the

Wednesday of week 1 before deciding that it simply wasn't for him. Another lasted until week 3 before being booted for not coming up to standard.

Instructors on the course are chosen based on their skills and experience (there is no such thing as an instructors course instructors course in case you were wondering!) and they employ a variety of methods to bring their students up to standard. One of their favourite tactics is to act as a "stooge" driver, when they will replicate the faults they've seen in other real-life students and then teach the students how to overcome them.

This is no small feat – those of you old enough to remember Les Dawson will remember his ability to play the piano very badly. In fact, this ability to play badly requires a very high level of skill and can only be carried off by someone who is an extremely skilled and gifted pianist. It's the same with driving – driving deliberately badly – replicating driving faults – is actually very difficult and requires a very high level of skill. It's a bit like being an impressionist, but instead of mimicking voices and mannerisms, the instructors mimic other people's driving style. And believe me – these guys are the Rory Bremners of the driving world.

A drive will start with a short introduction by the instructor – something like *"I'm a week 2 standard student, I've only held my driving licence for 6 months, I drive a diesel Ford Fiesta and I'm very nervous"*.

Worrying? Well, believe me, it's not as worrying as *"I'm a week 3 advanced student, I've been driving for 10 years, I've got a Subaru Impreza and I love going fast"*. That opening line is always sure to give you a sweat on your back like a layer of frost!

The trick with instructing – and the reason that the course is so demanding – is to ensure that you remain ahead of your students. An instructor should be able to spot a hazard earlier than the student, and then describe where they are looking, and what they want the student to do all before they arrive at the hazard. To improve your descriptive skills, students are discouraged from pointing and using hand gestures, and should give all their instructions verbally – something I found particularly difficult!

Towards the end of week 6, if you've lasted that long, the final testing begins. You're required to give an advanced level demonstration drive with full commentary, two final tests of your instructional ability – one standard and one advanced – and give a 45 minute presentation to a mixed audience (we got this out of the way in week 4 so we could concentrate on the actual instructing).

Pass all of those elements and you'll receive the highest car driving qualification available in the UK (and probably the highest standard of driving qualification available anywhere in the world) – a police car instructors certificate.

If I'm being honest, I don't think the achievement of passing the course actually sank in for a few weeks – I was just glad to get through it and come out of the other side!

Passing the course is just the beginning though, as I soon discovered when I was finally allowed to take real, live students out on the road. Staying alert and keeping ahead of students for the length of a driving course is unbelievably mentally exhausting – I thought working at the driving school would be a nice break from shift-work, but in reality, when I was instructing, I would be in bed for 9.00pm every night!

8

Time Constraints (and how to deal with other people's mistakes)

In my experience, one of the most stressful aspects of driving is having a time constraint. When I was a traffic officer, *the* most common excuse I used to hear when booking people for excess speed was "I'm sorry, but I'm late for work / a meeting / a fitting with my hat-maker / a funeral / a massage / an appointment with your Chief Constable Officer – if you look in the boot you'll see my collection of whips and lubricants.

Having a time constraint *always* magnifies small delays into major problems and creates tension. If you're out for a leisurely drive on a Sunday and you get caught up in some roadworks, it's not really a problem, but if you've set off for work at the last minute, only to find that a water main has burst and some 7-way temporary traffic lights have been set up, then your stress levels will understandably rise.

The most obvious tip to suggest here is to give yourself more time, but I think you'd find that a little patronising to say the least, especially coming from someone who knows the *exact* minute he has to set off from home in order to get to work *just* on time.

I think it's probably better to look at how to stop that additional stress from affecting your driving. I find that the best way to do that is just to accept that you're going to be late. These things happen, and getting stressed about it won't make the problem go away, or make the traffic move any faster. Make some phone calls *, let people know you're going to be late, and then just take your time. If you're unexpectedly delayed during a journey, and you decide to "try and make it", you're far more likely to start taking risks, and risks, at any level, are something a good driver should avoid at all costs.

Find a "happy place" in your mind – imagine you're on the beach, or skiing, and when the traffic starts moving again, think about your driving, and not about the time.

*Please note – Reg does not condone use of a mobile phone, hands-free or otherwise, whilst driving a car. As we all know, removing your hands from the steering wheel, even for a fraction of a second, could result in death, destruction, and global warming.

How do you react to the mistakes of others?

I'll be the first to admit my biggest fault as a driver. I am extremely intolerant of other people's mistakes, and this is the biggest single cause of stress to me as a driver. The best advice I was given in relation to this was from a senior instructor – "Reg, forgive them, for they know not what they do".

If you're ever in any doubt as to how inattentive and thoughtless the average driver can be, you should have a run out with an operational police officer for a few hours. At some point, the officer will be deployed to a "code 1 emergency", and the blue lights, flashing headlights and sirens will be switched on. Now, having worked for several years at a police driving school, teaching, amongst other things, probationary officers how to drive correctly on route to an emergency, you'd have thought I'd have seen it all by now, but more often than you'd think, someone will do something astoundingly daft.

If you're the police officer on the emergency shout, people will pull out from junctions in front of you, indicate right and then pull to the left, pull out to pass the car in front which has pulled over to let you past, or just sit there, in lane 3 of the motorway, at 85mph, without realising you're behind for 14 miles.

This is interesting – if there are a substantial minority of drivers out there who can't see a fully liveried Police car with lights and sirens on, what chance have you got of them seeing you in your ordinary, non-police liveried car? It's also the reason why I don't ride a motorbike.

So, what's the best way of dealing with these situations? Obviously, when you're in a Police car, people's reactions are fairly uniform if they realise they've made a mistake – they just want to curl up and die, and apologise profusely. If you're on route to an emergency, it doesn't really matter anyway, as you've got to continue to the job, and you just want the person out of the way.

If you're in your own car, however, how do you avoid getting stressed if someone cuts you up, forces you to take avoiding action, or blatantly attempts to kill you?

Let's go back to what the old sweat instructor told me – "Reg, forgive them, for they know not what they do". In the vast majority of cases, these people genuinely don't do these things deliberately. They make mistakes. Once the mistake is made, no amount of horn-blowing, headlight flashing, gesticulating, swearing, and fist shaking will make the mistake go away. It's done.

The best drivers I've sat alongside take other people's mistakes in their stride, shrug, and continue as though nothing happened. Unfortunately, I'm not wired that way, and for years, I was a fist-shaking horn-blower.

These days, I've learned that the best way for me to deal with these things is to laugh at them. Laugh at how stupid the other driver is – chuckle at their choice of car – snigger at the aftermarket spoiler they've fitted or at their choice of spouse – anything, in fact, that's remotely amusing about the person, car or situation. If you laugh at it, your stress levels drop almost immediately, and your ability to go back to concentrating on your own driving returns.

You can, of course, learn to spot the drivers who are going to make mistakes, before they actually make them, but I'll deal with that in chapter 10.

9

FORGIVE YOURSELF

There comes a point in a driving course when the nature of an instructors job changes. Take an advanced course for instance, which in my force is 4 weeks long. The first three weeks are very intensive for the instructor, who initially "drives" the car from the passenger seat, constantly staying ahead of the student, and issuing timely instructions designed to encourage the student to change their driving habits and improve their observations and planning.

Towards the end of week 3, however, the instructor starts letting the students have a go by themselves, and into week 4, they should be consistently producing drives of an advanced standard, without instruction. This is really the make-or-break point for the student, because it's the point when the instructor finds out whether all their efforts have been worth it, or whether they might as well have taken the opportunity to have the occasional drive themselves, because a student is hopeless when left to their own devices.

By far the most difficult task for an instructor is getting students ready for test. It goes without saying that driving tests of any description, by their very nature, are stressful events. Imagine, however, the additional stress on a student's shoulders if that test meant the difference between getting their dream specialist role and going back to their old job. That's why, on the lead-up to test day, the instructors role changes from teacher to psychoanalyst/coach/ego-booster/confidence builder/mind-reader and all-round shoulder to cry on.

The most difficult aspect for students to deal with is how to cope with their own mistakes. A common misconception is thinking that the examiner is looking for the perfect drive. Believe me - if the examiner were looking for a perfect drive from a student, they'd have the most disappointing job in the entire world. The thing is, you see, being human beings, none of us are perfect, and we all make mistakes.

Every *single* time I drive a car, no matter how far, I make a mistake or a series of mistakes. I could take you out and give you an advanced-level demonstration drive with full commentary, which to the untrained eye would be smooth, systematic, progressive and correct in every way, but there *would* be mistakes in there. I might allow my following position to slip back to 3 seconds a few times, or conversely, I might accelerate within my following position when overtaking. I could misjudge my acceleration sense and have to brake gently on a motorway, or I might position incorrectly in a following position and miss an overtake. You might miss all the errors because my commentary would be directing your attention further up the road, but I'd know they were there.

So what chance have students got then, after 4 weeks training, of producing a perfect drive?

None whatsoever. And this is what's difficult to get across to them on the lead-up to test day.

You *will* make mistakes during your drive, and the examiner isn't looking to fail you for those mistakes. What they're looking for is your ability to *recover* from the mistake, and for you not to make the same mistake again. The examiner's view is that everyone can make a mistake, but if you make the same mistake again and again, then it's not a mistake anymore - it's a fault, and faults will fail you.

So how does this translate to our everyday driving? Better than you might think, actually.

The trick, if you can do it, is in three parts.

1. Recognise the error immediately.

2. Make a mental note of it.

3. When similar circumstances arise again, don't make the same mistake again.

And above *everything* else, you must **forgive yourself**.

If you carry on with the drive, mentally beating yourself up about a mistake that you have made, your ability to concentrate on your driving will drop considerably. I've known students who, for the first half of a test, have produced a very good, advanced-level drive. They have then made a simple mistake around the halfway point, and spent the rest of the drive going over that mistake in their mind - the second half of the drive has then suffered dramatically and the student has failed, simply because they struggle with the mental process of forgiving themselves.

If you're out for a drive and you make an error, providing an accident doesn't occur, just forgive yourself, wave an apology to anyone else who might have been affected, and then leave the mistake where you made it.

Just remember to make that mental note, and don't make the same mistake again.

As your observation and planning skills improve, your ability to spot potential problems increases, and with that, your ability to avoid conflict with other road users grows. You *can* get to a point where you can spot most problems soon enough to avoid those "oh shit!" moments, but one thing you should *never* do is become complacent with your new-found skills.

I was out for a drive a while back, and I'd just lined up a perfect overtake on an old Rover. It was on a perfectly straight piece of road across an earth dam which separates two reservoirs. Obviously, there were no junctions left or right, there was no on-coming traffic, and it was a clearway, so there shouldn't have been any danger of the Rover pulling over to park anywhere. My closing speed on the Rover was approximately +30mph.

The Rover driver was happily bimbling along at about 30mph with no sideways weaving, no change in speed, and no indication that they were about to do anything other than continue bimbling straight on.

It was going to be a perfect "rolling overtake" with no need to slow into a following position and no need to alter my speed, my gear, or to accelerate - all I had to do was move sideways nice and early, and roll past it.

I was about 5 car lengths from the rear of the Rover when, in the space of less than a second, the driver put on a right indicator, braked, and pulled right across the road to park next to the offside kerb. This prompted some heavy brake application from me, and a very quick swerve to the nearside, followed by some selective Anglo-Saxon phrases.

My point is that it doesn't matter how good you are, or how experienced you become at spotting potential hazards, there are still things out there that can catch you out.

Incidentally, I looked in my mirror immediately after that little episode, and the driver of the Rover had her head down and was busy rummaging in her handbag, not only totally unaware of what had (nearly) happened, but blissfully unaware of my presence.

She's still out there, and she's out to get you!

The mistake was hers, but there was also an element of error on my part, as it is possible that I missed a clue that she was about to park on the offside.

To this day though, I'm buggered if I can think what I missed!

10

ANTICIPATION

I mentioned in chapter 8 that it is better to forgive and forget other drivers' mistakes, in order to keep your stress levels to a minimum, but how about if you actually knew what people were going to do *before* they did it? How much less stressful would driving be if you knew the vehicle you were approaching from behind on the motorway was about to move from lane 1 to lane 2, or if you knew the car in front was about to turn right, or if you were sure that the car waiting in a junction ahead was going to pull out in front of you?

If you knew these things in advance, then you'd be able to compensate for them before they even happened. You could move to lane 3 or adjust your speed on the motorway, slow down and move nearside for the right-turner, or adjust your safety position and be ready to brake for the car in the junction.

I can hear you - "don't be daft Reg" you're saying, "Who do you think we are? Derren Brown? We're not bloody mind-readers or paranormal mentalists or anything".

Derren Brown is an interesting comparison at this point. I'm not a huge fan of magicians or conjurers, but I do like to try to suss out how they perform their tricks. I'm always disappointed when I find out it's done with wires and mirrors, but Derren Brown performs much subtler tricks, involving mind-reading and mental manipulation. What's more, he'll often tell you how the trick is done. When he's doing the mind reading stuff, he isn't performing psychic miracles, he's just watching people, spotting tiny clues in their body language and facial movements, and interpreting them correctly.

Tiny eye movements, very slight head movements, hand rubbing, changes in respiration rate - such small things seem totally innocuous to most of us, but he's able not only to spot them, but to realise their significance, and make it appear as though he's "mind reading".

Drivers give off similar "body language", and you can, over time, learn to spot the signals that other drivers give off, interpret them correctly, and anticipate what they're going to do next.

Let's go back to the driver on the motorway first. One of the most annoying and potentially dangerous problems you will encounter when driving along the motorway is drivers unexpectedly changing lanes - but do they *always* do it completely without warning?

Usually, people will move from lane 1 to lane 2 in order to overtake a vehicle in front of them. If you extend your observations a bit further in front, you can train yourself to look for closing gaps, which indicate that one vehicle is catching up with another. If you spot one of these closing gaps early, you'll have plenty of time to move over to lane 3, or adjust your speed, before the inevitable happens, and the vehicle moves into lane 2.

You'll often get a wave of appreciation from the driver too if they're any good, as their plan would have been to wait for you to pass, and by spotting their intentions and adjusting your position/speed, you've made it a little easier for them.

There are other, even more subtle things you can look for which will warn you that a vehicle is about to change lanes. People generally drive in the centre of their chosen lane on the motorway, however, just before they change lanes, they make a slight, wandering move in the direction they want to go, then they move back to the centre of the lane, and then they change lanes.

I've considered this long and hard, and I think it's their physical reaction to their own mental planning process. They think about changing lanes, and as they're thinking, the vehicle wanders towards that lane slightly; they correct it, and then act on their decision and change lanes.

If you can spot this slight wandering move, you've enough time (less than with closing gaps, but enough nonetheless) to change lanes or adjust your speed. Don't just take my word for it though - next time you're on the motorway, look for that little move, and you'll see that Reg isn't feeding you bull - it really works.

Here's another good one - it's not motorway related, and will probably ring bells with any Police instructors who are reading this. If you're driving along, and a vehicle emerges from a junction on the left ahead of you, and travels in your direction, there is a *very* strong possibility that it will turn right at some point in the next mile or so. There's nothing particularly scientific about this - if a car is coming from your left, it'll generally be continuing in that direction, which means a right turn somewhere ahead.

It's a trick that Police instructors have used for years to impress passengers during a demonstration drive. They won't mention the vehicle pulling out, but after a few hundred yards, they'll include in their commentary "I'm anticipating that the vehicle in front will turn off soon, probably to the right".

Lo and behold, the instructor goes up in everyone's estimations when the vehicle does the (easily predicted) right turn.

So, that trick is good for showing off, but it's also very useful. If you can spot the ones that are going to turn off, it won't be a surprise when they do a lastminutebrakeandindicate, as favoured by a seemingly large number of today's drivers.

There are thousands more of these little "car body language" clues that you can pick up when driving around, and looking for them can really liven up a dull journey, and can genuinely improve you as a driver.

11

PLANNING

YOUTUBE LINK - **OBSERVATIONS & PLANNING**:

https://youtu.be/_9v6tk1HivI

By far the most valuable skill a driver can learn is planning. An advanced police student is taught a whole range of skills during a driving course - systematic driving, skid control, overtaking, cornering, etc. etc. but the one skill I want them to keep above everything else is their ability to make driving plans.

Roadcraft states that good observations allow a driver to make driving plans based on...

1. What you can see,

2. What you *can't* see, and;

3. What you can reasonably expect to happen.

Number 1 is easy, and shouldn't need any further explanation, unless you're a taxi driver or my mate Andy, who can't drive for toffee.

Numbers 2 and 3, however, aren't as simple, and could do with a little expansion.

A good driver isn't just someone who can react to what's happening in front of them. Young drivers naturally have very fast reaction times, and so, if fast reaction times were a measure of driving ability, young drivers aged between 17 and 23 would have the lowest accident rates. I don't think I need to dig up any accident statistics to show that isn't the case, do I?

Even the best drivers only have an average reaction time. I remember reading that Michael Schumacher had his reactions tested a few years ago, and had basic reactions that were no quicker than any other Joe Soap of a similar age. Reaction times are just that - the time it takes a person to react to basic stimuli. "So come on then Reg - stop mucking about - what *does* make a good driver then?" I hear you ask.

Two essential ingredients...

An active imagination and;

An ability to constantly ask yourself questions.

An active imagination is necessary in order to fulfil number 2 above - what you *can't* see. As you drive into a left-hand bend with a limited view, you can see lots of things - the limit point, the camber of the road, the condition of the road surface, the white line system, on-coming vehicles, etc. etc.

What you *can't* see are the car that's parked in an awkward position just out of view, the cyclist going in your direction (which is also going to pass the parked car), the dog off its lead, the bus coming in the opposite direction that will cut the corner, and Arnold Schwarzenegger in a Harrier jump-jet, who's about to land in the road.

All the things that are *out* of sight are the reason why the fourth principle of cornering is that you should always be able to stop on your own side of the road, in the distance you can see to be clear. But, having such a good imagination, you already knew that, didn't you?

The thing is, you have to be careful not to let your imagination run away with you. An *over* active imagination can be as much a hindrance as not having one at all. If you actually did think that Arnold was about to land after every corner, you'd never get above 5mph, and that would be bordering on tedious.

A good driver will combine their imagination with an ability to ask themselves questions as they go along. If there *is* a combination of parked car/cyclist/on-coming bus around this corner, what is my plan? Will I slow down and let them sort themselves out? Can I safely pass the cyclist before I get to the car? Do the wheels on the bus go round and round?

The most important question I teach people to ask themselves as they drive along is "what's next?"

What am I going to do next? What is the next hazard? After this corner, what's the next one like? When I've completed this overtake, what's next? I don't need to go on - you get the idea.

Start asking yourself "the question" and you'll find that your attention is drawn further up the road and your planning skills will improve no end.

12

THE ZONE OF RELATIVE SAFETY

YOUTUBE LINK - **POSITIONING FOR SAFETY:**

https://youtu.be/YPRUAeSbShM

Advanced driving isn't just about getting the car smoothly and quickly down the road – it's also (and predominantly) about safety. The safety of yourself and your passengers, and the safety of everyone else we're sharing the roads with.

Improving your observation and planning skills will allow you to spot dangerous and risky situations earlier and to make suitable plans in how to deal with these situations. But there is another principle which – if you add it to the mix – improves your safety even more and should help you to avoid being involved in somebody else's accident:

The Zone of Relative Safety

A zone of relative safety is an imaginary "bubble" or "area" around your car which you should aim to keep free of any other road users or other hazards.

Try to imagine that your car is surrounded by an invisible force-field. Or imagine that your car is actually a little bigger than it actually is. This, in essence, is the principle of a zone of relative safety.

The size of the zone is variable – it can be smaller on slower and congested roads and larger on faster, more open roads. Your plans can then be made with a view to keeping everything outside this invisible area – and so there is much less chance of anything colliding with your car.

Let's have a look at a few simple examples:

If you're driving along an urban road, you'll be scanning ahead and looking into each junction which joins the road you're on. If you see a car approaching one of these junctions ahead to the left, what would you normally do? The vast majority of drivers will do nothing – they'll just continue along, in the centre of their lane, and drive past the car in the junction.

A more advanced driver, however, will link their observations of the car with a possibility that it will pull out. As they get closer to it, they'll look for some other visual clues – are the wheels turning or stationary? Can they see the other driver? Is the driver looking in their direction?

Alongside these improved observations, using the zone of relative safety can give us just a little more time to react should the car start to move. Instead of continuing straight along in your lane, you should – if it's safe – move towards the offside of the road. Up to and sometimes over the centre-lines of the road.

If you make this offside move, you'll get a slightly better view of the car in the junction, they will get a slightly better view of you and you'll increase the space between the cars which would give you more time and space to react if the car suddenly pulls out.

It probably won't pull out, but if it does, the zone of relative safety can make the difference between an accident and a sharp intake of breath.

Here's another example. If you're driving past a line of parked cars, there is always a possibility that a pedestrian, child or animal may cross carelessly from behind one of the parked vehicles, or that someone may carelessly open their door into your path.

Most average drivers won't give this much thought – if they can get through the gap and past the parked cars, that's all that matters.

Advanced drivers, however, will be looking for a range of other visual clues. They'll be looking underneath the parked vehicles for movements and feet. They'll be looking for brake lights going off, which might indicate a door about to open, and they're looking to the left and right of the parked cars for inattentive pedestrians and animals.

If we introduce the zone of relative safety into the mix, the driver will imagine one of the car doors opening, and give enough space – if it's available – for a door to open without making contact with their car. The zone is easily defined in these circumstances – it is just larger than the length of an open door.

Cyclists are a good example too. Most drivers (unintentionally in most cases), pass too close to cyclists. Even if they look steady and experienced, it only takes a bump in the road or a pothole to set a cyclist wobbling and you should always take this possibility into account when passing them.

I imagine the cyclist laid on their side – which is where they'll be if they fall off. If I cannot pass a cyclist without leaving enough room for them to fall off without hitting them, I'll wait behind them until there is more space. So in this case, the zone of relative safety is the height of the cyclist laid width-ways across the road.

I'm sure you get the idea. Try using the zone of relative safety as part of your driving plans.

13

Car Balance

YOUTUBE LINK - **CORNERING BALANCE:**

https://youtu.be/NGJLNKQxZ98

What on earth do we mean when we talk about "balance" when driving a car? It's not like you can fall off it. Well, you can fall off the road of course, but not in the same way as the organ-donors who dust off their superbikes every April and throw themselves around the countryside in their ever-tightening leathers at warp factor 9.

Balance is an absolutely essential ingredient of high performance driving, and it's not a skill you can learn overnight. It's one that you need to practice, and occasionally get wrong in order to learn correctly.

But first off, here's my explanation of balance as applied to driving a car. And before any of you physics pedants start (you know who you are), I know the correct terms for this will include "mass", "acceleration", "force" and no end of other scientific terms, but I'll be sticking with "weight" for now, as I'm a simple man and it's a complicated subject.

Balance is the ability of a driver to control a car in such a way that the transfer of weight involved in accelerating, braking and cornering does not lead to a loss of control.

It's fairly obvious (and actually *is* written in Roadcraft) that a moving car is at its most stable when travelling in a straight line at a constant speed. Any action that the driver takes to alter that state - increasing or decreasing speed and cornering - will transfer the vehicle's weight around the car. Braking, for instance, will transfer the vehicle's weight forwards. This will have two fairly obvious outcomes - there will be more weight pressing the front tyres into the road, and less weight pushing the back tyres into the road.

Imagine for a moment that you're driving a car with two boots - a Mk1 Toyota MR2 for instance (if you're not familiar with the Mk1 MR2, it is a mid-engined car with a boot in the front and another, smaller boot right at the rear, behind the engine), or a Porsche Boxter. If you went out and bought a couple of sacks of potatoes and stuck them in the front boot, then the car would handle very differently than if you put them in the rear boot. If you're a fast driver, then you're effectively shifting those sacks of spuds into the front boot every time you brake, and chucking them in the back every time you accelerate.

Now, I'm not saying that the transfer of weight is a bad thing - far from it in fact. It's an utterly unavoidable consequence of moving a ton-and-a-half of car along a road. Without it, none of us would enjoy driving high performance cars, as it's the transfer of weight which produces the sensations of speed that we all love - the hard cornering, the shove in the back under acceleration, and the dive under braking.

No - the transfer of weight isn't the problem. What *is* the problem is *how* you transfer that weight.

Let's look at braking first, as it's a fairly simple operation in a car (none of this twiddling hand and foot levers that motorcyclists have to do) involving pressing a pedal. That's it - you just press a pedal and the car slows down.

Well, not exactly. If you just jumped on the brake pedal really hard every time you braked, you wouldn't last very long. You'd get a sore right leg, it wouldn't do your car much good, and I'd give you 10 minutes before a taxi ran up your rear.

The other problem when applying the brakes as though they are a switch is that pressing the brake pedal hard and fast transfers the vehicles weight forwards hard and fast. This can unsettle the rear end of the car and leave very little front-end grip left for steering.

The correct technique when braking is to start applying the brakes gently and then firm up the pedal pressure as you go. I'm not talking about building up the pressure over several seconds - you should be able to do it smoothly in less than a second. You can use this technique even when braking *very* hard - the amount of weight you're transferring forwards is just the same as if you jumped on the pedal, but if you're smooth in your brake application, that weight transfer takes slightly longer, and that's what allows you to keep better control of the car. This is what I'd describe as "balancing" the car under braking.

Whilst we're on the subject of braking, it's just as important to be smooth coming *off* the brakes as it is to be smooth when applying them. It's relatively easy to learn how to press the pedal smoothly, but when you're steaming on, your attention is always on "what's next?", and it's very easy to just jump off the brakes and move straight back onto the accelerator for the next corner.

Don't forget that you've transferred all that weight forwards when braking, and when you come off the brakes, it will settle rearwards again. Jumping off the brake will suddenly release weight from the front of the car, and if you're entering a corner, this can be disastrous. A much better technique is to *ease* off the brake pedal, which moves that weight rearwards at a slower rate, and helps to keep the car balanced. My instruction to students was never "off the brakes" – it was always "oooooofffff the brakes". They looked at me as though I was retarded - granted - but they got the idea.

The same is true for acceleration. If you just jump on and off the throttle, particularly if you drive a powerful car, then the resultant weight transfer can move around too quickly and unsettle the car.

Take lift-off oversteer as an example. If a driver is pressing on in a corner, close to the cars limit, and has to suddenly tighten their line, then the car is liable to start sliding.

If that driver then reacts badly and lifts off the accelerator in a panic, then the weight will inevitably move towards the front of the car and, more importantly, *away from the rear,* which will put the car into an oversteer situation that will take some skill and clear thinking from which to recover. The average driver's usual response at this point will be to hit the brakes, which, of course, transfers *more* weight forwards, and will pitch the car into a spin.

In a similar situation, a good driver will feather back slightly on the throttle, and use the accelerator to move the weight around to their advantage, rather than to their disadvantage. The key, as with most aspects of performance driving, is to do it *smoothly*.

It's the same with steering.

I reported a fatal accident a few years ago in which a young driver lost control of his car whilst negotiating a bend on an NSL road at high speed. As part of the investigation, we prepared a video of the scene to be played in court. I demonstrated that a similar car could be driven through the bend almost 20mph *faster* than the speed at which the young driver had lost control. It wasn't a problem because my style of driving is smooth, whereas marks at the scene showed that this lad had chucked the car into the corner, and the manner in which he'd done it had put the car out of control.

Here's another nice little line.

If you sneak up on your car and make it jump, it'll throw a strop, but if you tell it what you're going to do, and ease it into it, it'll do whatever you want.

What Wheel Drive?

The *driven* wheels are what give a car its tendency at the limit. As a general rule, rear wheel driver (RWD) cars tend to oversteer, front wheel drive (FWD) cars tend to understeer, and four wheel drive (4WD) cars react based on a combination of the layout of the car they are based on and the torque bias of their 4WD system.

Every car is different though - older FWD Peugeots, for instance, are very throttle-sensitive when cornering, and will oversteer quite easily. Conversely, modern RWD BMWs have a tendency to initially understeer when approaching the limit.

Another essential factor to consider is the position of the engine and gearbox. Older Audi Quattros used to have their engine way out over the front axle line, whereas we all know about the handling idiosyncrasies of the Porsche 911 with its engine mounted a few inches inboard of the back bumper.

Every car has different tendencies, and a different "feel" to them. Even identical cars can feel quite different to drive. The essential technique across all car types, though, is the smooth use of the controls, and the gradual, rather than sudden application of inputs.

Jackie Stewart used to teach smooth driving using a big shallow bowl-type-thing attached to a cars bonnet with a tennis ball in it. He used to teach people to drive around a racing circuit without allowing the ball to come out of the bowl. I thought it was a very nice teaching aid.

Or you could drive round with a bowl of water on your knee and try to stay dry.

Whilst I'm on the subject of Jackie Stewart, although I'm of the view that a lot of track techniques should stay on the track, I am a big admirer of Sir Jackie. He has always maintained that good driving is based around a smooth driving style, and he has some very nice ways of teaching the principles of smooth driving and vehicle balance.

There is an old episode of Top Gear in which he taught James May how to improve his lap times around Oulton Park. There was a nice example when they were having a mid-session break - Jackie pushed May and he stumbled off balance, and then he leaned against him, pushing him just as hard, but building up gradually, and May tensed against him and didn't lose his balance.

Jackie's point was that if you sneak up on a car with an unexpected move, it'll go off-balance, but if you build up gradually into a move, the car becomes ready for it, and keeps its balance.

It was a nice visual example, and it's one I now use myself.

Juan Pablo Montoya was interviewed a few years ago, when he was driving competitively for Williams in F1 (no slouch, in other words!), and he told this story about Sir Jackie Stewart:

Montoya and Stewart were appearing at a corporate day at a British race circuit. The plan was for them to drive guests around the circuit in a modern road car - a Ford Escort Cosworth I believe - but first they were asked to do timed laps in the car together, each riding as the other's passenger.

Stewart drove first. On his hot laps, Montoya said, Stewart seemed to be taking his time, shifting gear in a relaxed way and taking nothing to the edge. Montoya said that, as he observed this display, he actually felt sorry for Stewart, thinking that it was a bit sad that this former world champion's ability to drive at the limit had deteriorated so much over the years.

After Stewart had completed his laps it was Montoya's turn. Montoya thought that he had a little something to prove to Stewart (racers being racers), so he went flat out. He said that he drove as hard as he could, slamming home the gear-changes, throwing the car into and out of the bends, using the throttle and brakes heavily and driving on the ragged edge of the cars limits.

After Montoya had finished his laps, he found that his fastest lap had been 8/10 of a second slower than Stewart's.

So there you go - keep your balance.

14

STEERING

YOUTUBE LINK - **STEERING**:

https://youtu.be/5M13T2rhYf8

Steering is one of those skills that we don't really think about. Turn the wheel a certain amount and the car points in the direction you want it to go - simple.

Isn't it?

Not if you read advanced driving manuals it's not - rotational steering is a no-no, push pull is best - or is it pull-push? But rotational steering *is* actually ok sometimes. What about an emergency though? What's the fastest way to put lock on if things go wrong? Isn't shuffling the wheel the preserve of driving schools and people who smoke pipes?

Questions, questions.

Allow me to simplify things for you. I don't actually care *how* you hold or turn the wheel, as long as you operate it in the correct manner.

I do care if you're trying to pass a Police course or one of the civilian advanced courses which require pull-push of course. In those circumstances, if you don't demonstrate an ability to use the prescribed technique, then you won't pass the course.

But in every day driving, trust me, I don't care one iota *how* you turn the wheel, as long as you turn it in the correct way.

But what *is* the correct way Reg?

Let's explain the terminology first…

Rotational steering is a technique whereby the driver grips the wheel in a set position, usually with their hands at ten-to-two or quarter-to-three, and keeps their hands in that fixed position on the wheel whilst steering.

Pull-push is a technique where the driver starts with their hands in a fixed position, as with rotational steering, but then move their hands around the wheel rim when turning the wheel.

If I'm being honest, in my every day driving, I use a combination of rotational and pull-push. Rotational for more open corners, and pull-push for tighter ones. It's just that, to steer smoothly requires more concentration with rotational steering than it does with pull-push.

I talk about vehicle balance in a previous chapter and the basic principles for steering are exactly the same as for any other driver input. If you're rough with the steering, you'll catch the car unawares, which is something cars don't like - roughness moves the vehicle's weight around quickly and results in the car feeling unsettled, and in extreme cases, can result in a loss of directional stability. Modern vehicles - even the more mundane family cars - have quite high grip levels these days, but you can easily use up all of a cars lateral grip very quickly just by being rough with the wheel.

The way to apply steering lock is to turn the wheel slowly at first, build up the speed of the lock application until you're close to having the right amount of lock applied, and then slow down the application again until the wheel is stationary. Starting with a slow, gradual turn of the wheel starts to gently settle the car onto its springs rather than suddenly chucking lock on and expecting the car to go immediately from travelling in a straight line, to turning.

I don't mean that you should be excruciatingly slow with the wheel - this technique can be used even at very high speeds and on the track. I just mean that at the point you start to turn the wheel, the speed of lock application should build up and then slow down again, rather than just being done at a constant speed.

Imagine a pendulum swinging from left to right. At the very far reach of its swing, it's momentarily stationary until gravity starts to swing it the other way. It then starts to accelerate - slowly at first - until it's travelling at a constant speed. As it swings through its arc, gravity starts to slow it down again until it becomes stationary at the other far reach of its swing.

Keep that swinging pendulum in mind, and now attach a steering wheel at its fulcrum (is that the right word? It's been a long time since I did secondary school physics). The pendulum can swing faster or slower, depending on the weight and it's length, but the manner in which it turns is still the same - slow at first, speeding up, and then slowing down again.

It's just as important to use that same technique when taking lock *off* as well. As you're taking lock off when you're coming out of a corner, the steering action should be accompanied by a degree of acceleration, so to keep the car balanced under that acceleration, the lock should come off slowly at first, then quicker, and finally slowing down until you're pointing straight ahead again.

Of course, this sounds simple enough when applied to a single corner, and in reality, when negotiating a series of corners of varying degrees of sharpness, it's more difficult to apply correctly, but all you're effectively doing is shortening or lengthening the imaginary pendulum to suit each corner.

There are techniques which make this type of steering easier to maintain. If you try pulling the wheel down at the start of a turn you'll usually naturally apply a pendulum effect, which is why the Police, IAM etc., recommend pull-push. You *can* steer correctly with rotational steering, but it requires a little more concentration and practise, particularly if you like to sit with a straight-arm posture. Straight-arm driving requires the steering input to come more from the shoulder, whereas sitting with arms bent means the steering input comes more from the wrists. If you steer from the shoulder, it's less sensitive, and can be rougher.

So, next time you're out for a drive, just pay a little attention to how you operate the wheel, and have a go at imagining the pendulum effect. If you apply it correctly, you should notice an improvement in the smoothness of your drive, and in the stability of your car through corners.

15

GEAR CHANGING

YOUTUBE LINK - **CHANGING GEAR - MANUAL TRANSMISSION:**

https://youtu.be/A4rs09AKBc8

Occasionally, friends ask me to take them out for a few hours driver training, so they can improve their skills and tell their mates they've been taught "by a proper Police Instructor".

If I get a full day with someone, I can give them a little taster of most aspects of advanced driving. A sort of Chinese buffet, starting with the basics of smooth car control, moving on to improving observations and planning, and then, if I've got some confidence with their ability, doing some higher speed cornering and overtaking. There's no way I could get anywhere near teaching someone everything they'd learn on a full course, but they get a small sample of most aspects, and I've never had anyone who doesn't think they've improved at the end.

Occasionally though, time will be limited, and someone will ask me to take them out "just for an hour or so" and teach them something. So I always teach them something with which they'll feel a difference immediately, and which they'll go away and practice.

It's also something that their regular passengers will notice immediately (a number of wives have already thanked me) and it's something they can show off to their mates if they are so inclined.

I teach them to change gear.

"Teach them to change gear Reg? Don't be daft - everyone knows how to change ruddy gear. Except for the Americans."

Well, most people *do* know how to change gear in a manual car, and some people know how to change gear smoothly, but I can teach people to change gear so smoothly they can out-smooth Sean Connery (before he lost his hair and appeared in Highlander).

It's a well-established fact that you should operate a car's controls smoothly, but why? What difference does it make? To be honest, it doesn't make a great deal of difference at lower speeds - my mum used to be rougher with the gear-stick than Big Daddy used to be with Kendo Nagasaki, but she only trundled round at town speeds, so it never caused her a problem.

The point at which smooth car control *does* start to matter is when the speed increases. When a car is travelling at high speed, the potential weight transfer under heavy braking, hard acceleration, or high-G cornering is very high, and it's this transfer of weight across the car which can seriously unsettle the car if it's not done smoothly.

Changing gear is one way of transferring the vehicles weight backwards and forwards, and so, if you can do it as smoothly as possible, the weight balance of the car moves around in a more stable manner, and your progress will be safer. Plus, your passengers will appreciate it too.

So, what's the secret? Well, it's not one thing, but, as with most aspects of driving, it's a series of actions which must be coordinated and timed to perfection in order to get it right. I've seen grown men, some of them high ranking Police and Army officers, congratulating themselves, and feeling chuffed to pieces at getting *one* gear-change correct. Remember, these are people who make life-or-death decisions, and they were impressed enough with their own improvement in a basic driving skill, to say "let's do it again" with a big grin on their faces.

In true driving school style, I'll split the subject into two sections. Predictably enough, they are...

1. Changing up through the box.

2. Changing down through the box.

But before I move on to the more advanced sections 1 and 2, let's start with how you move the gear stick.

HOLDING THE GEAR STICK

Most people simply change from the gear that they are in; to the gear they want to be in. But in reality, it's slightly more complex. What you're doing is taking the car out of the gear it's in, putting it into neutral, taking it out of neutral and then putting it into the next gear.

I know they sound the same, but there's a very subtle difference, and if you can get into the habit of pausing for about 1/2 a second whilst in the neutral phase, you will give yourself enough time to operate the most important pedal for smooth gear-changes - the accelerator.

Police driving schools teach the "thumb up and thumb down" method for holding the gear-stick and I quite like it, as it encourages you to place sideways pressure in the correct direction, and helps to avoid selecting the wrong gear. Basically, hold the gear stick with the palm of your hand, and if you're selecting first or second, point your thumb down. If you're selecting third, fourth or fifth (or sixth!), point your thumb upwards. If you place the pressure on the gear-stick with your palm, you'll always move the gear-stick in the right direction.

This is one of those elements which can be demonstrated in 10 seconds, but is very difficult to describe, so here's a couple of pictures I've just taken, to demonstrate (Yes, I know it's a semi auto, but you get the idea)

Thumb down, for 1st and 2nd:

Thumb up, for 3rd, 4th and 5th (and 6th):

I'm now somewhat concerned as to how fat my hand looks in that second picture!

Although it's a "thumb-up/thumb-down" technique, the key is actually in the position of your palm, rather than the position of your thumb. If you position your thumb correctly, your palm will naturally be in the correct position to apply pressure to the stick in the correct direction.

Most gearboxes are sprung so that the stick "rests" in neutral between third and fourth gears, so sideways pressure is only ever needed when selecting first, second and fifth (and sixth) gears. Changes to third and fourth just involve a movement either straight forward, or straight back from the neutral plane.

Right - back to 1 and 2.

Changing Up

In explaining how to change up through the 'box, I'm going to assume that you'll move the gear-stick correctly, as described above and, most importantly, include that essential pause in the neutral phase.

The most important aspect of changing up correctly is what you do with the accelerator pedal. A lot of drivers will press the clutch and completely release the accelerator pedal whilst they change gear. They will then release the clutch prior to re-applying the accelerator. This technique will usually result in the car jerking forward when the clutch is released because the engine speed doesn't match the road speed for that gear. This jerk is more pronounced in lower gears than it is in higher gears.

The way to avoid this jerk is to release pressure on the accelerator before and during the gear-change, but not to release it *completely*. I'll talk you through it.

Let's assume we're about to change up from 2nd to 3rd in an average car, at about 40MPH. In this imaginary average car, the engine will be doing 5000RPM at 40MPH in 2nd gear and 3000RPM at the same speed in 3rd.

Before you start to change gear, ease off the accelerator slightly so the *rate* of acceleration slows. *Then* press the clutch and change gear as described previously. Whilst you're changing gear, ease the accelerator back until the revs have dropped from 5000 to 3000, and then release the clutch.

You shouldn't be *holding* the revs, you should be just letting them drop to the right point before releasing the clutch. If you're holding the revs, then the clutch will be taking some punishment, as the road speed will be higher than the engine speed for those revs, and the clutch will have to take up that difference in speed.

A colleague of mine taught it by getting students to curl and un-curl their toes inside their right shoe.

Once you've released the clutch, *squeeze* the accelerator, and continue accelerating. Allowing the revs to drop correctly will remove that jerkiness from the up-change, and you'll notice the difference immediately.

Changing Down

Changing down is very similar, but the process involves raising, rather than lowering, the revs. Racing and competition drivers "blip" the throttle on down-changes to match engine speed to road speed, but I'm talking about road driving, which is slightly different. A blip is only suited to very fast gear-changes, which aren't necessary on the road, so in advanced road driving, the revs are *raised* during the down-change, and not blipped.

As you're changing gear, squeeze the accelerator gently to raise the revs from 3000 to 5000, release the clutch, and then continue accelerating.

On the subject of raising the revs, as you go down a gear, try just holding the accelerator pedal exactly where it is. Pressing the clutch releases the engine from the effort of moving the car, and generally raises the revs just enough to make for a smooth down-change.

I do appreciate, however, that there are huge differences between different cars. A tuned 4-cylinder engine with a lightweight flywheel and clutch, for instance, can be much more responsive to the throttle, and will lose or gain revs much more quickly than a large capacity V8 with a heavy clutch and driveline.

The basic technique is still the same though - it just needs tweaking for different cars.

Many drivers "blip" the throttle when changing down through the gears. A blip is a quick, momentary press of the accelerator which results in the revs rising and falling quite quickly. Now, I don't want to get too "Open University" over this, but I've drawn a couple of graphs to help me explain.

Imagine, in this case that you're changing down from, say, fourth to third. The engine speed in fourth is 3000 RPM and the engine speed in third will be 4000 RPM.

Your objective during the gear-change is to bring the clutch up at, or as close to 4000 RPM as you can, in order to smooth out the change. The first graph shows a throttle blip, where the revs rise and then fall quite quickly:

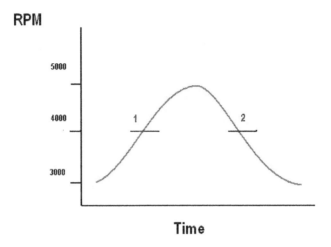

As you can see, the engine is at 4000 RPM twice during the blip, at 1 and 2. However, the time that the engine is at 4000 RPM is only momentary, and if you release the clutch at the wrong time, you're going to catch the engine at the wrong revs.

Here's the graph showing a sustained-rev gear-change...

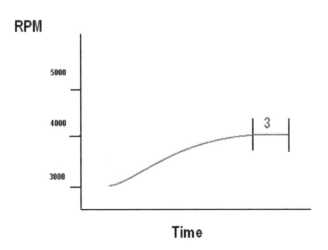

As you can see, the engine is held at 4000 RPM, which allows you to time your clutch release much more easily and accurately - the time available for releasing the clutch at 3 is much longer.

It's taken me ages to explain something which can be done in around a second and it's far easier to teach by demonstration and then trial and error than it is to write it out, but I think that's my best explanation.

Practice

Have a go tomorrow when you get a chance. Don't just change from 2nd to 3rd - I always get students to drive along a straight piece of road at 50MPH, and change randomly through the 'box, without losing road speed. The gear-change will always be *heard*, but the point is that it shouldn't be *felt*.

All the actions involved in the gear-change should seamlessly flow into each other. This isn't easy when you're practising at first, as you need to think about each action separately, but with practise, it should all come together nicely.

Then, when you've practiced for a bit, see if anyone notices.

Clutchless Gear-Changing

It is entirely possible to change gear in a manual car without actually using the clutch.

There isn't an advantage to clutchless gear-changes. I have used it in the past as a teaching aid to help students learn how to time their gear-changes and match engine revs properly, but it's no more than an interesting exercise these days.

ADVANCED & PERFORMANCE DRIVING

If you're smooth and positive with the gearstick and you're accurate with your rev-matching, gears can be selected just as smoothly without the clutch and with just as much mechanical sympathy, but one slip or mistake and you'll be grinding and crunching, so it's usually best to stick with the clutch for gear-changing under most circumstances.

It could come in useful if you ever have a clutch failure of course – it's much better to be able to limp home rather than wait hours for an expensive recovery truck.

If you have to come to a stop, slip the car into neutral before you roll to a stop, turn off the engine, select first, set off again on the starter motor as you would if you were doing a stall-retrieve in a 4X4 and you're away!

You do look a bit of a tit kangarooing away from the lights, but needs must when the devil piddles in your kettle.

16

Automatic Gearboxes

Youtube Link - **Automatic Gearboxes**:

https://youtu.be/ujwVkxDeim0

Autos are dead simple aren't they? Stick the car in drive, press the right pedal to go and the left pedal to stop. Piece of cake. In fact, there's no need for a section on automatic gearboxes in this book is there? It's an *advanced* driving book after all, and *advanced* drivers like to change gear themselves don't they?

Well, hang on a minute. Although in the UK, we've traditionally preferred manual gearboxes, they're getting more and more popular these days as manufacturers have developed more efficient and effective automatic gearboxes.

When I was a teenager, one of my mates had an automatic 998cc Mini. It was unbelievably woeful - the torque converter was sloppy, the drive was vague and the gearbox seemed to sap at least half of the engine's power & torque, which was lacking in the first place. That car was slow with a capital *zzzzzz*.

In the 80's & 90's, automatic gearboxes only really suited large, heavy cars with large capacity, torquey engines. Range Rovers, Ford Granadas & Dorchester Hearses.

Whenever you read a review of a car which was available with both manual & automatic gearboxes, the auto version was always slower to accelerate and less fuel efficient than the exact same car with a manual gearbox

In more recent times however, car manufacturers have put a huge amount of effort into developing automatic gearboxes which are way more efficient than they used to be and which are even more efficient than their equivalent manual gearboxes. I would even go as far as to say that modern automatic gearboxes are getting better to drive than their manual equivalent.

Modern torque converters are tight and responsive, and modern autos have more ratios - 7, 8, 9 and even 10 speed auto gearboxes are becoming commonplace & you don't need to be a qualified mechanical engineer to realise that more ratios will make a gearbox more efficient.

So, how should you use an automatic gearbox? What's the best approach? And how does it fit with the system of car control & advanced driving?

I'll get on to those points in a minute, but let's be clear about the subject of this chapter first. In this chapter I'll be talking about what I refer to as "traditional" automatic gearboxes, by which I mean gearboxes where the drive from the engine to the gearbox is controlled by a torque-converter and not a mechanical clutch.

A torque converter in very simple terms is a fluid coupling - imagine two dishes with some propellor-like fins fixed inside them. Fill the dishes with light oil, put them together with their rims touching and spin one of the dishes around. The movement of the fins will turn the oil, which in turn will turn the fins in the other dish. That's how a torque converter works to transfer the turning motion of the engine across into the gearbox without you having to operate a clutch.

In this chapter, I won't be talking about semi-automatic, DSG, Dual-clutch. DCT, or PDK transmissions. These have mechanical clutches and I'll cover them in a later chapter. Nor am I covering electric or hybrid vehicles which, again, are covered in a later chapter of the book.

Now that's all been said, how should you use an automatic gearbox? Let's start with the basics.

When you get in an automatic car, you'll see that, instead of a normal gear stick in the centre console, there is, instead, a gear *selector*. In older automatic cars, this was a mechanical lever which was directly connected to the gearbox under the car, but these days it is just a switch which electronically selects the drive mode for the car.

Some manufacturers have kept the gear selector looking something like a gear stick and kept it where you would expect to find it, whereas other manufacturers have moved it to a different part of the cabin & made it in a different form. Some cars, for example, have the gear selector on a stalk next to the steering wheel, and others have turned it into a rotary dial on the dashboard.

Whatever it looks like, however, the purpose of the gear selector is the same - it allows you to select the drive mode (advanced stuff eh?!)

On the whole, with a few exceptions, the gear selector will have the drive modes in the following order:

P (Park)

R (Reverse)

N (Neutral)

D (Drive)

Below "D" you may see an option for **"S" (Sport), "M" (Manual)** and possibly a little snowflake symbol **(Winter)**.

Let's go through each of those drive modes & explain what they mean.

P (Park)

As with all these drive modes, the clue is in the name! Park is the equivalent of leaving a manual car in gear when you leave it parked up. Park mode engages a mechanical "pawl" in the gearbox which locks the driveline and prevents the car from rolling away.

Of course, you should always engage the handbrake/parking brake when you park your car, but you should always have two methods of holding the car stationary in case one fails, or in case you leave the handbrake off by mistake, as I did with my Toyota MR2 when I was 19. It somehow managed to roll across both live lanes of the A6 without hitting any other cars and rolled gently into the wall across the road, but trust me, it's an experience you should try to avoid!

Many modern cars won't actually let you leave the car without engaging park - some will engage it automatically and some will bing and bong until you remember, but it's pretty difficult to leave a modern automatic car in anything other than park these days.

One other thing to note - Park can be selected whilst the car is running and will keep the transmission (and the driven axle) locked even whilst the engine is on. In a manual car you would only take a gear to hold the car with the engine off, but in an auto you can use Park irrespective of whether the car is running or not.

R (Reverse)

Again, this is pretty obvious, but the next gear down from Park is R for Reverse. As with manual cars, autos only have one reverse gear and it makes the car go backwards. Any further explanation necessary? No? Good. Carry on.

N (Neutral)

As with manual gearboxes, autos have a neutral position, where the engine's drive is disconnected from the gearbox.

Unlike manual gearboxes, however, neutral doesn't seem to be very useful in an automatic car. As you'll see when I describe how to drive an auto, the car can effectively remain in drive for the whole of your journey - if you come to a stop, the torque converter slows right down and allows the engine & gearbox to be separated by the fluid coupling. When you press the gas pedal, the torque converter moves the car away from stationary, so unlike a manual, there is no need to ever put the car into neutral during a journey.

So what's it for then?!

The most important reason for automatic gearboxes having a neutral position is to give the gearbox a little "rest" in between reverse and drive. If you were to change directly from reverse to drive, the change in direction within the gearbox would lead to a nasty mechanical "shunt" which would be uncomfortable in the car and likely to cause unnecessary wear to the gearbox. Having a neutral position introduces a slight pause between forward and reverse gears and prevents this unnecessary mechanical shunt.

So neutral is actually for the car and not for you!

Having said that, there are certain circumstances where you might want to select neutral.

If the car has a problem & needs to be pushed or towed, you should put the gearbox into neutral so it will effectively "freewheel".

If you're stuck in mud or snow & you need to be pushed or towed out of your predicament, again, put the car in neutral until it's moving then engage drive or reverse.

And if you use those automatic car washes where the machine pulls the car through, again, you should engage neutral to prevent damage to your car.

Other than that, neutral is very rarely used in an auto.

D (Drive)

So, you're in your car and you want to go forward to your destination? Drive is for you!

For most of the time, on most journeys, you'll be in drive. This is the beauty of an automatic gearbox isn't it? In drive, the car will set off smoothly from stationary, change up through the gearbox as you're accelerating, cruise in an appropriate gear, and change down as you slow down. It'll even "kick down" to a lower gear if you press the accelerator hard (more of this in a bit).

In short, drive is where you want the gearbox if you're, erm, driving.

S (Sport)

Sport setting effectively makes the gearbox behave in a similar way to how you would behave if you're having a "sporty" drive in a car with a manual gearbox.

As such, it will hold lower gears for longer so that the engine revs higher before changing up, and it will kick down to a lower gear more readily when you press the accelerator, for example when you want to overtake.

Contrary to some people's suggestions, it doesn't give you any more power or torque - it just ensures the car is kept in a more responsive gear for longer, prioritising performance over economy.

M (Manual)

It's worth noting that engaging manual mode doesn't suddenly transform your automatic car into a manual. It doesn't make the car sprout a clutch pedal or flick a gear stick out of a secret compartment.

"Manual" in the contact of an automatic gearbox just allows you some control over the choice of gear and prevents the gearbox automatically changing up or down.

In older automatic cars, below "D" on the gear selector were the numbers 3, 2 & 1 (depending on how many ratios the car had - a 3 speed would just have 2 & 1 under D and a five-speed would have 4, 3, 2 & 1).

These selectable gears allowed you to simply "lock out" the gears above them. So if you selected "2" in a 4 speed auto, the car would change between 1st & 2nd gear, but go no higher.

There are distinct advantages in some situations, to holding the car in a lower gear. If you're approaching a series of bends, for example, you might want to hold third to maintain flexibility, rather than having the car change up to 4th. If you're planning an overtake, you might not want a delay whilst the car kicks down to a lower gear, so you might manually select a lower gear for maximum vroom factor!

Additionally, on a long downhill run in a 30 or 40 speed limit area, holding a lower gear will give you more retardation and allow you to keep within the speed limit with minimal brakes.

The "lock-out" function was not, however, designed to allow you to drive the car up & down through the gears like a normal manual gearbox. They were purely there to allow you a little control under very specific circumstances.

Modern automatic gearboxes, however, have a much more sophisticated "manual" mode which allows selection of chosen gears through either the gear selector or, more popularly these days "flappy paddles" behind the steering wheel.

The best way to use this function is not, however, to drive the car up & down through the gears like a manual. Instead, as with the older "lock-out" functions, the manual setting allows gears to be held longer, and selected earlier in anticipation of a corner or overtake. Once the situation is over, I like to revert to automatic mode, rather than leaving the car in manual indefinitely.

W (Winter)

Some automatic cars have a winter setting on the gearbox. This usually just makes the car set off from stationary in 2nd gear, rather than 1st, reducing the amount of torque to the driven wheels and minimising wheelspin. It also tends to default to the highest available gear whilst driving for the same reasons.

How to drive an automatic

OK, so I've explained how the gear selector works, and how & when to use the different functions of an automatic gearbox. How, then, do you actually drive an automatic properly? And how does it fit with the system of car control?

I'm a Creep, I'm a Weirdo…

The first thing you should know about "traditional" automatics is that they are designed to "creep". That means that if the engine is running & either drive or reverse are engaged, the car will slowly creep backwards or forwards at about 2 or 3mph *without any pressure being applied to the accelerator*.

So, if your automatic car is running, drive is selected & you put both of your feet flat on the floor, away from the pedals, the car will roll forward on a relatively flat surface at 2-3mph without any inputs from you.

To counteract this & to make sure you are always in full control, it is very important to remember the number 1 rule for driving an automatic car:

Everything starts with the brake pedal!

The first thing you should do when you get in an automatic car is put your foot on the brake pedal. That's the **VERY FIRST THING** you should do!

Before you switch on the ignition, before you put on your seatbelt, before you even close the car door - **PUT YOUR FOOT ON THE BRAKE!**

If your foot is pressing the brake pedal, there is very little chance that the car will roll away or creep forwards or backwards when you start the car up. A foot on the brake pedal will always overcome any element of creep designed into the gearbox & getting in to the habit of always holding the brake when you get in to your car will mean you never forget!

So you're in the car, foot on the brake pedal - what next? Do you need to select neutral before starting the car?

No - start it in Park. Starting the car with Park selected means the pawl is still engaged in the gearbox & the car should be held stationary with the handbrake, footbrake and park function.

Remember though - **KEEP YOUR FOOT ON THE BRAKE!**

You'll feel the brake pedal "drop" slightly when the engine is started, but don't worry - this is just the brake servo (designed to make pressing the brakes easier) coming to life with the engine.

Now - **with your foot on the brake** - move the selector through "R" and "N" and into "D for "Drive".

You might feel a very slight movement of the car as drive is selected - this is the torque converter starting to transfer drive to the wheels and making the car try to creep forward.

But it won't creep forward will it?

Because you've still got the brake pressed, haven't you?!

HAVEN'T YOU?!!

Of course you have.

Right then - release the handbrake and then gently start to release the brake pedal. Once the brakes are almost fully released, you'll feel the car start to gently creep forward. Take your foot completely off the brake & the car will accelerate very gently to about 2 or 3mph - no more. If you're manoeuvring out of a parking space or in another tight area where you need to move the car slowly backwards & forwards, you should do all your movements off and on the brake pedal - there is no need to use the accelerator when you're manoeuvring an automatic car - just do it all on and off the brake pedal.

It's worth mentioning that, if you're on an incline, the car may not creep as gravity will do the job of the brakes, but if the car is in drive facing uphill, the creep function should prevent t from rolling backwards, and vice versa if the car is in reverse facing downhill.

When you're ready to set off, however, press the accelerator and the car will start to accelerate (who would have thought eh?!). As the car builds speed, it will change up through the gears very smoothly until it is in an appropriate gear for your speed. You don't need to do anything other than press the accelerator.

Need to slow down? Well, in manual cars, lifting off the accelerator will stop fuel going into the engine and the car will start to slow down due to the compression in the engine. Modern autos will do the same, but with less retardation. Older autos will feel as though they just want to run on and so the brakes tend to be used a little more for slowing in an automatic than in a manual.

Press the brakes & the car will slow as normal whilst the gearbox very smoothly changes down through the gears.

Need to stop? Keep the brakes on until you stop. The torque converter will allow the car to come to a nice, smooth controlled stop - but don't take your foot off the brake pedal! Remember the car still wants to creep forward & you need to hold it on the brakes until you're ready to set off again.

What should I do when I'm stopped in traffic?

I see loads of people faffing about with the gearbox whilst the car is stationary in traffic - they come to a stop, put the handbrake on, put the car in neutral or park, take their foot off the brake, then back on the brake, engage drive, handbrake off & move off.

There is no real need for any of this. In an auto, just come to a stop on the footbrake, leave the car in drive, hold it on the footbrake until you're ready to set off again & then release the brake. In police training we were taught to leave the car in drive, keep the foot brake applied & put the handbrake on, but I'm really not convinced this is necessary. Being stationary in traffic means you're still driving the car & the foot brake is still the most effective way of holding the car stationary for short periods of time.

There is an argument that holding the car on the footbrake can dazzle drivers behind with the brake lights, particularly in the dark, but I would argue that it makes it more obvious to drivers further behind that you're stopped and less likely for them to run in the back of you.

Either way, I'm a big believer in reducing your workload behind the wheel, so it makes perfect sense that you should just come to a stop on the footbrake & hold it there until you're ready to move off again.

When you're on the move, you may want to accelerate quickly if, for example, you've spotted an opportunity to overtake a slower-moving vehicle. In a manual car, you just select a lower gear which raises the engine's revs & gives you maximum acceleration, but what should you do in an automatic?

Can I kick it? Yes you can!

Automatic gearboxes have historically been fitted with a "kick-down" function. This used to be a physical switch underneath the accelerator pedal which was triggered by pressing the pedal to the floor - this caused the gearbox to change down a gear and would give much stronger acceleration due to the higher torque at higher revs.

These days, kick down is still designed into automatic gearboxes, but the switch is effectively built into the car's software. If the car detects a significant press of the accelerator, it will make the car kick-down. The harder and/or faster you press the pedal, the lower the gear which is selected, but there is no need to press the pedal all the way to the floor - unless, of course, it floats your boat!

Putting the gearbox into sport mode will make the car hold lower gears for longer, to allow for better acceleration, and will also make the car kick down more readily, and often to a lower gear than it would in normal drive mode.

Automatics and the system of car control

I'll examine the system of car control in greater detail in a later chapter, but let's have a quick look at the schematic of system & see how it fits in with automatic gearboxes:

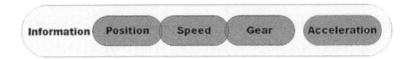

As you can see, the fourth phase (or the third action phase, depending on how you prefer to read the system) is "gear". In a manual car, you should be looking to have finished braking for a hazard *before* you select an appropriate flexible gear for the hazard. As such, braking is generally finished early, to allow time for a nice, smooth rev-matched gear change.

In an automatic, however, you don't need to physically change gear yourself do you? The car does that automatically, so surely you don't need to leave any time for the gear change? Do you?

This is where a great many advanced drivers - including some extremely competent & experienced ones - get it wrong. They think that you don't need to leave time for a gear change because the car is doing all the work, and so they leave the brakes on right up to the hazard & then go almost immediately from brakes (the speed phase), to gas (the acceleration phase).

Now, in theory, that shouldn't be a problem should it? They don't need to physically change gear themselves, so they don't need any extra time between the speed and acceleration phases to change gear do they?

Well, no they don't, but the mistake they're making is forgetting that there is another fundamental benefit in building in a short delay between brakes and acceleration - *it allows the car to settle back on it's suspension off the brakes before starting to accelerate.*

In other words, it allows the car to enter the hazard in a more settled & balanced state, by allowing the weight to transfer from the front axle to the rear axle in a more steady manner.

So if you drive an auto, the best way to get this right is to remind yourself that, after the speed phase, the car needs a little time to get the gear. In reality it doesn't need much time, but thinking about it in that way will ensure that you build in a slight pause between the speed phase and the acceleration phase where you're off the brakes, but not accelerating. The result will be a much smoother, more balanced approach to hazards.

So there you go - automatics & how to use them.

I should add that this technology is continually evolving & although I've tried to cover the most common types of traditional torque-converter automatics in this chapter, I accept that it won't be long before someone asks me how to operate their 14-speed pre-selector automated hybrid continually-variable transmission.

In which case, I suggest you RTFM (read the flipping manual!).

17

SINGLE CLUTCH SEMI-AUTOMATIC GEARBOXES

This is something you won't find in Roadcraft - a guide to using single-clutch semi-automatic gearboxes. I've never read a *proper* guide to using them, so the advice I'm giving is based solely on my own experiences. Obviously, every manufacturer's systems are slightly different, and have their own idiosyncrasies, and technology is changing and improving all the time.

Let's set the guidelines for this chapter first. I'm not going to be writing about switchable automatic gearboxes. A traditional fully automatic gearbox works via a torque converter, and I've covered those in great detail in the previous chapter.

What I *am* writing about are the slightly more modern style of semi-autos, which incorporate a mechanical clutch and a traditional gearbox which has automatic (usually hydraulic) operation of the gear-change and clutch.

They are two-pedal cars in which the gear-change is operated with either a gear-lever style switch on the centre console, or "paddles" behind the steering wheel, or a combination of the two. The gear-change is generally sequential (i.e. you have to go through each individual gear on the way up and down the 'box), but there are ways to effectively "miss" gears out, which I'll cover.

Now, my experience of these gearboxes isn't vast, but I used to own an E36 BMW M3 with the SMG1 gearbox, and I've had a reasonable amount of time behind the wheel of other BMWs with SMG gearboxes, such as E46 M3s and E60 M5s. I've also driven an F1 gearbox-equipped Ferrari 355, so I suppose I'm reasonably well qualified to talk about these types of gearbox.

Setting off

The first thing to remember with gearboxes of this type is that they are *not* automatics. They have a mechanical clutch, and you should drive them with as much mechanical sympathy as you would a manual car.

In a traditional automatic, the car is happy to sit on a hill with a small amount of power applied, keeping it stationary or just moving forward slightly - that's because the drive is being transmitted through a fluid coupling, and it creates no wear whatsoever if you drive it in that manner.

Try that in a semi-auto, however, and you're effectively slipping the clutch. Drive like that all the time in traffic and you'll need a new clutch fitting *much* sooner than you'd like.

Semi-autos don't "creep" either. Put a traditional automatic in drive, and its tendency to creep allows you to carry out almost all your low speed manoeuvring by just releasing and pressing the brake pedal.

If you put a single clutch semi-auto car in gear and release the brake, nothing will happen. That's because the car has, in effect, pressed the clutch, put the car into gear, and is waiting, clutch down, for your next input. The car requires you to actually press the accelerator and apply some revs before it will release the clutch and start to move.

This is another area where you need to demonstrate some mechanical sympathy, and not quite in the way you might think. If you apply a small amount of throttle, the clutch will be released gradually and the car will slip the clutch for you. This is fine on the odd occasion that you're doing some parking or manoeuvring, but if you set off from stationary like that every time, again, you'll quickly wear out the friction plates of your clutch and face a large bill.

I find that it's actually more mechanically sympathetic to set off with a little more throttle, so that the car almost immediately fully engages the clutch, rather than slipping it. I'm not saying you should set off with full-bore acceleration every time, but rather with a positive press of the accelerator, as opposed to feathering the pedal.

Most semi-auto cars have some form of "launch control" system built into their software. In the M3, I think it's called "race start" or something similar. It requires the driver to push and hold the gear lever forward, which holds the clutch down, and then apply 4,000 to 5,000 revs with their right foot. Releasing the gear lever effectively "sidesteps" the clutch and the car takes off like a rocket.

Now, don't get me wrong - it's an effective system, and it's great for impressing/frightening passengers, but it feels very rough on the whole transmission and in an RWD car, it can kick the rear-end sideways on all but the driest, best-quality tarmac. Other than trying it out a few times, I don't use it on the road, and I don't recommend it for anywhere other than the track.

So the best advice I can give you when setting off in a semi-auto car is to remember that it's a manual gearbox with a proper clutch, and to drive it like that.

Changing up

I've discussed the merits of smooth gear-changes in a previous chapter, so I won't flog that dead horse any more, but new users of semi-auto gearboxes (myself included), find that the quality of gear-change is a little poor. I suspect (as was the case with me) that that's because they don't drive it like a manual, and expect the cars elastictrickery to sort it all out for them.

I'll refer you back to the advice I gave before - drive it like a manual.

If you don't adjust your throttle position during an up-change, then the engine speed won't match the road speed for the next gear, and there will be an inevitable jerk when the clutch is released and the engine speed is brought back down through the transmission.

So, the trick for up-changes is to release the throttle a bit during the gear-change. It doesn't have to be much, but allowing the revs to drop slightly during the up-change nicely matches engine speed to road speed, and eliminates almost all the jerkiness from the change.

This is obviously easier with slower gear-changes than it is with quicker ones. My SMG 'box was an early one and only had one speed of gear-change, which was quite slow. It suited my driving style, and allows me to change nice and smoothly - almost seamlessly. Newer SMG set-ups, together with other manufacturer's systems allow the driver to choose the gear-change speed.

In those cars, I'd recommend perfecting your changes in a lower-speed setting, before turning the gear-change speed up. In the fastest settings, I think you'll always lose some smoothness, and these are best suited for track use, or spirited drives on your own.

The lift on upshift is obviously driver choice - I prefer a smoother change, but keeping the throttle pressed throughout a gear-change can feel more sporting. Some people prefer that kick in the back that comes with the up-shift.

There are some benefits to smoothing out the gear-change though, particularly in road driving. The weight balance of the car is moved around more progressively during a smooth gear-change, which has obvious positive implications for the overall balance of the car. If you ever take a gear whilst cornering, smoothness is also essential to keep the car settled in a corner.

Changing Down

Down-changes in semi-auto cars are much easier to perfect, as the car's software usually incorporates a system which raises engine revs - "blips the throttle" on down-change. The SMG system is very good, and I've heard open-exhausted Ferrari 360 CSs running at Fiorano, and they sound like they match the revs on down-change seamlessly.

One aspect which will be alien to the more traditional advanced drivers is that semi-auto cars - particularly those with paddle gear-changes – make it much easier for the driver to change gear whilst braking.

One of the main reasons that Roadcraft recommends separation of braking and gear-changing is that it allows the driver to keep both hands on the wheel whilst braking. Paddle-shift setups obviously allow the gear-changes without removing the hands from the wheel.

Despite that, though, I drove my M3 *almost* to the Roadcraft system, in that I left my gear-changes to the end of the braking period, as I'm still a big believer in separation for all the reasons outlined in the previous chapter.

Automatic Mode

Apparently these cars have a fully automatic mode.

I've never tried it.

(I have, of course, but I never liked it. Just remember, even in automatic mode, to drive it like a manual when setting off).

18

Dual Clutch Semi-Automatic Gearboxes

YOUTUBE LINK - **DOUBLE CLUTCH TRANSMISSIONS:**

https://youtu.be/IUdZoUxwGiI

Let's bring this book more up-to date with a chapter on dual-clutch semi-automatic gearboxes, shall we?

With a few small differences, the previous chapter was written around 10 years ago when single-clutch semi-auto transmissions were used in a small variety of high performance cars and dual-clutch transmissions were quite new technology.

In the 2020's, single-clutch semi automatic gearboxes have been and gone, and most manufacturers now fit dual-clutch systems. Some examples are Porsche's PDK gearbox (Porsche Doppelkupplungsgetriebe), VW/Audi's DSG gearbox (Direktschaltgetrieb) and BMW's M DCT transmission (M Double-Clutch). These all sound very complicated, but work in almost exactly the same way as each other.

Although originally designed for high-performance cars, some manufacturers, especially VW/Audi, fit their dual-clutch transmissions across their entire range.

So, apart from the obvious point that these gearboxes have two clutches, what is the difference between these transmissions and single-clutch transmissions?

Firstly, it's worth noting that most single-clutch transmissions are simply modified versions of the original manual gearbox. So closely related are they, in fact, that it's relatively easy to convert a single-clutch semi-auto gearbox into a full manual gearbox. The internals are all the same, the only difference being the automatic operation of the clutch & gear selection. When I said "drive them like a manual", I was pretty close to the truth!

Dual-clutch transmissions, on the other hand, are designed from the ground up to be a stand-alone type of gearbox. It would be pretty much impossible to convert one to a manual, because the clutches operate in a very different way to that in a manual or single clutch semi-auto transmission.

A dual-clutch gearbox is almost two gearboxes in one. One clutch controls the odd-numbered gears (1st, 3rd, 5th etc), whilst the other clutch controls the even numbered gears. The gearbox is designed in such a way that the gears are permanently engaged via what is known as a two-part transmission shaft. Because the gears are permanently engaged, when the gearbox changes from one gear to another, there is effectively no delay, and no pause in drive from the engine to the wheels as the car changes gear.

Gear changes in a dual-clutch car are computer-controlled, and the only delay in the gear change is the movement from one clutch being engaged, to the other clutch being engaged. In fact, the gearbox isn't really changing gear - it's just selecting which gear to take drive from & engaging it via the appropriate clutch.

One other thing to note is that the clutches in dual-clutch transmissions are usually "wet" clutches. In a similar way to most motorbikes, the clutches run in a bath of oil, which helps with efficiency & reduces wear rate. It is still very important to remember though, that they are still a mechanical clutch and can still wear out, so as with single-clutch transmissions, it's best to avoid holding the car on the gas pedal on a hill & to avoid creeping along at very slow speeds in traffic. Don't treat it like a traditional auto, or it's cost you a fortune in new clutches!

From the driver's perspective, these cars offer two fundamental ways of driving - automatic & manual. Let's take a look at both of them.

Automatic Mode

In the previous chapter, in a tongue-in-cheek fashion, I suggested that full auto modes in single-clutch semi-autos were terrible.

They were.

I've never driven a single-clutch car which didn't lurch about & give horribly-times and rough gear changes in full auto mode. In all honesty, they were old technology & were much better suited to drivers who took control & drove them in manual mode. That way it was easy to smooth out the gear changes & anticipate when the car was going to change gear.

Dual-clutch transmissions, on the other hand, are much *much* better in full auto mode.

My current car is now a BMW M2 Competition, with BMW's M-DCT dual-clutch transmission fitted. In that car, if I'm bimbling around, or on the commute, or just doing the sort of everyday normal driving that we all do most of the time, I use the car in automatic. It's smooth, easy to use, consistent and efficient and the car effectively glides around effortlessly.

As I've mentioned previously, it's important to remember that the car has mechanical clutches, so I don't hold it on the gas pedal on inclines or in traffic & I try to set off from stationary in a positive manner, to minimise clutch-slip, but other than that, the auto mode is excellent and works in very much the same way as a traditional automatic gearbox - including kick-down, sports modes etc.

Manual Mode

If, on the other hand, I'm out for a drive for my own enjoyment, or looking to make greater progress & I want more control over the car & the gearbox, I'll put it into manual mode & change gear myself.

In the M2, you can change gear either using the gear selector (forward to change down, backwards to change up - other cars are different in this respect, but it feels right to me!), or using the paddles behind the steering wheel - pull the left paddle to change down and the right paddle to change up.

Manual mode gives me really quick, snappy gear changes which are perfectly rev-matched by the car's software and which do not require a lift from the gas pedal when changing up. Gears in these gearboxes are selected sequentially. So there is no neutral phase between gears, but it is necessary to change up & down the box by going through every gear. The software does effectively skip gears if you pull one of the paddles several times in quick succession, but at the same time, it will not allow you to select a gear which is too low & which might risk engine damage through over-revving.

When changing down, the rev-matching allows braking and gear changing to be overlapped, but my preference is to brake first, and remove most of the required speed on the brakes, before changing down to the appropriate lower gear.

In some respects, this is very similar to the approach taken on motorbikes, where application of the system of motorcycle control allows overlap towards the end of the speed, or braking phase.

I suppose I've tried to keep most of the information I share with you as factual and objective as possible, but it is worth noting that, in a purely subjective way, I think double clutch transmissions are excellent pieces of kit & really fun to use when you're pressing on!

In no way, however, do they make you feel like an F1 driver.

None at all.

Honestly.

19

Electric cars

YouTube link - Advanced Driving in a Tesla Model S 90D - Full Electric Car:

https://youtu.be/SPhbZ33eU-I

Electric cars are the future aren't they?

Well, no, actually they're not. They're the present. They're here now, in the present day and you can buy a full electric car from almost all the major car manufacturers these days. You can buy economy city cars, SUVs, family hatchbacks and full-on supercars, all powered by batteries & electric motors, without an exhaust pipe, petrol cap or spark plug to be seen anywhere.

You might be a full-blown petrolhead & love the sound & smell of a V8, but there is no denying the onslaught of electric cars is well underway and that at some point in the not-too-distant future, you will no longer be able to buy a car with any kind of internal combustion engine. The days of petrol & diesel cars are numbered.

Is this a bad thing? I don't think so - it's progress, it's better for the environment & car manufacturers can still make electric cars which are fun to drive, so for us enthusiasts, there is probably a lot to look forward to.

I'm writing this in 2020 and the charging infrastructure definitely isn't currently where it needs to be in the UK, but that will change, and it won't be that long before battery range has been increased, the cost of electric vehicles has come down & we're all wondering what the fuss was all about.

But how should you *drive* an electric car? What is the secret to getting them down the road in a safe, efficient, progressive & smooth way?

Stay with me for the rest of this chapter & I'll tell you. First of all though, here's a really important thing you should know about electric cars.

They're just cars

By which I mean that, other than the motor & transmission operating in a slightly different way, every electric car you can buy is just that - a car. They don't hover above the ground on anti-gravity, they don't materialise magically out of thin air and they don't dive underwater. In other words, electric cars are not the thing of science fiction.

They have doors through which you get into them, controls like steering wheels & pedals just like other cars, suspension & brakes which are no different to anything else and wheels & tyres which you could swap with a normal car without noticing any difference.

Obviously, manufacturers want to make these cars attractive to customers, so they market them on the basis that they're "high tech". They add fancy coloured LED interior lights, multiple LCD computer screens, fancy graphics & seamless integration with your mobile phone to make you feel like the car is some fantastic piece of future-tech. But it's not really - it's still just a car, and it needs to be driven like any other car.

The first thing you'll notice when you get into an electric car for the first time is that there is no starting procedure. The car is either "on" or "off". You switch it on by unlocking it with your key (which isn't really a key these days, but you know what I mean), get into it and it'll be ready to go.

The Controls

The controls will be very familiar - electric cars don't have joysticks or gesture-controlled steering or holographic mirrors. They are fitted with a steering wheel, two pedals and a drive selector, very much like a traditional automatic car. So, just like a normal automatic car, it is very important that you do everything from the brake pedal. When you first get into the drivers seat of an electric car, put your foot on the brake pedal and leave it there till you're ready to drive off.

There will be no need to start the engine. The car is "on", and all you need to do is select the drive mode & set off.

Some electric cars will creep off the brake pedal like traditional automatics and some (most) will not. So once you've selected drive for the first time, gently release the brake & see if the car creeps. If it does not, squeeze the accelerator pedal gently to move off.

Once you're on the move, on the whole, the car will feel like any other - it will go & stop & steer just like any other car, but with a couple of differences which will stand out at first.

The first thing you'll notice is that the car is pretty much silent. The motors aren't completely silent, but with only one moving part and no combustion, electric motors make no more than a slight whining noise. A bit like Piers Morgan, but less irritating.

The second thing you'll probably notice is that electric cars don't really have a transmission as such. The motors in electric cars are effectively connected directly to the wheels (For the engineers amongst you, I know it's not quite that simple, but go with me on this). They do not change up and down through the gears like a manual or automatic car because they don't have any gears. Or they have one gear, depending on your point of view.

And the nature of how the wheels are driven is what makes electric cars so quick under acceleration. Electric motors can produce maximum torque at pretty much any speed, so from stationary, they will instantly give maximum torque; on the move at any speed, they will also give maximum torque, so an electric car always feels "on the boil".

There is no need to rev the engine and wait for it to reach its most efficient rev-band, no need to wait for the turbo to build up boost and no need to use the gears to make sure you keep the engine in the sweet spot. An electric motor is always in the sweet spot and with no transmission or clutch or torque converter, it's ready to give maximum acceleration in any situation, with pretty much no effort from the driver.

Drive 'em like a sewing machine

The final and most noticeable difference you'll notice the first time you drive an electric car is that you can pretty much - 99% of the time - drive them with one pedal.

My old Mum used to have an ancient sewing machine with a pedal switch on a wire that made it speed up & slow down. Just the one pedal - no brakes. Driving an electric car is very similar to using my Mum's old sewing machine.

Not that I ever did use it…

Can I get a reeeee-gen?

The accelerator, of course, when pressed will make the car accelerate, but lifting off the accelerator will put the motors into regeneration or "regen" mode, where they effectively work in reverse and become generators, using the momentum of the car to put some charge back into the batteries when the accelerator is lifted.

Most electric cars allow you to choose different levels of regen, but the effect is very similar to applying the brakes. They will actually operate the brake lights above a certain level of regen even though the car isn't actually slowing on the brakes.

This regen facility effectively gives you a hugely enhanced ability to operate the car using acceleration sense almost all the time - the brakes generally are only needed when coming to a complete stop, or in an emergency.

One of the really surprising things about this kind of car is that most people become familiar with them almost straight away. Driving the car using just the accelerator, silently whizzing away from traffic lights & maximising the regen become second-nature in less than an hour.

The acceleration can be addictive as well. I borrowed a Tesla Model S for a weekend a couple of years ago and I honestly never got tired of its instant, relentless and effortless acceleration. I didn't really warm to the car if I'm being honest - it wasn't very engaging to drive and the tech didn't really appeal to me, but I can see why they are so popular.

Downsides?

So what are the downsides? Well, the charging infrastructure issues and range anxiety are well documented elsewhere, so I'll leave those to the proper motoring journalists, but the thing you must remember above everything else is that electric cars - or to be more specific, their huge batteries - are very heavy. The Tesla Model S weighs 2 1/4 tonnes, about the same as a full-fat Range Rover, and even though it doesn't initially drive like a heavy car, that weight becomes apparent when you start pressing on. The car starts to develop secondary movements on its suspension & it doesn't react well to mid-corner bumps, which can be a little disconcerting.

It's also worth noting that, unlike internal combustion engined cars, electric cars are most efficient when they're being driven in a continuous start/stop environment. On a long motorway run (when normal cars are at their most efficient), electric cars get very little chance to regen because the driver is continually holding the accelerator pedal down, so the batteries don't get topped up. Around town, however, the car is constantly accelerating & decelerating, putting juice back into the batteries every time it slows down & actually increasing the battery range as it does so.

Electric cars and advanced driving

"That's all well and good Reg, but I want to do my advanced driving test in my Tesla. What do I need to know?"

Good question. In simple terms, the only real difference when it comes to the system of car control is that these cars don't have a transmission, and so there is no gear phase. Here's that schematic of the system of car control for internal combustion-engined cars again (because I haven't shown it for at least a dozen pages):

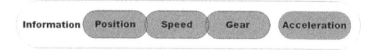

And here - thanks to my extremely competent photoshop skills - is the system of car control for electric cars:

The sharp-eyed amongst you will see that I've subtly removed the "gear" phase. Because there isn't one in an electric car.

Other than that, the application of system is exactly the same in a battery powered car as it is in a petrol or diesel-powered one.

As is pretty much everything else. As I mentioned before, they are still just cars like every other car on the road and need the same approach I've described elsewhere in this book when it comes to steering, braking, accelerating, cornering, overtaking, approaching hazards and everything else.

It is still worth including a little pause between the speed phase and the acceleration phase, just to let the car settle after slowing down, before you start to accelerate, but don't think of this as a phase - just think of it as a slight delay - 1/2 a second to a second. Remember these are heavy cars and that weight is still moving around when you operate the controls, so it's much better to smoothly stir the weight around the car, rather than chucking it around with gay abandon.

Introduce the controls - accelerator, brakes & steering - *taper* your inputs - don't surprise the car with a sudden demand for tyre grip that it won't be able to deal with.

If you get a chance - go and try an electric car. You'll be pleasantly surprised how easy they are to drive & impressed by the performance.

I'm just not quite ready for one yet...

20

OVERTAKING

YOUTUBE LINKS - **OVERTAKING**:

https://youtu.be/SjFWKVYfkpE

Scottish Overtakes:

https://youtu.be/pp4rzmCQAgM

More Scottish Overtakes:

https://youtu.be/NLB_C7HgG3Q

If there is one skill that is misunderstood, badly practised and which frightens and intimidates drivers more than anything else, it's overtaking.

This doesn't have to be the case - there's no big mystery to overtaking, and when it's carried out correctly, it's no more dangerous than any other manoeuvre that we carry out whilst driving. For some reason, however, the general motoring public (bless 'em) seem to view overtaking as a potentially disastrous move only carried out by idiotic johnny-boy-racers.

You only have to see the adverse reactions I sometimes get from other drivers when I've carried out perfectly safe overtakes, to realise how many people have an unnecessary aversion to overtaking.

This "overtakaphobia" seems to be a particularly English problem too. I've driven in France, Italy, and extensively in Scotland where

I've found the locals far more inclined to assist you in overtaking by moving nearside or giving a helpful indicator when it's safe to go.

I'm of the opinion that this particular phobia stems from two sources - the unnecessarily over-pressed "speed kills" message, and the fact that no-one is ever taught how to overtake properly (unless they take further driver training, and unfortunately, that's only a *very* small percentage of drivers at the moment).

Now, I can't do much about the first point, other than to say that excessive speed is only a small factor in accident causes, particularly when compared with driver error, but I'm afraid I'm powerless to change the government's stance on speeding, so I can't help there.

What I *can* do, however, is give you a few pointers on how to overtake safely and efficiently, with maximum control and minimum fuss. So here goes...

The Following Position

By which I mean a nice, safe following position from the vehicle in front – about 2 seconds if it's a car in front.

The following position is a vital element in safe overtaking, and it's where the majority of overtakes start from. There are two main reasons for this - it's far enough *back* to give you a good view of the road ahead, and it's far enough *forward* to allow you to quickly move into the overtake if it's on.

If you sit two seconds behind the car in front (slightly more if it's a larger vehicle), then it won't be filling too much of your field of vision - you'll still have a reasonably good view of the road in front of that car. If you move your car sideways at the appropriate times, you can vastly improve your view of the road ahead, but the key is knowing when and where to move your car.

How many times have you seen drivers looking for an overtake by moving their head to the right to improve their view? In most cars, you can only really move your head by a maximum of about a foot, so the improvement in view by moving a foot to the right is fairly minuscule.

It's much better to move the *whole car,* as the distance you can potentially move the car sideways is much greater and so, subsequently, is the improvement in your view.

So, where should you be moving to? That depends entirely on what the road is doing.

Let's start with a straight piece of road, as that's the easiest. Move your car towards the centre line whilst in your following position, and look into the distance. If it's safe to do so, you can then move your car across the centre-lines, over towards the offside of the road.

This offside move is very alien to some people, but believe me, it's by far the best way to see if the road ahead is clear. The amount of sideways movement can vary from having your offside wheels on the white line, to straddling the white line, to moving completely over to the offside of the road, dependent on the available view.

Don't get sucked into the old "right and wrong side of the road" stuff - unless white lines dictate otherwise, it's perfectly acceptable to use the full width of the road if it's safe to do so. You pay your road tax don't you? Well, get your monies worth & use all of it – not just half of it!

The most common mistake people make when moving offside for a look is this...

They look with their right foot.

To expand on that, people confuse the move offside with the start of an overtake, and, even if they *know* that they're just trying to improve their view, they accompany the offside move with a slight inadvertent squeeze on the accelerator.

They look with their right foot.

This is a problem if the overtake isn't on, because when you move back to the nearside, the inevitable result of looking with your right foot is that you close up your following position to less than 2 seconds. Do this several times, and without realising it, you can end up *very* intimately involved with the car in front, if you get my meaning.

So the sideways move should be just that - a *sideways* move for a look, and not accompanied with a *forwards* move.

On a left hand bend, the series of moves required to obtain the optimum view start with a move to the nearside to obtain a view of the bend down the left-hand side of the car in front.

Once you've got that nearside view, it can be improved as you get closer to the corner, by moving the car offside. There's no prescriptive distance that you should move offside - just move enough to improve that view down the left-hand side of the car, without going so far that you end up blocking it.

I've just read that back, and it sounds complicated, so I'll try to simplify it...

Approaching the corner, move nearside and look nearside. As you get into the corner, move *offside,* but keep looking nearside.

There - that's better!

As you round the bend, you'll get a brief view of the road ahead as it straightens up, and if it appears clear, this view can then be confirmed with a move further offside, the outcome of which will finalise your decision as to whether to go or not.

For right-hand bends, the process is to initially move offside on the approach to the bend, and then, on entering the bend, to move as far nearside as it's safe to go. This move nearside should be accompanied with a slight closing of the following position to about 1 1/2 seconds (the only time I advocate getting closer than 2 seconds), and you should then obtain a good view down the offside of the car in front.

As you round the bend, from this position, you'll obtain a good, early view of the road as the bend straightens, and if it's safe, you should be able to get out into the overtake nice and early - often whilst still negotiating the bend.

Again, that reads quite complicated, so I'll simplify it...

Approaching the corner, move offside and look offside, and then on entering the corner, move nearside, *close up,* and look offside.

Don't forget, though, that if the overtake *isn't* on from the right-hander, you should drop back to a 2-second following position.

So, that's how to move your car around from the following position to obtain a good view, but what else is there to consider?

Other considerations

This list could go on and on, and I'm in no doubt that I'll miss some things, but here goes...

Are there any junctions or entrances ahead?

If there are, the car you're intending to overtake could possibly turn right, or something could emerge from the junction and come towards you.

If you can get your overtake in well before you get to the junction, then fine, but if not, you should wait until you can see that nothing is going to emerge, and you're happy that the car in front isn't going to turn right.

Is there a faster moving vehicle behind that could overtake you?

Motorcyclists are notorious for this, as nothing's faster than their Tamajaki 900RSR is it?

Your sideways movement looking for a view should be a good visual clue that you're looking for an overtake, but motorcyclists aren't usually too bothered about the complexities of overtaking - breath in and wind it on is the normal motorcyclist's overtaking technique, so us drivers have to compensate for them.

A mirror-check is a vital part of the overall planning process for an overtake. Don't go if you're about to be overtaken yourself.

And with that in mind...

Is the vehicle you're looking to overtake also looking to overtake?

Do the movements of the vehicle in front suggest they're also looking for the opportunity to go?

An un-trained driver will follow the next vehicle quite closely, and their decision to overtake will generally be made much later than a more advanced driver. They usually accompany this with an inability to check their mirrors before overtaking, which means that whilst you may have decided that it's safe to go, and started overtaking, their later decision making could mean that they move out and accelerate just as you're passing them, which isn't good.

Trust me - it's *really* not good.

What is the performance potential of your car?

This may be an obvious one, but it's always something to consider. My plans for overtaking in an M3 differ considerably from my plans for overtaking in an MX-5. It's actually a good exercise to learn how to overtake in a slow car, as the planning required for overtaking is much more intense than if you drive a fast car.

Have I got somewhere to land?

Landing space is essential, as you shouldn't be forcing other cars to slow down or alter their position just to allow you to overtake. If the car in front is a tailgater, but they're not actually overtaking, then your plan should always be to overtake both vehicles rather than to take one, and force in between them.

If you're overtaking in a line of vehicles, it's much nicer to use acceleration sense to slot into your chosen gap than to over-accelerate and then come in under braking.

How much space you need is mainly dependent on how fast your car is. I'm not going to commit myself to any set distances - as with a lot of aspects of driving, that distance can be an ever-changing thing, dependent on how large a vehicle you're overtaking, how good the road surface is, what the weather conditions are, etc., etc.

But the biggest deciding factor is definitely the performance of your car.

I'll leave the judgement of the distance up to you.

Is there a vehicle that you can't see which is currently out of view but travelling towards you?

I'll use motorcyclists as an example for this one too, as they're the fastestthingontheroad (tm). Imagine that there's a motorcyclist travelling at full chat towards you, but currently out of view. Can you complete your overtake before coming into conflict with them?

If you can, then all well and good, but if you can't, then wait. This is another example of when a good imagination is important to an advanced driver.

When planning an overtake, I much prefer to have an on-coming vehicle in sight, because you can assess your closing speed against something real, rather than trying to assess against something which may or may not come into view at an unspecified speed.

This method of planning is somewhat arse-about-face to less experienced drivers, who prefer, on the whole, to have no oncoming vehicles in view before overtaking.

Have you selected the correct gear?

Gear selection is critical when overtaking. You need a gear which will give you the correct degree of acceleration when you start to go, but not one which is so low that you'll need an up-change halfway through the overtake. I prefer to have both my hands on the wheel whilst overtaking, thank you very much.

That correct gear selection should also be considered when you're in the following position. The entry to corners should be accompanied by a change to a flexible gear in anticipation of an overtaking opportunity. If it turns out the overtake *isn't* on, then you should change back up again and wait for the next one.

Do I have an alternative plan?

If things go badly wrong, what are you going to do? Can you brake and get back in behind the vehicle? Is there somewhere else you can go to avoid a collision? Did you put clean underpants on this morning?

As I said, this isn't an exhaustive list - take each overtake as it comes and consider every possible scenario as part of your planned approach.

Completing the overtake

In my mind, once you've weighed everything up and decided to go, that's it - the overtake is done and dusted, and mentally you should be moving on to the next hazard. Physically, you'll be accelerating and completing the overtake, but mentally you should be *waaay* ahead of that and well into the planning stage for your next manoeuvre, whether it be another overtake, a corner, a roundabout or any one of the other million things we have to deal with as drivers.

The overtake should be completed with a minimum of fuss, and should be started with a move offside, **which should not be accompanied by any acceleration.** This is very important, as you shouldn't be getting any closer to the vehicle in front than 2 seconds (or 1 1/2 on a right-hand bend). Once you're out, then you should accelerate to pass the vehicle.

You should aim to come back nearside leaving at least a 2 second gap between the overtaken vehicle and yourself. I find that the easiest way to get this right is to wait until you have a full view of the overtaken vehicle in your *centre* mirror before moving back to the nearside.

Of course, we know that information changes all the time, and once you're out on the overtake; you might decide that there is another one on. Mentally assess each overtake individually, taking account of all the points above, and if it's on, stay out and continue to overtake. My record was a memorable 18-vehicle overtake on a single-carriageway A road, carried out in perfect safety by one of my students.

Rolling Overtake

There is another method of overtaking which I call a "rolling overtake".

These are performed in a situation where you have "plus speed" on the vehicle you're planning to overtake, and the overtake is carried out in one move, without first settling into a following position.

They don't come up very often, and you have to be very sure of your observations and your plan before committing yourself to one, but when performed correctly, a rolling overtake can be a very satisfying move.

Remain calm and level-headed when planning overtakes and never base any of your decisions on anger or aggression, or on the fact that you're late - this will affect your ability to make a rational decision and could introduce the one thing that you should always try to keep out of driving - an element of risk.

Don't Look Too Hard For the Overtakes

Don't look too hard for overtakes. If you sit in the correct position, in the right gear and look in the right place, overtakes will *present* themselves to you. All you have to do is accept the invitation

The "don't look too hard for overtakes" is a line I used to calm students preparing for test. The point being that if you look too hard for overtakes, your following position will suffer, you'll lose smoothness, and your overall awareness of what's happening all around is reduced. That's because a student on test often makes the mistake of thinking an examiner is just looking for a maximum number of overtakes.

What they're actually looking for is a progressive mind-set combined with restraint. A student can earn as many points by positioning correctly for an overtake and not taking it (for the right reasons, of course) as they can for actually getting the overtake.

This translates across to everyday driving quite nicely when you're starting to get cheesed off behind a slower vehicle. If you look too hard for the overtake, you can end up getting too close, driving roughly, losing awareness etc.

However, if you just concentrate on positioning for the view correctly, looking in the right places, and changing to a flexible overtaking gear when you anticipate that an overtake *might* be on, then you'll stay more relaxed, your overall driving won't suffer, and overtakes will, quite literally, present themselves to you. The actual overtake is the easy bit - it's the preparation and planning that takes up the most megabytes of a driver's RAM.

21

Cornering Part 1 – Assessing the Bend Using the Limit Point

YOUTUBE LINKS - **CORNERING:**

https://youtu.be/nJgll4p9QJc

Limit Points:

https://youtu.be/OWD7SNU4eXs

I've decided to start by looking at something else that is considered a bit of a "black art" - assessing the severity of bends. There's not really any secret to it, but I've heard some ruddy complicated explanations in the past, so it's not surprising that some people think it involves voodoo.

I'll try to stick to my mantra of KISS - Keep It Simple, Stupid - and you'll probably find that, actually, it's quite straightforward and that you probably use a lot of these skills already.

The Limit Point (Sometimes Referred to as the Vanishing Point)

Let's deal with this little chestnut to start with, as it's the one that most people struggle to get their heads round. Have a look at this picture of a section of road - you can see a straight piece of road over a motorway bridge, followed by a left-hand bend in the distance:

Now, there's plenty to look at - it's obvious we're coming off a left-hand bend with double white lines, there are some NSL signs, the road goes over a bridge, there are some street lights on the offside, some rumble-strips which are, presumably for traffic travelling towards us, a change from double white to hazard lines, and, right in the distance, you can see the limit point for the left-hand bend.

What? Oh, sorry - I didn't explain - the limit point has been described to me as "The furthest point at which you have an uninterrupted view of the road surface", which sounds a little pompous, and "The point at which the nearside and offside verges seem to meet", which is a bit better, but the opposite verges of a road don't actually *meet*, do they? That'd be silly.

A better description would be "The furthest point you can see the road surface" - less pompous I think, and straight to the point. Straight to the limit point, in fact.

For the next few pictures, however, I've recruited an assistant in the form of the Finger of Destiny which will point out the limit point for you.

Anyway, here's the same picture again, with the limit point indicated:

As you can see, the limit point is *waaay* in the distance, but although the driver may be performing other actions at this point on the road, such as changing to a flexible gear, checking the mirror and preparing to accelerate, they'll be paying some attention to that limit point, as it will help them to determine the severity of the next bend, and assist them in mentally preparing a plan as to how to drive through the corner.

The thing to look for with a limit point is its position relative to you as you approach. If you seem to be getting closer to it as you approach the bend, then the bend will be quite tight. If it seems to be remaining a constant distance from you, as, for instance, a rainbow does as you move towards it, then the bend isn't getting any tighter. If the limit point seems to be going further away, then the bend is opening up and the road is straightening.

Let's recruit the Finger of Destiny's help again, and look at where the limit point is after we've moved a short distance up the road:

We've moved forwards onto the bridge now, the driver will be accelerating at this point, and their focus will be towards the corner. Look left from the bend, across the adjacent fields, to see if there is a view of the road, as this can assist in assessing how tight it is.

In this case, there isn't a view to the left, so we're relying on the limit point to show how tight it is. With help from the Finger of Destiny you can see that we appear to be getting closer to it.

Let's move a bit further forward:

We're halfway across the bridge now and we're still getting closer to the limit point. There are some other clues as to how tight the bend is though, and they're in the form of what you *can't* see, more than what you can see.

You can't see a triangle warning sign for the bend, you can't see a chevron board to the left, you can't see a change back to double white lines and you can't see a "SLOW" painted on the road. The fact that you can't see these things is an indicator that the bend won't be particularly tight.

One other thing - take notice how many lamp-posts you can see to the right in this picture, as it'll give you a guide to how far forward I'm moving, and what the limit point is doing. In the above picture, you can see four lamp-posts.

Let's move on again - Finger of Destiny, it's over to you:

From this one, you can see that I've moved forward by one lamp-post, and now the limit point has started moving forwards too. This is a critical point, as, when you're driving through this bend, the limit point is now acting like a rainbow and moving away at the same rate as we're driving towards it. As we're still a distance away from the bend, this means that it's going to be a quite open corner, so we're unlikely to have to lose much, if any speed to negotiate it.

On to the next one:

We've only moved forward another lamp-post, but things have changed quite dramatically on the limit-point front. So dramatically, in fact, that in that short distance, the limit point has shot off away from us, and no longer exists, so we've nothing for the Finger of Destiny to point at any more.

Look at where we are on the road - we're only just entering the bend, and yet the limit point has gone completely, and we can quite happily accelerate through the corner.

Obviously, it's very easy from that position to see that the corner is nice and open, but if you've paid attention to the limit point from when it first becomes visible, then you can work out how open or tight the bend is from *much* further back, which obviously helps you to make your all-important driving plans.

There are many more ways of assessing the severity of corners, and I'll look at some of them in the next chapter.

22

Cornering Part 2 – Assessing the Bend Without Using the Limit Point

If you were wondering where the road went in the previous photographs, wonder no more - a short straight, followed by a right hander:

Now, let's consider this next bend - as with the last one, it'd be fairly easy to assess using the limit point - I've got the Finger of Destiny to point it out again:

In this case, however, if you extend your observations a little bit - "look outside the box" a little, you'll pick up enough clues to allow you to assess this bend properly without having to use the limit point at all. The next picture is the same as above, but with the essential area circled:

ADVANCED & PERFORMANCE DRIVING

In the circle, you'll see the road continuing uphill to the right, and you can also see a car travelling towards us. This shows you, almost immediately, the angle of the upcoming corner. It allows you to plan your position on approach, to get your speed and gear correct for the corner, and to plan the line you'll take as you drive around it.

Let's move a bit closer to the bend:

Now, we're getting to a point where you'll be getting your speed and gear correct for the bend, and planning your line through it. Two potential hazards have come into view though - can you see them?

ADVANCED & PERFORMANCE DRIVING

There is an entrance to the left, right on the corner itself, which has a very limited view into it, and further up the road, there is a line of fencing which indicates a possible road off to the right. The presence of this road is confirmed by the small white car which is driving along it, towards our road.

Let's consider the entrance on the left first. Even without that entrance, if there are no on-coming vehicles, my plan would be to go offside through this corner - it gives you the benefit of making the radius of the turn as large as possible, so your car will remain as stable as possible through the corner.

Another advantage of going offside through the corner is that this road appears to have been built with crown camber (raised in the middle and lower towards the edges to aid drainage). Now, crown camber can be a disadvantage when negotiating right-hand bends, as the slope to the nearside can destabilise a car, forcing it out towards the nearside. If you take an offside position, however, the crown camber actually helps you through the bend, keeping the car more stable.

There would be a third major advantage from taking an offside position through this bend. Remembering that we should always keep a zone of relative safety around us when we're driving, a move offside would keep you away from the entrance, and away from any vehicles which could potentially emerge.

Clearly, the plan would be different with on-coming vehicles present, and in that case, you'd have to lose more speed for the corner to allow you to remain safely on the nearside of the road, albeit towards the centre-line, away from the entrance on the left.

As for the junction to the right further up the road - it shouldn't alter our plan for this corner - if the white car emerged and turned left towards us, it wouldn't be anywhere near the bend when we negotiate it, but it could have some implications. Approaching it after the bend, you should be wary of other vehicles emerging from or turning into the junction, and you could end up coming up behind the white car if it's turned right, so an overtake might now form part of your future plans.

As far as this single corner goes, however, it's not really too relevant, but it does show the benefit of an extended view.

As we get to the bend itself, it all becomes clear and the plan should fit into place nicely:

The muddy tyre marks coming out of the entrance on the left confirm that it's used regularly, so we're absolutely correct to move away from it. In the distance, you can *just* make out the white car which has turned left towards us, so we've got a nice clear run through the bend, and plenty of time to return to the nearside, from where we'll consider the next hazard.

Before I move on to cornering lines, it's important to make reference to how we actually use the information we've taken in whilst assessing the angle of the corner.

Assessing the limit point or using other methods to work out the angle of the corner allows us to decide how much speed we need to lose for each particular corner.

It may, for instance, need just a brief lift off the accelerator if it's a nice open bend. Tighter corner, however, may need a good, long press of the brakes to lose 10, 20, maybe 50 or 60mph to negotiate the corner safely.

The most important thing is that we get the car down to the right speed *early*, so that we've then enough time to come off the brakes and select an appropriate gear *before* turning the steering wheel.

What is an appropriate gear? In my view, it's a gear which will be low enough to give you nice, responsive acceleration through the corner, but high enough to take you all the way round the corner before running out of revs and requiring a higher gear.

So, get your speed correct, select the appropriate gear – it's now time to drive around the corner...

23

CORNERING PART 3 - PICKING THE RIGHT LINE

YOUTUBE LINK - **CORNERING LINES**:

https://youtu.be/4w5IjyNIFbE

So you've seen the corner in the distance, you've used your observation skills to assess the severity of the corner, you've positioned your car correctly on the approach, reduced your speed appropriately with the brakes, changed down to the correct gear…

What next?

It's just a case of turning the wheel and steering round the corner isn't it?

Well, in the simplest of terms, yes, it is, but this is an advanced and performance driving book and you'd be disappointed if I left it at that wouldn't you?

In fact, there's quite a lot more to think about – when to turn the wheel, how to plan your line through the corner, how to maintain vehicle balance with the throttle, when to press the accelerator, how to make best use of the roads camber, where to look, how to use your exit from one corner to best advantage when planning the next corner…

Like I said – there's a lot more to think about, so let's start with how to pick the best cornering line.

I'll use a nice, straightforward 90 degree corner as my example, but these principles can be used for any corner of any degree of tightness. So, let's look at our corner:

Like I said – a nice, straightforward 90 degree right-hand bend. Now, if this corner were on a racetrack, our choice of line would be simple – if you can use the full width of the road and you've no fear of anything coming the other way, the ideal line would start from the extreme left-hand side of the road, cut right over to the offside at the corner's apex, and then go back out to the extreme left-hand side of the road on the exit of the corner. This would allow us to use the minimum amount of steering by turning the car through the shallowest arc. Just like the grey line in the picture below:

As you can see, the grey line is a much wider arc than the corner itself, and would allow us to carry more speed whilst maintaining maximum balance. It would also give us the benefit of the crown camber if that's how the road is constructed.

If you've got a full, unobstructed view of the road on the approach to this corner and there are no other hazards, then the above line is perfectly acceptable. The white centre-lines are only hazard lines, so there is no legal requirement to stick to the nearside. There are no "right" and "wrong" sides of the road in the UK, so where circumstances allow, "offsiding" on right-hand bends is a good, advanced technique.

Having said all that, it's not often that offsiding will be appropriate – it's rare that you'll encounter the combination of a fully-sighted corner and no traffic which would allow you to take this line.

In most cases, our plan should be to keep mostly to the left of the white centre-line, and so the more obvious line would be as per the picture below:

In this case, our position on entry and exit is well over to the nearside, but within the more restricted available space, we've still taken a line which prescribes the widest possible arc.

So – that's that then. Simple.

Slow and late in – Quick and straight out

Come on – you should know me better than that by now! That line might be an ideal competition or racing line, but things are different on the road – we have many other pressing priorities than simply carrying maximum speed and balance through the corner. On the road, each corner is effectively new to us, we're constantly evaluating the angle, camber, road surface condition, view, oncoming traffic, preceding traffic and nearside & offside hazards whilst looking as far ahead as possible to start the same assessment on the *next* bend, and even, occasionally, the one after that.

So with all those additional considerations, our line in most corners needs to change slightly to allow us to also maximise our view around the corner. The principle is quite simple – you use your own positioning to slightly "re-prescribe" the arc of the corner so that, in most cases, every corner "opens".

Let me explain a bit further – some corners are designed with a constant arc, like the one in the picture above, whereas some corners "tighten" as you drive around them (the curve becomes tighter) and some corners "open" as you drive around them (the curve becomes less tight).

The corners which "open" are always easier to negotiate. If, for instance, you're using the limit point method to assess the tightness, you'll slow down to an appropriate speed for the entry of the corner, which is the tightest part and then as you turn in to the corner, it will start to become less and less tight and you can increase your acceleration through the corner, which keeps the car balanced and allows you to make nice, smooth progress.

The corners which "tighten" are less easy. On the approach, you'll be assessing your speed against the more open part of the corner, and if you're pressing on a bit, this will mean that, as the corner develops, your entry speed will turn out to be too high for the tighter part of the bend, so you'll need to lose more speed, which – in turn – unsettles the car, weights up the steering and forces you to wait much longer before you can apply some throttle and start to straighten the steering wheel. This is not a recipe for smooth, advanced driving.

The principle we'll apply to cornering lines on the road will mean that we'll try to turn every corner into an "opening" corner by using a slightly different line from the traditional "racing" line. It will feel a little odd at first, and it's not an easy technique to adapt to – particularly if you're an experienced driver – but the benefits will, with time, start to become clear.

The technique for a right-hand corner is to stay tight into the nearside for a bit longer than you normally would, before turning in to the corner with an initial turn which is slightly tighter than normal and aiming for an apex which is slightly later than you might normally aim for.

This "late turn in" will help to give you a better view of the corner as it develops and will allow you to see, at an earlier point, when the corner is starting to open up, so that you can start winding off the steering and start applying a firmer throttle. In very simple terms, it's just a development of the old adage "slow in, quick out". I call it **"slow and late in, quick and straight out."**

ADVANCED & PERFORMANCE DRIVING

For those visual learners amongst you, below is a picture of the line in white, with the traditional "racing" line in black for comparison:

As you can see, the initial turn is sharper, and will require a slightly lower speed on entry, but that sharper turn very quickly starts to open up, and you'll be straightening the car before you reach the apex and accelerating earlier out of the corner.

Going in slower really does allow you to exit faster!

So to summarise, for a right-hander, stay nearside for a little longer before making the initial turn. When you do turn in, turn a little sharper at first, aim for a later apex, and then accelerate out of the bend.

But what about a left-hander?

Well, the principle is exactly the same. In the UK and any other country which drives on the left, a left-hand bend will always be tighter then when travelling in the opposite direction.

But there is an advantage to left-hand bends. You've got much more room to adjust your position on the approach to a left-hander than you have on the approach to a right-hander. Let me explain a little further.

Approaching a right-hand bend, the best position is towards the nearside (left) side of the road. In reality, you're never that far from the nearside anyway, so a move to the nearside is usually only quite a small one – maybe a foot at most.

But when approaching a left-hand bend, the best position is towards the offside (right) of the road. So we've actually got much more space to play with on the approach – the full width of the road in fact. If it's safe, there is nothing wrong with taking a fully offside position on the approach to a left-hander. It will greatly improve your view on approach and help you to assess the tightness of the bend.

It's not usually safe or appropriate to stay offside right up to a corner though, so the advice is to take a position as far offside as is safe when you're a good distance away from a corner, but to move your position gradually back over the centre line as you get closer to the corner. If you use this gradual, diagonal approach to left-handers, you'll not be caught out by any oncoming traffic, and more importantly, you won't frighten the oncoming traffic!

Something like this:

ADVANCED & PERFORMANCE DRIVING

Your position on approach very much depends, of course, on traffic conditions, so if it's perfectly clear, the above position will be fine, but should be adjusted to take into account any oncoming traffic so you may be straddling the centre-line or sitting just to the left of the centre line on approach.

As you get up to the corner, use the principle of slow and late in – quick and straight out, to take a line something like this:

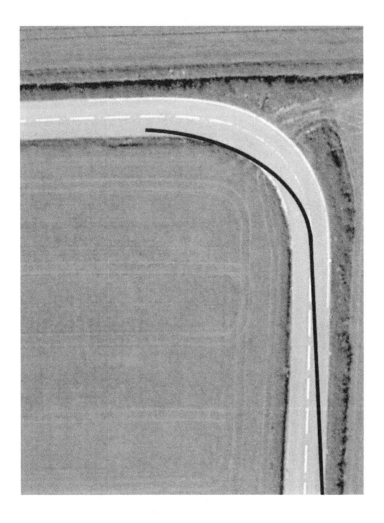

Now, you'll notice I've left out the final exit line – this is because the exit of left-handers – just as with the entry – allows you more choice, depending on traffic and other hazards.

If your space is limited on the exit, you can stay to the left of the centre line:

ADVANCED & PERFORMANCE DRIVING

Or if your view opens up to a nice, empty road, then take full advantage of it:

Now, it's fairly unusual just to have one single bend like this – our British roads are far more complex than that, so you should keep your observations as far ahead as possible to try to identify the next corner, and the one after that. The important thing to consider is that your exit from one corner should be adjusted to give you the most appropriate entry to the next corner. Just remember the key principle: ***Slow and late in – Quick and straight out.***

24

Cornering Part 4 - Controlling the Car Through the Corner

YOUTUBE LINK - **CORNERING BALANCE:**

https://youtu.be/NGJLNKQxZ98

In this chapter, I'll look at how you should operate the car's controls as you drive through the corner. I'll start by assuming you've done everything else – assessed the corner, brought the car down to the correct speed, selected the right gear, picked out your line – and you're now just at the point where you need to drive the car through the corner, following your chosen line.

Let's make this as simple as possible. There are only two main controls you'll need to operate.

1. The steering.
2. The accelerator.

In operating these controls, the key aim is to maintain vehicle balance – we want to accelerate out of the corner as quickly as possible whilst maintaining grip with the road surface. This involves balancing the two main forces which are competing for the tyres grip – turning the car and accelerating the car.

When you first turn the wheel, bear in mind the principles which I describe in the steering chapter – start the turn of the wheel slowly to "hint" to the car that you're about to start turning, and then when the car starts to turn and the suspension has "taken up the slack", you can increase the speed at which you apply the steering lock before slowing the application when you've applied the right amount of lock.

One thing to bear in mind is that a car's suspension isn't just designed to give a comfy ride or to keep the wheels attached to the car. Suspension – particularly rear suspension – is designed to help the car to negotiate corners as safely and efficiently as possible.

Using some very clever links and angles, engineers nowadays design rear suspension to include a small amount of "passive" rear-wheel steering, which means that when the car is cornering and the suspension is compressed by the cornering forces, the rear wheels will steer slightly and help the car through the corner.

It's very subtle, but has a very real effect, and to take full advantage of this effect, it's important that whenever you steer through a corner, you should accompany the steering with a press of the accelerator. Many people know that you should accelerate *out* of a corner, but most people don't know exactly *when* you should press the accelerator.

The answer to that question is very simple:

You should start to press the accelerator at *exactly* the same time that you start to turn the steering wheel.

ADVANCED & PERFORMANCE DRIVING

This might seem too early – if you've any track driving experience, it will definitely seem too early, as a good track driver may still be braking when they start turning the wheel – sometimes right up to the corners apex.

But, as I've said many times before, driving on the road is not track or competition driving, and on the road, we should have sorted our position, speed and gear *before* actually getting to the corner.

So, the instant you start to turn the wheel, you should balance the steering by pressing the accelerator. In a tight corner, you should only press it gently at first, to balance the car and make use of the passive rear-steering. As you approach the apex, and the corner starts to open, you can press the accelerator a little harder, and as you start to take the steering lock *off* and the road starts to open right up, you can press it harder and harder to match the straightening of the front wheels.

I used to tell students to imagine there was a piece of string connecting the steering wheel with the accelerator. As you turn the wheel – the accelerator is pressed – almost as though they are one single control which applies steering and accelerator simultaneously.

In a faster, more open corner, you can press the accelerator harder and fire the car through the corner with a good amount of firm acceleration. Trust me on this – it's one of the most satisfying feelings it's possible to obtain whilst holding a steering wheel! The key – as with tighter corners – is to start pressing the accelerator as soon as you start to turn the wheel – *immediately* when you start to turn the wheel.

The slowest point in a corner should be the point where you turn in. From there, pressing the accelerator will gradually build up speed whilst settling the car on to its rear suspension, taking full advantage of the passive rear-steer and giving you maximum steering effect.

Try it next time you're out for a drive. Take a bit more speed off for the corners, and accelerate earlier – you'll be surprised how much better your car will feel through the bends!

25

Cornering Part 5 - Linking Corners

As I hope I've shown in the last couple of sections, assessing the severity of bends is reasonably straightforward, but does take some practise, particularly if you're relying on the limit point. Over time, however, you should be able to get to a stage where you can consistently assess corners for severity, which obviously greatly assists in your ability to formulate driving plans.

It couldn't just be that simple though, could it? A good driver should be like a good snooker player - whilst they're playing one shot, they're planning the next one, and thinking two or even three shots in front of that one. So if you've reached the stage where you can consistently assess individual corners, the next stage on the road to driving greatness (it's a *very* long and *very* winding road, trust me), is to start thinking beyond the corner that you're currently dealing with, and start thinking about the next one, and the one after that.

You see, getting one corner correct is all well and good, but if you're on a road with a series of corners, which would be pretty much every single carriageway road in the UK, then your position as you exit one corner greatly influences your position into the next one, and as you're probably aware, your position on the approach to a corner is vitally important in terms of improving your view, maximising the radius of the turn, and keeping the car stable and well-balanced.

I'm again going to use a series of photographs - quite a long series this time - to demonstrate what I'm on about. It's not a particularly fast set of bends, but they are varied, and I'd use different methods to asses each corner. It's not so much how we'd take these corners that I want to look at - I'll cover that later - it's more about where you should be looking as you're driving along, and what your thought process should be as the view of the road changes with our progress.

Here's the first view:

As far as assessing the first couple of bends, our work is pretty much done for us - we've got a very good view of the left and right handers, with just one small zone of invisibility to the nearside which we could easily deal with by moving offside slightly.

But we're moving on a bit from just looking at the next bend, and so our attention should, in this case, be on the third corner - the left-hander which goes out of sight at the top of the rise. Just to help out, I've used the Finger of Destiny again, just this once, to point out the limit point for that corner:

I'll not use Finger of Destiny again, as I'm assuming you've already read and understood the chapter on limit points, and you'll know what I mean when I refer to it.

So, in this case, we'd move offside a little to improve the view to the nearside, but our attention is already on the limit point for the left-hander and what its position is in relation to us as we approach it. Let's move forward a bit:

So, the view has opened up nicely, we can easily plan for the left and right handers (I'd be looking to move offside to straighten the bends, but with a cautious eye out for on-coming vehicles), and our attention is mainly focused on the next left-hander.

As you can see, despite moving forwards, the limit point hasn't moved, so we should already be thinking that it's a tighter corner than the other two.

As we move further forward, you can see that we've actually lost some of the view we had, behind the banking on the right. It's not really a problem, as we've already looked there, but if you go back to our limit point, it's still not moving. One little thing to note - there's a finger-post sign indicating an entrance or footpath off to the right. It's difficult to see from here, but it's indicating an area which has now gone out of view, so it's something I'd keep half an eye on. It'll become clearer in the next picture:

There's the finger-post, and we still can't quite see what it's pointing at (although the view would obviously be better in real life).

The limit point for the left hander still hasn't moved though, has it?

At this point, however, the limit point has started to move away from us, so we've potentially reached the point where we know roughly how tight the bend is. We'll keep an eye on the limit point as we turn in to the bend, but let's keep our observations in the distance too - remember to look outside the box a bit, and not just concentrate on the limit point.

Oh, and we can now see the little entrance to the right, and give it a quick visual check.

Back to the left hander:

Yes - I'm happier with this one now - as we enter the bend, the limit point is going away from us at a consistent rate, so we've assessed it correctly. Keep looking elsewhere though - I want to know what's next, and there are no clues yet…

Still no clues as to what's next, but that limit point is getting further away now, so the bend is opening up…

Yup - still opening up, but look at the hedge - it's on the offside of the road, so the corner continues for a bit further yet...

Still in the corner, but a hint of straightening from the hedge-line. Still no idea what's next though. Remember the safe stopping rule? It's vitally important here.

Right - this is where we can start planning again. We're still negotiating the left-hander, but in the distance we can see some easy-view railings, which you'll only ever see next to a corner or a junction. They're a little rusty here (they *should* be painted white), but they've a distinctive shape, and their name is a clue to their function - they allow a good view through them of on-coming vehicles.

If you're in any doubt, here's the same picture, with the railings highlighted:

So, we now know that, up ahead, is either a junction or a right-hander, but which one? It's impossible to tell from here, so let's move on a bit more…

Well, we can see that the road tightens considerably, and that the junction/corner is fairly tight, so we'd be slowing quite a bit going into here.

No other clues yet as to what's coming up though. Having said that, it would appear to be a neighbourhood watch area. Which is nice…

Right, now we've got it - the vital clue as to whether it's a junction or a right-hander. You have seen it, haven't you? Haven't you? Go on then - I'll show you...

Not easy to see, granted, but it's there nonetheless - a chevron board showing a bend to the right. I'd still be cautious about the hidden area behind the hedge on the left, mind, but we know that the road's going to the right…

Moving closer to the bend opens the view up to the right, so, as you should with any corner - if the road goes right, look right...

Looking off to the right will give you a nice early view of any oncoming vehicles or other hazards, and *may* give you a view of where the road is going next.

We can, of course, use the limit point at this stage, to assess the angle of the bend, but the railings are doing that job for us.

Although we can't see the road itself, they're giving us a very good idea of how sharp the bend is, which in effect, renders the limit point useless.

We'd have gone nearside by now, as that's the best position on approach to a left-hander, but we should also be conscious of the little entrance on the left that's just popped into view.

It's not caught us by surprise - we identified the possibility some distance back - but its existence has now been confirmed, and our move nearside should incorporate a zone of relative safety to deal with anything which may emerge from the left.

Looking right again at this point confirms the severity of the bend, and gives us a couple of other visual clues. There's another finger-post, which will be opposite another entrance or footpath, and we can see the end of the railings, which would indicate the end of that particular corner.

We can see a continuation of the fence-line, showing that the road goes straight, at least for as far as we can see from here…

We're just entering the bend at this point, and it's a good example of how an extended view can improve your ability to plan. From this point, we've a very limited view, and a driver who only looks in front of themselves would have absolutely no idea of how tight the bend is, or what's coming next.

Because we *have* looked outside the box though, we know exactly what's coming up, and we'd be driving into this corner with a little confidence about what's next…

Thinking in terms of the limit point, you'll see that it's now a consistent distance away from us, so we've "found" the tightness of the bend. It's irrelevant to a certain degree though, as we've already assessed the bend using other means.

Things are getting interesting again now. OK, we've got an oncoming car (it wasn't possible to show it before this, as I was stationary when I took the pictures - you wouldn't want me to take pictures when I'm driving, would you?) which, in reality, we'd have seen some time back. But look beyond it.

There is a hedge line going off to the left which, to me, would be a very strong indicator as to where the road goes next…

And, as if by magic, all our predictions come true at this point. We've got the road bending to the left, the short straight, and even the footpath off to the right.

This is a really good example of how forward observations and planning works. We've spotted several visual clues, worked out what they mean, and decided what the road is going to do before we get there. It's a huge part of advanced driving, and something that gives me just as much pleasure as driving at speed.

Having your predictions come true can be hugely satisfying, and can turn even the dreariest drive into an interesting one.

26

How to Stop Things Getting Worse (skid control)

We all get things wrong sometimes. It's the nature of being a human being - *no-one* is perfect (except Mrs Local of course, but I wouldn't dare say otherwise, would I?), and we're all disposed to getting things wrong once in a while.

I wrote in chapter 9 – Forgive Yourself - about how a good driver learns from and remembers prior mistakes, without dwelling on them, and uses them in their future driving plans as what *not* to do in similar circumstances.

There are occasions, however, when you can get things wrong, and your actions in trying to correct that mistake can either save the situation, or bugger things up even more than you already have. I'm talking, of course, about skidding.

Now, there's some very good advice in Roadcraft, and I've taught and stood by its principles for a long time now, but there's one area where I feel that Roadcraft is fundamentally lacking, and that's the books teachings on certain aspects of skid control.

It's not that the book is *wrong*, exactly, it's just that it's teachings on skid correction are just too basic for what is supposedly an advanced drivers manual (bible, even). Of course, most people don't get the benefit of some skid training (although a damn site more, and - dare I say - all new drivers should), and so you could argue that any skid training is advanced, in that it's beyond what an ordinary driver would get, but for me, some of the techniques it recommends are clumsy, basic, and in one case actually *dangerous* if you're travelling at high speed.

Reg looks up to a room of silence - you could hear a pin drop. An ex-police instructor who doesn't agree with Roadcraft? What the chuff is going on?

Let's start with some stuff that I do agree with, just so you know I haven't gone *completely* mad.

Roadcraft's description of skids, how they occur and its advice that the best option with skidding is to avoid getting into skids in the first place is all spot on, and not worth repeating here.

Where it is lacking, however, is in its description of how to control certain kinds of skids - specifically situations where a driver is experiencing oversteer and understeer.

Now, there are two main errors that a driver makes which induce oversteer and understeer. One is accelerating too harshly when cornering, with which Roadcraft deals, shall we say, adequately. The other one is by cornering at excessive speed, which is where I feel the book's advice is flawed.

Oversteer

Let's start with oversteer, and for my example, I want you to imagine that you're driving a rear-wheel drive car without traction control. *Reg sees the TVR drivers' ears pricking up*

The advice in Roadcraft if you've started to oversteer is to first of all release the accelerator or declutch *and* release the accelerator. Now, if your oversteer is being caused by excessive bootage of the right pedal, then this advice is entirely correct - releasing the accelerator or pressing the clutch and lifting off will almost immediately stop the rear wheels from spinning, regain you some road grip, and providing you've counter-steered correctly, then you should have yourself back on the straight and narrow in next to no time.

But what if your oversteer is caused by travelling excessively fast for the corner? Let's start by having a look at what's happening to the car as it starts to break traction.

As the car travels round the corner, its weight is moving over the wheels which are on the outside of the corner. The more speed you carry into (or build up during) the corner, then the more weight is transferred onto the outer wheels.

At the same time, the tyres on those outer wheels are trying to counter the cars natural tendency to travel straight on, by holding lateral (sideways) grip with the road surface. Now, as I've mentioned before, there's only a certain amount of grip available to the tyres, and by cornering harder, you're getting less grip from the inside wheels (because the weight transfer to the outside ones means there's far less weight pressing the inside wheels down), and you're demanding more grip from those outside tyres.

And breathe

The sum total of all that is that when the speed becomes too much for the corner, the car will start to slide. The natural tendency of the majority of rear-wheel drive cars is for the rear to start sliding first, so that the car starts to turn in towards the inside of the corner more than the driver wants it to, hence it's *over*steering.

And what is Roadcraft's advice in this situation? The same as before - release the accelerator, or declutch and release the accelerator.

Let's think about that for a minute shall we? In a situation where the rear-end of a car is losing grip, Roadcraft is advising us to perform an action which will transfer weight towards the front of the car, and more importantly *away* from the rear of the car, thus removing grip from the rear at exactly the time when you want *more* grip, rather than less.

Not the best advice in my opinion.

So what *should* you do then Reg, you smartarse?

Don't lift off for starters - not completely anyway. The idea is for you to correct the skid using the steering and throttle by not adding any more speed, and by counter-steering.

When I say "by not adding any more speed", think about what you do when you're in a 40MPH speed limit area - you accelerate up to your chosen speed, and when you've reached it, you relax the pressure on the accelerator slightly so that the car remains at that speed. Note the wording - you relax the pressure on the accelerator - you *don't* release it. If you released it, the car would start to slow down, whereas you just want it to stay at that speed, so you relax your pressure, but you definitely keep some pressure on the accelerator.

That's what you should do - relax the pressure on the accelerator just slightly, so that the car isn't gaining any more speed - it's what I'd describe as a slight feathering back on the throttle. Certainly *not* a release of the throttle.

At the same time, you should steer in the direction you want to go.

The steering part isn't any more complicated than that. I could harp on for ages about steering in the direction of the skid, counter-steering and opposite lock, but all you need to know is that you should steer in the direction you want to go.

You should, of course, be careful not to steer *too* far in the direction you want to go, as this could induce a secondary skid, and these are, on the whole, much worse than the primary skid, and your trousers probably couldn't cope with the additional stress.

So steer *just enough* in the direction you want to go, and no more.

Understeer

What about understeer then Reg? Some of us drive Astra VXRs and Golf GTIs - what about us?

Patience my children.

If you're understeering due to excessive acceleration, then, again, Roadcraft's advice is sound. Release the accelerator, or declutch and release the accelerator, take a little steering off, and you should be all smiles again almost instantly.

But again, Roadcraft is lacking somewhat when it comes to understeer due to excessive speed. Many front-wheel drive cars will react to a lift on the throttle in a similar (although not identical) way to a rear-wheel drive car. They will pitch into oversteer as a reaction to the transfer forward of the cars weight which is associated with a lift on the throttle.

This FWD oversteer can be even more difficult to catch than in a RWD car, and so, unless you're playing on a circuit or skidpan, should be avoided at all costs.

So, you've carried too much speed into a corner, the car is running wide and not responding to extra lock, and you're suddenly becoming very concerned about an imminent expensive alloy wheel / kerbstone interface - what do you do?

As explained earlier, don't lift off the throttle completely, but feather back on it slightly. In this case you *do* want to lose a little speed, so that feathering back should be a little more than you would in the over-steering TVR.

The reason you want to lose speed is because this will transfer some weight back onto the front wheels, regain you some front-end grip, and, together with steering towards where you want to go, will have you pointing back in the right direction presently.

To De-Clutch or Not To De-Clutch

I've mentioned Roadcraft's advice to de-clutch (press the clutch) when a skid is developing, but I have one serious issue with this advice. If your car is fitted with traction control, de-clutching completely takes away any effect that the TC would have.

Traction control systems are becoming more and more sophisticated – many of them will actually brake individual wheels to help you keep control. However, if you dip the clutch, the systems won't kick in, so in my considered opinion, you're best leaving that clutch pedal well alone.

Driver Aids

One of the most significant developments in motor car design in the last 20 years has been the introduction and improvement of "driver aids". It started with anti-lock brakes, which then developed into traction control, and then into much more sophisticated systems designed to assist drivers in keeping control of their vehicles when things are going tits-up.

I've been lucky enough to experience some of these driver aids first hand in a safe environment, and they're very good. I'll not go into all the different acronyms on here, as each manufacturer seems to come up with a new one every month and I don't want to start getting my ESPs mixed up with my DSCs.

Needless to say, these systems work in similar ways, with a combination of wheel sensors, pitch sensors, yaw sensors, roll sensors, and other such electric trickery which all link into a central unit which constantly monitors what you're doing with the car. If things start to go wrong, this unit can take control of various aspects of the cars controls, such as throttling back and even applying individual brakes, in order to bring the car back under control.

As an example, if a car starts to oversteer in a right-hand bend, the unit can apply the rear offside brake individually, which helps the driver to regain control of the car.

It's all very clever stuff and having tried it in the same car, switched off and then on, I can say it works brilliantly. Well, as good as a very good driver anyway.

Just remember though, as mentioned above, if you take the option of pressing the clutch, the majority of these driver aids won't work properly, as you'll take away the drive from the wheels. So if your car has these aids, bear that in mind.

Here's a little story for you (completely true, as I dealt with the accident, so I promise you it's not one of those Policeman's urban legends).

I went to deal with an accident once, I think it will have been in about 1997 or 1998. The driver of a 2.5 litre Vauxhall Omega had lost control on a right-hand bend, skidded through a 180 degree rotation, and then left the road on the offside, landing in a ditch. The car was written off, but the driver, although shaken up, was uninjured.

I spoke to him about what had happened, and I expressed some surprise, as I knew that Omegas were fitted with traction control.

He agreed with me, especially as he said "I know - and I religiously turn it on every time I get into the car".

I asked him if he had read his owner's manual, and if he knew that the switch which turned the traction control light on actually turned the system *off*.

I've never seen anyone do a better Homer Simpson "D'OH" in all my life.

Quick lesson there for everyone there – RTFM.

Read The Flippin' Manual!

If Nothing Else Is Working

If you've tried everything else, and you're still heading for the scenery at a strange angle, I have two final tips for you which may keep the subsequent damage or injuries to a minimum.

Firstly, press the brakes - hard.

Muller that brake pedal like your life depends on it (this may actually be the case!). If you are going to hit something, it's best to do it at the lowest possible speed, so the harder you brake, the slower you'll be going when the collision occurs.

Secondly – look at the gap, not at the tree.

There is a phenomenon "target fixation". It refers to the common habit of looking at something, and automatically driving towards it. It's the reason that so many people manage to easily miss the huge gaps between trees and always seem to hit the (relatively) small trees themselves (or lamp-posts or telegraph poles – you get the idea).

It's because they look at the tree, which causes them to unconsciously steer towards the tree.

So please – if everything has gone horribly wrong, look at the gap. Because, trust me, it's always better to hit the gap!

Practice

I'd better just add that practising this stuff on the road isn't to be advised. You *could* find a quiet roundabout somewhere and have a go, but there's always the possibility that something could go badly wrong and you may well end up with a dented car, a dented ego, a dented driving licence, a dented wallet and.... I'm sure you get the picture.

My advice if you want to have a go at this stuff is this - pay out a few quid and have a half-day at a skid school. It'll be in someone else's car, so your car won't get dented, you'll have someone who *really* knows what they're doing sat next to you, so your ego will remain intact, it'll be off-road, so your licence is safe and although the cost might dent your wallet a bit, the pay-off may well come back and save you a fortune at some time in the future.

Go on - you know it makes sense!

27

A Question of Speed

YOUTUBE LINK - **SPEED**:

https://youtu.be/4U1AM0428P0

Without a doubt, one of the most contentious subjects related to driving – and in particular to driving performance cars - is that of speed. If there's one thing which is guaranteed to generate endless internet debates, it's speed and speed limits.

Spend just a few minutes on any motoring related website or forum and you will find discussions about how fast cars accelerate, what their top speeds are and how fast people have travelled on track and on the public road.

And then there's the dreaded speed enforcement threads. How much do we hate speed cameras? What is it with safety camera partnerships? How long till I get an NIP? Have the Police nothing better to do? Etc., etc.

It's a wide-ranging subject which has been discussed at length in countless other forums, but I'm going to add my thruppence on the subject of speed when applied to advanced driving.

The first thing I'll emphasis, before I go any further, is that the views expressed in this section are my own personal views only. I know it's a generally accepted principle but with a subject as contentious as speed, I think it's important to press the point.

So, now that's out of the way, it's confession time...

I speed.

There - I feel better now I've got that off my chest.

It's true - I speed. I'm a speeder. I have been since I passed my test twenty-something years ago and I probably always will be. Speeding is as integral a part of my driving habits as putting my seatbelt on and regular mirror checks.

Does this make me a bad person? I don't think so. Does it make me a child killer? Not so far, no. Does it make me more likely to have an accident? No. Should I be taken out at dawn and shot like a dog? I'd prefer not, thanks. Have I ever had any points on my licence? *touches wood* No.

The reality is that I always, **always** stick to **posted** speed limits, i.e. those speed limits which are "red ringed" (20, 30, 40, 50 and occasionally 60 mph speed limits), and I limit my excursions above the speed limit to national speed limit roads.

Why's that then? Why do you choose to break one speed limit, but adhere to another? Surely, if you're a speeder by nature, you'll break every speed limit? After all, the penalty is similar if you get caught, irrespective of the actual limit, isn't it?

My reasoning is this - if everyone drove correctly, according to the road and traffic conditions, and according to what actual and potential hazards existed, there wouldn't actually be any need for speed limits *at all.* People would appreciate what problems existed on a particular road, and would drive at a correct speed in relation to them.

With that in mind, I find that most posted limits are generally correct. 30mph in a busy, built-up area with all its associated hazards is just about the right speed. 40mph on a main road lined with residential properties is, again, just about the right speed. 20mph on a council housing estate, where Chesney and Tyrone's parents don't take proper care of them is also the right speed.

Posted limit areas are also the areas where you're most likely to be caught and prosecuted for exceeding the speed limit. The **vast** majority of fixed camera sites in my local area are in posted limit areas, and I can only think of 2 or 3 locations on national speed limit roads where mobile enforcement cameras are used, and even then, only infrequently. This is still the case in many other areas too, but not all.

Now, let's bust a myth before we go any further. It's not absolutely necessary to break speed limits in order to enjoy driving. Of course, there are many enthusiastic drivers, driving high performance cars and the concept of actually ***not*** breaking speed limits will be quite alien to those people, but bear with me a minute.

Some time ago, Mrs Local and I went to North Wales for a few days. We drove down in an M3, but I was paranoid about North Wales's reputation for excessively zealous speed enforcement, so I decided to stick to the national speed limits as well as the posted ones. The roads are lovely in North Wales and, believe me, I could have gone a *lot* faster, but rolling along at 60ish, combined with accelerating hard out of slower sections, planning and executing overtakes and cornering briskly, without approaching the cars limits made for a quite enjoyable journey. Not exciting, of course, not adrenaline pumping or tyre-screeching, or eye-widening, but enjoyable nonetheless.

On the way home, however, I took a different route, along very lightly trafficked roads, and I pressed on a bit more than I did on the way down. Well, a **lot** more if I'm being honest, and the drive was also very enjoyable, but in a different way. My concentration levels were much higher, as was my state of awareness. Driving at speed gives me a feeling of connection between myself, the car and the road, and it's a difficult feeling to describe to non-enthusiasts.

So what *is* the correct speed to drive at on NSL roads then?

Sorry - you're not going to catch me out with a question as simplistic as that I'm afraid. The answer to that question is based on so many variables that I couldn't even begin to list them all. I'll just stick to the absolute basics for now.

Firstly, it depends on *you*. You should have a *realistic* assessment of your own driving ability. Be honest with yourself - how good are you? Really?

If you drive on the road at a speed where you're approaching the limits of the car, then you're driving too fast. If you don't *know* when you're approaching the limits of the car, then you really need to take stock. If you have an unexpected moment, again, you should be taking stock and re-considering what your *actual* ability level is.

It's not necessarily something you need to feel embarrassed about, but if people, in general, stopped thinking that they were God's gift to driving and accepted that there's always more to learn, then the roads would be a safer (and less law enforced) place.

The next major thing to think about is *why* you're travelling at speed. If the answer is because you're late, or because you've got a time constraint, then back off and consider what I wrote in Time Constraints in chapter 8.

Time constraints add additional stress to a journey and if you combine that stress with driving at excessive speed, then you're introducing an unnecessary element of risk into the equation.

If, however, the answer to why you're speeding is "because I enjoy it", then you shouldn't be stressed by outside influences. Keep the enjoyment element in the forefront of your mind, and remember that you're driving at speed for the enjoyment of the sensations it brings. You're not trying to set a lap time or reduce a stage time by a few seconds - you're out to enjoy yourself, and there should be no risk involved in what you're doing.

Remember that, to the majority of road-users, the roads *aren't* there for enjoyment, but are merely a transport option, so your enjoyment isn't high on their list of priorities. Don't start feeling that other drivers are ruining your day, but instead, use your planning and anticipation skills to look for a nice, safe overtake.

A few notes on speed limits in the UK:

Speed limits are an interesting subject (well, relatively anyway - I don't think you'll pick up many young ladies (or gentlemen, depending on your preferences) by demonstrating a comprehensive knowledge of the history of speed limits in the UK).

Some highlights? Well, between 1930 and 1935 there was no speed limit for cars and motorcycles *whatsoever,* and during that time, road casualties *fell* by nearly 800 per year.

In 1935, a 30mph limit was introduced in built-up areas, but everywhere else remained free from any speed limits. At this time, I understand that the white circle/black diagonal line sign which we now recognise as an NSL sign was first introduced, but back then it was used to indicate the end of a built-up area and the start of a "de-restricted" or more correctly, an "unrestricted" section of road.

On the Isle of Man, these signs still have this meaning.

1935 also saw the start of police driver training and the development, firstly by Sir Malcolm Campbell and then further by the Earl of Cottenham, of a "system of car control" and the early stages of Roadcraft.

Police training, and especially advanced police training, made full use of unrestricted roads and their lack of speed limits to train advanced students in higher speed driving. In built-up areas, however, police drivers were expected to set a good example and comply with the 30mph limit.

The national speed limit was introduced as an experimental measure in 1965 and then permanently in 1967. When introduced, all previously unrestricted sections of roads, including motorways, dual carriageways and single carriageways were subject to a 70mph limit.

The national speed limit has varied since its introduction - the oil crisis in 1973 saw it dropped to 50mph (apart from motorways), and then finally set at 60mph on single carriageways and 70mph on dual carriageways and motorways in 1977.

Throughout this time, and up to the present day, the police have trained drivers at speeds above the national speed limit, but within the "red ringed" limits.

Police driver training has for a long time set the standard for civilian advanced training and this crossover has probably led to the commonly held opinion that it's more acceptable to exceed national speed limits than those in built-up areas.

In theory, the Government had it right all the way back in 1930. If everyone drove according to the hazards and risks present at the time, there would be no need for speed limits. Unfortunately, life isn't that simple, is it?

One last note on the subject. If you get caught, take it on the chin.

I know full well that I'm risking prosecution every time I go over a speed limit, and I'm well aware of the consequences of being caught. I try to pick the right time and place, and drive safely, without upsetting anyone else, but there's always the possibility that I'll be caught at some point.

If (or when) I do, I'll take it on the chin, pay the fine, take the points, and I won't whinge about it.

If you choose to break a speed limit, and the worst happens, I suggest you do the same.

28

DRIVING COMMENTARY

YOUTUBE LINK - **AN INTRODUCTION TO COMMENTARY:**

https://youtu.be/eaootQjPpGc

Commentary is one aspect of advanced driving that students seem to dread, mainly because there are some unnecessary pre-conceived ideas about what commentary is and how it should be applied.

Let's look at it from the perspective of a Police driving course - I'll use an advanced course as an example, but in most police forces, some commentary is also required on standard courses too.

Back when I did my advanced car course [Uncle Albert] during the war [/Uncle Albert], students were expected to commentate for 10 to 15 minutes during both of their final drives (which are both generally 40 - 45 minutes long). Back then, you'd be expected to point out upcoming hazards, both actual and potential, talk through the five phases of the system as you applied them to those hazards, point out road signs, describe the actions of other drivers, etc., etc.

On top of that, at relevant points, you were expected to introduce various definitions from Roadcraft, which required us to literally learn them parrot-fashion, from the book every evening. Many of them have stayed with me today.

Acceleration sense is an easy one "the ability of a driver to adjust the speed of the vehicle to meet changing road and traffic conditions by accurate use of the accelerator".

Braking sense took me a couple of nights to get spot-on "the ability of a driver to appreciate a situation correctly and apply the brakes in a gradual and timely manner, to stop, or reduce the speed of the vehicle, where this cannot be achieved by deceleration alone."

For some reason I've never understood, we learned the old *and* new definitions of the system of car control (it used to be a system or drill, and then it became a method of approaching and negotiating hazards), the definition of concentration, the full description of the tyre-grip trade off, the rules for gearchanging, the four principles of safe cornering and a shed-load of other minor definitions.

Our instructor, Dicko (bless him) also insisted that we learned, verbatim, several rules from the Highway Code, including the rule number. I can recall to this day that rule 172 of the Highway Code used to be that in built-up areas, you should give priority to buses which are signalling to pull away from stops - its rule 198 now, before you correct me, and yes - I know the wording has changed.

Did learning all this stuff parrot-fashion make us better drivers?

I don't think so, no.

In fact, part of me thinks that it detracted from the most important aspect of the course - learning to drive at an advanced level.

Does this mean that I don't approve of commentary?

No - it just means I think it should be different from when I did my advanced course, and fortunately, the majority of Police driving schools these days agree with me and have relaxed the requirement for a definition-centred driving commentary in exchange for a slightly more relaxed, but more relevant commentary.

These days, certainly in my force, and in many others, a student on test will still be asked to commentate for 10 to 15 minutes during a final drive. The difference nowadays is that an examiner just wants to know what problems the driver has seen or anticipated, and what they are going to do about it.

Crucially, the students need to remember this - if their driving is up to standard, they won't fail if they give a poor commentary. In addition, having tested at advanced level myself, a *good* commentary can *lift* an average drive.

So how should an advanced-level commentary go?

It's traditional, and appropriate for the driver to start with a description of what they can see in the far distance, and then work back through the middle distance, the foreground, then the sides and finally to the rear.

As they describe what they can see, they should also be talking about what their plans are - this is very important as it shows the examiner what their mental processes are, and allows them to see the thinking behind the driver's actions.

"Looking into the distance, I can see that the road bends to the left, out of sight, so I'm looking to the left of the road, along the hedge-line, to see if there are any hazards. I can see a couple of triangle warning signs for double bends, the first to the left, which we've already seen, and for a

junction to the right, for which I might need to adjust my position for safety."

"In the middle distance I can see that we're approaching a slow-moving HGV, for which I'll have to slow to get into a following position. I'll be looking to overtake it when appropriate, and as the left-hander is followed by a right-hander, I'm planning to look for an opportunity to overtake off the right-hander."

"In the foreground is a cyclist, for whom I've already moved towards the offside to pass safely."

"To the sides are fields and hedges, it's a rural area, so I'm anticipating there might be tractors pulling onto the road at some point."

"To the rear is a fast-approaching motorcycle, which is something I'll have to consider when I'm looking to overtake the truck."

So, no definitions - just a straightforward description of what you can see and what you're going to do about it.

It's not easy at first - any instructor will tell you that if they've got a student who's getting ahead of themselves, the easiest way to slow them down is to ask them to commentate. Because they're concentrating on what they're saying, their speed drops almost instantly.

With practise though, commentary can come quite naturally, and even with all the bumph I had to learn on my advanced course, I was disappointed when the examiner told me to stop commentating.

In a nutshell then, keep your commentary simple, [catchphrase]*"say what you see,"* [/catchphrase] and say what you're going to do about it.

Urban Commentary

When you're in a busy, built-up area, there is so much going on that you'd have to be some kind of freakish speed-talker to fit in everything. Instead, just concentrate on what is the most relevant.

Far distance stuff isn't *as* relevant in city driving, but it can be useful in identifying junctions or other situations that might cause you problems in the future. Most of your commentary, however, will centre on what immediate hazards you've got to deal with. Which pedestrians are going to step into the road, which van is going to cut you up, which cyclists are going to be a problem, which delivery vehicle is going to stop with little warning, etc., etc.

Just identifying observation links, pointing out the immediate hazards and stating what your plans are should keep your commentary flowing nicely when it's very busy.

Including System in Commentary

One thing that examiners certainly appreciate is an ability to "talk system" through a hazard. Take a straightforward left turn into a minor road. "I'm planning to turn left into the junction ahead. I'm taking in information by looking at the junction, the traffic and any warning signs for the junction and by checking the mirrors for following traffic. I'm using that information to formulate a plan and I'm giving information by putting on a left signal for the vehicle behind".

"I'm now adjusting my position towards the best part of the nearside, staying out of the grids."

"I'm now on the speed phase, reducing my speed with progressive, smooth braking."

"Now the speed is correct, I'm selecting second gear."

"I'm now turning into the junction, giving a quick mirror check and applying the correct amount of smooth acceleration to leave the junction."

"In the distance I can see..."

It's often good to throw in a quick 5 phase commentary for simple hazards like a parked car. Remember that the 5 phases of the system only have to be *considered* for each hazard...

"I'm taking in information about the parked car on the left, looking for feet movements underneath it and for anyone who may open a door, and checking my mirrors."

"I'm adjusting my position out to the offside, leaving at least a doors length between the parked car and me"

"I'm considering my speed and gear, but they're already correct and there is no need for any acceleration."

Another nice flourish to commentary is to make some observation links. They don't have to be immediate, either. If you drive into a rural area, mention that you're expecting to see slow-moving agricultural vehicles or animals in the road. 10 or 15 minutes later, if you see a tractor, mention it "ahead is a slow-moving tractor, as anticipated earlier".

If a car joins the road in front of you, mention that it may turn off in the next mile or so. If it doesn't, then there's no harm done. If it does, then remind the examiner "The car in front is now turning right, as anticipated." Junctions are always a good opportunity for a little link, especially if you're in a line of traffic. "Ahead is a primary route board indicating a junction to the right. I'm anticipating some of the vehicles will turn off." A pound to a penny that at least one will turn off and even if they don't, nothing is lost.

On one of my advanced final drives, *Harumph* years ago, I remember seeing some big dusty tyre tracks on the road, which I linked with a quarry entrance and slow moving tipper trucks. Sure enough, there was a laden tipper round the next corner.

Above all, don't bore them - keep them interested, and don't be afraid of introducing a little humour every now and again.

Cockpit Drill

A cockpit drill is a series of actions which drivers carry out at the start of every journey. Some advanced driving organisations can be very prescriptive on this subject, and some are more relaxed, but I thought it may be useful to share my thoughts.

One advantage of learning a cockpit drill parrot fashion is that it gives a student a few minutes of "settling in" time in the car when they're on test. It allows them to go through a well-rehearsed routine which ensures that they don't miss any essentials through nervous forgetfulness before heading out on test.

I don't for one minute think that students carry on doing a full cockpit check after finishing their course, but hopefully they'll consider a few more things when they get in the car than the traditional CID starting drill of "we're in, we're off".

When I did my police car instructors course, we had to give a demonstration drive with full start-to-finish instructional commentary, which differs from advanced level commentary in that you should talk about what you're going to do, rather than what you're doing.

The starting drill we had to learn was two full pages of A4 in a small font, incorporating a full description of not only what you were doing, but also why.

I can still remember it now if it's of any interest...

"I've just completed an exterior check of the car, during which I've checked that all doors, boot and bonnet are closed securely, all four tyres appear in good condition and inflated and there is no recent damage to the car. I'll now carry on with the interior checks."

"First I'll check that the handbrake is on. I check the handbrake first because I'll be putting the car in neutral shortly and I don't want the car to roll."

"Then I'll check that the driver's door is securely closed by first pulling it, and then pushing it - I won't start with a push as I don't want to accidentally open the door into passing traffic."

"Next I'll adjust the driver's seat. I'll adjust the seat base so that my leg is still slightly bent when the clutch is fully depressed. Then I'll adjust the seat back and steering wheel so that, with my arms out straight, my wrists rest on the wheel rim."

"Then I'll put on my seatbelt and make sure all my passengers are wearing theirs."

"I'll then adjust my interior mirror. Keeping my right hand on the steering wheel, so that my head remains in the correct place, I'll adjust the mirror with my left hand holding the edge of the mirror so as not to mark it. I'll line up the top edge of the mirror with the top edge of the rear window."

"Next I'll perform a static brake test. I'll press the brake pedal firmly and there should be plenty of resistance in the pedal. If the pedal is spongy or goes to the floor, that could indicate a serious fault with the brakes and I won't take the car any further."

"I'll now press the clutch, put the car into neutral, and start the engine with the clutch depressed. I keep the clutch down whilst starting because this removes the weight of the gearbox from the engine and makes it easier for the starter motor to turn the engine over, especially if it's cold. It also ensures that the car doesn't jump forward or backward if I haven't taken it out of gear properly."

"Then I'll check the instruments and warning lights. I'll make sure there is enough fuel for the journey, check the engine temperature and other gauges, and make sure all the warning lights go out, except for the handbrake light."

"The next items to consider are the vehicles auxiliaries. Starting from left and working across to the right, I'll adjust the nearside mirror, set any heater or air-conditioning controls, consider wipers and headlights, and finish off with the offside door mirror."

"I'm now ready to move off, so I'll check my mirrors, select first gear, check my mirrors again, give a right shoulder check and move off when it's safe."

"I should always remember that no starting drill is complete without a moving brake test. I'll accelerate up to 20MPH, check my mirrors, make sure nothing is close behind and **stand by**... I'll brake firmly down to 10 MPH, checking that the brakes are pulling firmly and evenly, and it's safe to continue."

The instructors' demonstration drive would then continue with full commentary.

A student's starting drill would be exactly the same, but just accompanied with brief or even one-word descriptions...

Exterior check complete;

Handbrake

Door

Seat

Seatbelt

Mirror

Static brake test.

Clutch down, into neutral

Start engine with clutch pressed

Check instruments and warning lights

Auxiliaries from left to right

Mirror check, first gear, mirrors and shoulders

Move off when safe

Moving brake test

29

MOTORWAY DRIVING

PART 1

YOUTUBE LINK - **MOTORWAY DRIVING:**

https://youtu.be/kWQzlWZG-lI

Very few people are ever taught how to drive on motorways, so I thought it would be useful to write a few chapters on motorway driving.

Provisional licence holders are specifically prohibited from motorways, and apart from a small element of the theory test, drivers in the UK aren't tested on motorway driving. This seems odd to me, as motorways are very different from any other roads that a learner will have encountered, and they're the fastest roads in the country, which in my view, isn't somewhere we should be allowing untrained, inexperienced drivers to go.

Most new drivers will, of course, take their first venture onto the motorway in company with a more experienced driver – my dad took me on the motorway for the first time on the day I passed my test, and I've since done the same for my eldest stepson. Others will take the Pass Plus course, which is a nice introduction to motorways.

In these particular chapters, I'm going to assume no prior knowledge on the part of the reader. I make no apologies for this – I want it to be helpful for everyone from brand new licence-holders, through to advanced drivers. I've tried to include something for everyone, so it should be useful if you only ever use a motorway every other month, or if you do 70,000 miles a year. There will be a section which covers driving at very high speed on the motorway for those who are interested – it has its own little introductory passage, so that you don't read it out of context, even if you skip the other stuff.

Most articles I've ever read about motorway driving always seem to start with a very patronising piece about making sure your car is fit for the journey, ensuring you've enough fuel, that your tyres are in good condition, that you've planned your route, polished your glasses, readied your pipe tobacco and correctly adjusted the position of the tissue box on the back shelf.

I think I'll skip that bit, to be honest, as it's a bit egg-suckyish even for a beginners guide, so I'll assume you know how to read a map and how to put petrol in.

So, in the first instalment, I've given a brief introduction to the subject, and then written about how to enter a motorway correctly…

Introduction

Before I go any further, I'll start with a description of a motorway, and a quick look at some of the terms I'll be using.

A motorway is a special road.

That was easy, wasn't it?

But what's special about a motorway? Well, let's expand my description a little. A motorway is a dual carriageway road, usually with two or more lanes in each direction. It is bordered to the nearside by a hard shoulder and to the offside by a central reservation and barrier. There are small exceptions to these rules, of course, but that description will fit for 99.9% of UK motorways.

Motorways do not have traffic lights, T-junctions or roundabouts, and to enter or leave a motorway, you have to negotiate slip-roads, which usually connect to the nearside of the motorway.

Motorways also have special rules, mostly centred around who *can't* use the motorway.

So, if you're out for a walk, cycling, out on your invalidity scooter, driving a tractor, riding a horse or a moped, or you haven't passed your driving test, you should stay off the motorway. If you're one of those road users, and you even **consider** using the motorway, then you're clinically insane, and you shouldn't actually be allowed out of the home for the terminally stupid, but that's by-the-by. As well as being bloody daft, you'll also be committing an offence.

So there.

There are some other rules about who can and can't use certain lanes, stopping on the motorway etc. and I'll cover those as I go along.

To start with, here's a picture which my production team (me, playing with Photoshop) have made, showing a few of the basic descriptive terms I'll be using…

As you can see, there is no such thing as a slow lane, middle lane, or fast lane. The correct designations for the lanes start with lane 1, which is the first lane to the right of the hard shoulder. It's bordered to the left by a solid white-line and red cats-eyes and to the right by a broken white line and white cats-eyes. The only time the line to the left of lane 1 becomes broken is when it's next to a slip-road, at which point the cats-eyes will be green.

Lane 2 is then the next lane to the right, lane 3 is to the right of lane 2, etc. etc. The right-hand lane is bordered by a broken white line and white cats-eyes to the left, and a solid white line and yellow cats-eyes to the right.

Having given you that information, henceforth, anyone referring to slow lanes, fast lanes etc. will be summarily executed by being ignored to death.

So, if you're able to keep you vehicle in a lane, with red cats-eyes to the left and yellow ones to the right, you're part-way to being competent at driving on motorways.

Also labelled in that picture are an ETB (Emergency Telephone Box), marker posts and a gantry sign, all of which I'll cover a bit later. For now, though, I'm going to move on to (quite predictably really)…

Entering the Motorway

Motorway driving, as with any other type of driving, is based around making driving plans. Planning for a motorway entry starts well before you actually get onto the slip-road itself. Your planning starts on the approach to the motorway junction.

Look at the photograph below. From this distance – several hundred yards from the junction – we've already got a good view of the traffic on the motorway. We can see if it's free-moving or snarled to a standstill (in which case, you might choose to take a different route).

On some motorway junctions (usually those with a roundabout junction built over the motorway and downhill slip-roads), we can have a quick look onto the motorway itself, and possibly plan which vehicles we're going to emerge alongside at the end of the slip road.

Anyway – back to the pic…

As we get a bit closer to the junction, we can see the route board for the roundabout. As the road we're on is not a motorway, the majority of the route board is white with black markings, but the roundabout exits which lead to the motorway, are indicated with blue signs and white markings...

From here, I'll assume that you know how to negotiate a roundabout, and in this case, we've turned right and taken the 5th exit from the roundabout.

As we leave the roundabout, you can see two blue signs. The smaller one to the left confirms which motorway you're entering and indicates the start of motorway regulations. The larger one to the right is a more general directional finger-board giving the direction of the motorway and the other motorways which lead from it. In this case, we are entering the M65 in the direction of Preston, from which we can also reach the M61 and the M6. There is also a triangle sign warning that our lane converges ahead (in case you hadn't already guessed).

There is a bit more information available here too if you're prepared to look outside the box slightly. Towards the end of the slip-road, we'll be looking to match our speed to the speed of vehicles in lane 1, to allow a fuss-free entry to the motorway. At the point shown in the picture below, we can actually see the motorway itself going from right to left. It's not possible to see any cars yet, but larger vehicles would be visible, and that view can greatly assist your planning. In this case, we're entering on an up-hill entry slip, but on down-hill entries, this view is much better and allows for a nicely planned entry.

So, after exiting the roundabout, we then need to accelerate firmly to enter the motorway. But how fast do we accelerate? And to what speed?

Well, as for acceleration, you can increase your speed as quickly as you like. Full-bore acceleration up a slip road can be fun, but it's your speed when you're adjacent to lane 1 that's important, so it's best not to overdo it. As I said before, you should be matching your speed to the speed of vehicles in lane 1. If those vehicles are large articulated LGVs, then they're unlikely to be going much over 60mph, so bear that in mind – if you accelerate up to 100mph on a slip-road, you'll probably have to brake again to join, so it'd be a waste of time. It's much better (and kinder to your passengers) to use acceleration sense and join without braking.

In the next picture, we're reaching the point where the slip-road and motorway meet. We should be paying plenty of attention to what's happening in lane 1, particularly *behind* you in lane 1, so there should be plenty of mirror checks (both centre and offside) and some shoulder checks too – there is a nasty blind-spot just over your right shoulder which usually manifests itself when joining a motorway.

We're looking for a suitable gap to pull into at this point. I don't generally signal when I'm entering a motorway unless it's particularly busy, in which case I'll stick an indicator on more as a way of asking the driver behind me in lane 1 to allow me to enter. 9 times out of 10, I find that a signal *isn't* necessary – especially if I've matched my speed correctly. It should just be a case of sliding smoothly but positively into lane 1.

In the next picture, we're reaching the end of the slip-road, and we should have picked our gap in lane 1 and matched our speed correctly.

We won't be moving sideways yet, though, as there is a chevron area (called the bull-nose) to the right, bordered with a solid white line. Crossing this line for an early entry onto the motorway is an offence. It's also a bit daft, as the traffic on the motorway won't be expecting you to enter at that point, so wait for the broken lines…

That's better – we've moved sideways into lane 1 smoothly and with a minimum of fuss. We haven't caused anyone to alter their course or speed and everyone is happy:

However, I like to drive progressively when it's safe, so at this point, I'm already looking for the opportunity to overtake. A mirror and shoulder check reveals that lane 2 is clear, so from that entry to lane 1, I'm almost immediately moving out into lane 2 to overtake…

Now, one thing I should emphasise here is that I always teach people to take one lane at a time when entering a motorway. It *is* possible to enter a three lane motorway and keep accelerating until you're almost immediately in lane 3, but it takes considerable planning and practice, and even if I *do* enter a motorway in that manner, I'm still considering each lane separately in sequence. Also, each initial move to a lane (to the right) should be accompanied with a shoulder check to eliminate the possibility of something lurking in your blind-spot.

It takes a short time to become accustomed to the vehicles that are around you when you first enter a motorway, so try to take a little time to work out their relative speeds and possible intentions, before barrelling straight into lane 3. I'm not saying that you definitely *shouldn't* go straight into lane 3 when joining a motorway – but you should carefully consider each lane separately if you do.

A few other notes on motorway entries…

Many slip-roads have two lanes, which allow you to overtake slower moving vehicles prior to entering the motorway. Now, overtaking on a slip-road is fine, but you **must** plan to have completed your overtake before the slip-road becomes one lane. This sounds like obvious advice, but I've seen countless idiots performing badly-planned overtakes on slip roads, only to end up having to brake hard to enter the motorway.

The tendency is to think too much about the overtake, and not enough about the entry until it's too late. There is also a possibility that you could end up being badly squeezed at the end of the slip-road if you're not careful.

On a similar theme, if it is a two-lane slip-road, my preference if it's busy, is to move out to lane 2 on the slip-road nice and early. There are two advantages to this – firstly, it puts you right next to lane 1 early, and gives you a little more time alongside that lane to match your speed correctly.

Secondly, as there *are* plenty of people who execute badly-planned overtakes on two-lane slip-roads; an early move to lane 2 prevents them from blocking you from entering at the correct point. Keep an eye on your mirrors, and don't let anyone stuff you.

It is common courtesy, if you're driving along the motorway, to give assistance to joining drivers if it's safe to do so. If traffic allows, you should try to make allowance for the joining drivers by moving to lane 2 and/or adjusting your speed.

However, as a joining driver, you should never *expect* people to make these allowances. It's become all too common these days for drivers to simply expect people on the motorway to make allowances for them. Always remember that the onus is on the joining driver to make the allowances – *not* on the drivers who are already on the motorway. If, for whatever reason, someone doesn't or can't make allowances for you, then make another plan.

30

MOTORWAY DRIVING

PART 2

YOUTUBE LINK - **MOTORWAY DRIVING**:

https://youtu.be/kWQzlWZG-lI

Driving along the motorway

Sounds simple enough doesn't it? I mean - motorways are just big wide straight roads where you just go in one direction. This should be a piece of cake to write.

Before I go any further, let's take another look at the photo from part 1:

This photo shows a few of the terms I'll be referring to and the correct terminology for motorway lanes.

So, we've joined the motorway. What next?

I'm going to make an assumption here - I'm going to assume that you want to make some reasonable progress. Motorways are the main arteries of our road network and we generally use them when we want to cover longer distances. There is nothing wrong with wanting to make some decent progress where it is safe and appropriate.

So, having joined the motorway and having slotted in to lane 1, what's next? Well, if the motorway is clear and there is no traffic ahead, it's simple. Stay in lane 1.

Lane 1 is the default "driving along" lane and your overriding plan whenever you are driving on the motorway should be to return to lane 1 whenever it is appropriate. If you read the motorway section of the Highway Code, it is very clear that lanes 2 and 3 (and 4 etc.) are for overtaking only. I'll cover lane hogging etc. a bit later, but all I'll say at this point is that you should always try not to be "that" driver.

A quick general note on driving along here - motorway driving can be bloody boring. Modern cars are comfortable and cosseting and generally nice places to sit and at 70mph most cars are as comfortable as your sofa at home. Combine this with an unchanging, unremitting wide stretch of grey tarmac with nothing to look at for mile after dreary mile, and you've got a recipe for becoming bored, distracted and even sleepy if you're not careful. I believe this is a major cause of poor motorway driving (and particularly of poor lane discipline) - people are bored.

Once you've read this chapter, you should go away with a few tips and techniques which will engage you in thinking creatively and planning your motorway progress. In turn, this should keep your interest levels up and prevent you from becoming bored. You'll be better able to spot situations before they actually occur and although it's unlikely you'll ever look forward to a long motorway drive, you will at least have some things to practice.

Here's another thing to consider. The Red Arrows choose only the best fast jet pilots and even then, they require months of training before they can fly in close formation.

When you're driving on the motorway, you're travelling in close formation at relatively high speeds alongside people who you've never met and of whom you have no clue as to their competency.

As another instructor once described it to me, motorway driving is "formation flying with idiots".

Not everyone is an idiot of course, but just have a look around you next time you bob in to a motorway service station for a pee. Not when you're peeing of course - this is the time to stare at your boots only - but on your way in and out of the building, have a look at the people around you. You will be in no doubt that some of them are idiots. The same idiots you've just been driving alongside at 102 feet per second. This exercise alone keeps my attention on every motorway journey I take.

Consistency of speed

Consistency of speed is something I always try to achieve on a motorway journey - I pick a speed and try to stick with it. This sounds a very simple concept, but it amazes me how many drivers are inconsistent with their speed.

They will accelerate on downhill stretches, but then fail to compensate on the uphill bits. They will dawdle in the middle lane, but then unexpectedly accelerate as you're about to overtake them. The worst ones will continually (and generally obliviously) overtake you and then slow down. You'll pass them and they'll disappear into a dot in your mirror, only to reappear 2 or 3 miles later at warp speed and pass you like you're standing still, only to slow down again and repeat the cycle.

Returning from a recent trip to Scotland, I overtook the same driver eight times in less than 50 miles without changing my speed. He had no idea that I even existed.

A consistent speed is also much more fuel efficient on a long journey than a pattern of acceleration and deceleration, so if you're a skinflint you'll benefit from this tip.

So, pick a speed and try to stick with it, preferably using acceleration sense as discussed in "Acceleration Nonsense" elsewhere in the book.

Many people choose to use cruise control on long motorway journeys. Cruise control is very good at allowing you to maintain a constant speed, but in my view it's a bit of a blunt tool and is only really any good when the traffic is light. It also encourages drivers to switch off a little more than usual, when in fact; using cruise control requires just as much planning as driving on a normal throttle.

I will, however, reserve judgement on more modern "adaptive" cruise control systems which use radar to maintain a constant following position in traffic. I've not tried one of these systems yet, so I'm not in a position to comment.

Approaching and overtaking slower traffic

So, you're approaching some slower traffic. All you have to do is move in to lane 2 or 3, pass the traffic and move back into lane 1.

Simple.

Except it's never that simple is it? There is a much more extensive planning process which starts with considering the domino principle. This is the fairly simple premise that vehicles moving from lane 1 to lane 2 have a domino effect on vehicles in lane 2 which will generally move to lane 3.

A good driver will be able to spot this situation before it occurs by looking out for one simple clue...

Closing gaps.

Say you're driving along in lane 1 at 70 and you're approaching a "clump" of slower moving traffic ahead - again in lane 1 (traffic tends to travel in clumps on the motorway - I've no idea why). Keeping with my advice to maintain a constant speed, you will move out to lane 2 and continue past the traffic.

But - have you ever been surprised by one vehicle within the clump suddenly deciding to move out into lane 2?

Usually in front of you? With no prior warning?

My advice is to look for the closing gaps. Don't just view the clump of traffic as a single item to be overtaken, but instead recognise that it is a collection of individual vehicles, whose drivers all have different agendas.

The most obvious would be a car behind an HGV. Goods vehicles are mostly speed limited these days and the drivers tend to sit on or near the 56ish mph permitted by the limiter. Look again at the car behind the lorry - don't just glance at it - look at it and work out if there is a difference in speed between the two vehicles. If the car is catching up with the HGV, the likelihood is that the driver will want to overtake it.

Most drivers don't plan too far ahead, so it's usually at the point when the car is right up with the HGV when the driver decides to overtake.

If you've recognised this situation early, you've two options. Either move out early into lane three if it's clear, or if lane 3 isn't clear, you can lift off and allow the driver to move out in front of you to pass the HGV. Either of those two options avoids a confrontational situation (even though the root cause is the other driver's poor planning and observation).

This is easy when it's just a car and a lorry, but less so when there is more traffic across several lanes. The key is to look carefully at each vehicle and try to work out its intentions.

There is some clear "car body language" which drivers display when they intend to change lanes on the motorway - even if they don't indicate their intentions.

Closing on the vehicle in front is the most obvious one, but here's another - ***the swerve and return***.

When a driver is thinking about moving into a lane to their right, it is very common to see them make a small move to the right within their lane, then return to the centre of their lane, and then indicateandchangelanes all at once (exactly as written).

It's very subtle, and I don't really know why they do it, other than my own theory which is that they're giving away their own intentions with a slight physical reaction. It is, however, a very real phenomenon and one to watch out for on your next motorway journey.

"Asking" Drivers to Move

What should you do if there is an inattentive driver ahead, travelling slower than you in an overtaking lane? How do you get their attention and "ask2 them to move over?

There is nothing wrong with a headlight flash to encourage an inattentive driver to vacate an overtaking lane - it is a technique I used to teach standard and advanced police students. There are a couple of things to bear in mind though.

Firstly, don't flash someone if they're clearly overtaking or have nowhere to go. It's pointless if the car in front is alongside another vehicle or will obviously be overtaking another vehicle very shortly. Save the headlight flash until they have a clear gap to their nearside into which they can safely move.

Once they have a clear gap to the nearside, but they're obviously not budging, give them a 2-3 second *single* headlight flash, but without encroaching within your 2 second following position. A longer flash seems to appear less aggressive than a series of shorter flashes, especially from a consistent following position.

If they move, accelerate smartly past and give them a courtesy signal - a quick wave of thanks clarifies that you weren't acting aggressively.

If they stay put, keep your distance & give a second 2-3 second burn.

If there is *still* no reaction, give a third flash, still from a 2 second gap.

If at that stage they haven't moved, they're either deliberately blocking or they haven't looked in their mirror since a week last Tuesday.

At this point, I just switch my headlights to dipped beam, leave them on and sit 2 seconds back - they might see you in the next 10 miles, so sit it out & try not to let yourself get too wound up.

On the legality of a headlight flash, it's a perfectly legitimate signal to inform other road users of your presence and I honestly can't think of a more appropriate use of the signal.

Rear observations

So, there is plenty of stuff to look out for in front, but what about behind?

Just as important - if you want to avoid being the swerve and return driver - is what's happening behind you. The centre mirror is the most useful one most of the time, but not just for a quick glance every 20 seconds or so. Some drivers and riders (either legitimately or not so) travel at very high speeds on the motorways. In the past I've legally seen in excess of 160 whilst covered by a police exemption and at those speeds, you're "on" other road users very, very quickly.

So mirror checks on the motorway should be a good second or so long - long enough for you to really take in what is happening behind and what is catching up with you. And regularly too - at least every 10 seconds and even more frequently when it's busy or your speed is high.

Look in the mirror in exactly the same way as you look out of the windscreen. Scan into the far distance for approaching vehicles, and then take in the middle distance and the foreground. In much the same way as you do when looking forward, it's very important to assess the information gained from your mirror check, such as the relative speeds of all the vehicles you can see, not just the one behind you.

Use this information to plan your progress. Move out early to obtain a lane well in advance or lift off early if you're approaching a slower vehicle but the lane to your right is full.

Changing lanes

If you're going to move out and pass a slower vehicle, my first piece of advice is not to leave it too late. If you move out early you're effectively stating your intentions early and "claiming" your place in the overtaking lane.

Before changing lanes, check your centre mirror and your offside (right) door mirror. In addition, it's good practice to give a right shoulder check. There is a very distinct blind spot just over your right shoulder and some drivers have a very annoying habit of finding it and sitting in it whilst matching your speed.

Not just a quick glance either - a good sustained gawp over your right shoulder through the rear offside window (if you've got one).

When you actually change lanes, move smoothly but positively straight into the centre of your chosen lane. Too quickly and it'll look and feel like a swerve. Too slowly and it'll look like an indecisive move- it shouldn't look indecisive because you've already made a positive decision to change lanes, so go with it.

Should you signal? This is a moot point in advanced driving circles. My personal approach is that I only signal if I believe someone will benefit. So a faster vehicle approaching from behind will benefit from a signal under some circumstances, but I pick and choose.

If you're in the habit of always signalling, then stick with it. Better to give the occasional unnecessary signal than to miss giving one necessary signal.

Once you've passed the slower moving vehicles, check your mirrors and wait until you have a full view of the vehicle in your centre mirror before moving back to the nearside lane. It's also important to check your left shoulder at this point in exactly the same way as described above, just in case an overtaken vehicle has decided to accelerate.

Three Vehicles Abreast

When I undertook my police advanced course in 1995, "avoiding making a line of three vehicles abreast" was a key ingredient of advanced motorway driving. Even when travelling at very high speeds, you were expected to time your approaches to vehicles in lane 2 to avoid passing them when they were alongside vehicles in lane 1.

If your observations were good, you could do it through acceleration sense only and it didn't really impede your progress, but it did start to become more difficult as the volume of traffic increased.

When I applied to take my instructor's course four years later, I had to carry out an assessed drive with full commentary. I included the three abreast rule, but was pulled up during the debrief. The school had decided that the general increase in motorway traffic had made keeping the three abreast rule increasingly difficult and they no longer expected students to apply it during high speed motorway runs. The fact that you're travelling at a much higher speed than the overtaken vehicles means that your "time alongside" is reduced to a minimum.

For general driving in heavy traffic, however, I still strongly advocate the "three abreast" (or four abreast, etc. depending on the number of lanes) rule.

As mentioned in my original post, there is a domino effect on motorways where movements in lane 1 affect vehicles in lane 2 etc. if traffic is heavy and there is an HGV in lane 2, I tend to fall into a following position just longer than the HGV and only start to pass it once the vehicle in front of me has moved forward enough to allow me to pass the HGV and sit in a following position without being alongside the HGV.

It's not a "rule" per se, - more of a general guide. Sometimes (often in heavy traffic), it's impossible to avoid three or four abreast, but it's good practice where possible.

Travelling at very *high speed*

I'll start this section with a disclaimer. I've previously been in the privileged position of having a speed exemption for police training purposes. This allowed me, when it was appropriate, to drive as fast as was considered safe. At times, it would be perfectly safe to travel in excess of 150mph for considerable distances.

This was, however, under very controlled and justifiable circumstances and as part of my duties as a police driver and instructor.

I do not in any way condone breaking any laws and this part of the book is in no way an encouragement for anyone to go out and floor it to Vmax on a motorway.

It is, however, an insight into how police officers are taught to drive at very high speed on the motorway. It may also be useful for anyone who drives, or plans to drive at high speed on unrestricted sections of autobahn or any other unrestricted sections of road.

I'm sure that many of you will, at some point, have been driving on a quiet and un-policed stretch of motorway and been tempted to put your foot right down to see what your car will really do. Many of you will have succumbed to this temptation and exceeded 110, 120, or 130.

I'll bet, however, that you reached your maximum speed for less than a mile before backing off with a slight giggle and bringing your car back to a more sensible speed.

High motorway speeds can be intoxicating and exhilarating and those brief bursts of (highly illegal) speeds that many of us have explored will leave you with dilated pupils and a raised heart rate.

Here, however, is the truth about *sustained* high speed driving.

It's a bit boring.

This will, of course, sound daft to most readers - how can driving a considerable distance on the motorway at 140 or 150mph be boring?

Well, firstly, when you're legally exempt from speed limits, the "naughty" element doesn't exist. There is no danger of you being prosecuted because what you're doing isn't illegal, so that element of excitement just isn't there.

Secondly, you very quickly get used to the high speeds. Modern high performance cars do not need working very hard to achieve high speeds, so there is no extra effort required in the part of the driver, and no real specialist car handling skills either. On a completely empty and spacious road, almost anyone could sustain high speeds until they ran out of fuel.

In fact, I would commonly tell advanced car students that their speed - by which I mean the actual numbers on the speedo - was irrelevant. As long as the speed was appropriate to the circumstances, the numbers didn't matter a not. I had a couple of students who had a real mental block about going over 100mph. We'd accelerate nicely up through the gears, but as soon as they saw the needle go into three figures, they would involuntarily lift off.

We cured these drivers of their phobia by covering the speedo with a beer mat whenever we were on a motorway or NSL road. That's how irrelevant the actual speed is when you have an exemption.

Extended observations become absolutely vital as your speed goes well into 3 figures. If you're travelling at 150 and approaching a car doing 70, it's the same as approaching a stationary vehicle at 80mph. It's much more difficult to focus on things close to you when you're travelling above 100mph, and so you must look further down the road, as this is where you can focus. Excellent forward planning is essential and will allow you to make decisions well in advance of an evolving hazard.

Scan right to the distance and look very carefully for closing gaps. Spotting one truck closing on another on the distant horizon can become a truck moving in front of you within a few seconds.

Don't forget that other road users never expect you to be travelling at very high speeds. I would always use dipped headlights at high speed for extra visibility.

Make all your inputs very slowly and smoothly. All the stuff about keeping your driving smooth suddenly makes complete sense when you're moving along in the hundreds.

Your choice of lane is slightly different too. It's highly unlikely that you'll be holding anyone up at 140 or 150 (although mirror checks are still required at high speed), so I would usually stick to lanes 2 and 3. There are two reasons for this. HGVs mostly use lane 1 and over time they can create distinct tyre tracks in that lane. These aren't usually a problem at 70, but can cause extreme tram lining at 140, so stay out of lane 1. Secondly, you're not likely to be impeding anyone's progress, so lanes 2 and 3 can be used as driving - as opposed to overtaking - lanes at high speed.

Here's something else to bear in mind on this point. Motorways are designed by engineers so that the radii of bends are safe at up to around 100mph. They are not designed to be travelled at top speed, and so the wide open bends you're used to become very distinct corners at high speed. Left handlers can be particularly uncomfortable when you're in lane 3 as the central barrier can feel perilously close.

In dealing with motorway corners at high speed, bear in mind that the basic principle of cornering with a little acceleration still applies if you want to keep the car well balanced. This means that you shouldn't approach a motorway corner at top speed, because you'll have nothing left with which to accelerate. Instead, lift off slightly on approach, lose around 10mph and then reapply the speed as you drive around the corner. This is a very subtle technique, but makes a world of difference.

Is there anything else to bear in mind? One overriding rule...

Always be prepared to sacrifice speed for safety

It's not a willy waving contest out there and even the very best drivers can get caught out at high speeds. The fact that sustained high speed driving can become boring makes it even more dangerous if that in turn reduces your concentration level. You need to be **EXTREMELY** alert to drive at these speeds.

One other thing - it's very, very easy to break the speed limit when you leave the motorway after sustained high speed driving. After 10 miles at 150, 100 can feel like 60 and 60 can feel very dangerously like 30.

31

Motorway Driving
Part 3

YOUTUBE LINK - **MOTORWAY DRIVING**:

https://youtu.be/kWQzlWZG-lI

We've covered motorway entries and some stuff about driving along the motorway and making some progress, so it's now time to cover a few additional things about driving on the motorway - specifically roadworks and stopping in an emergency.

Before I go any further though, I'll just stick this picture up again, for reference:

I'll start with everyone's favourite aspect of motorway driving...

Roadworks

Our motorway network is knocking on a bit these days, with some sections dating back to the late 1950s. Bearing in mind the massive increase in traffic, it's no surprise that motorways require a constant program of maintenance to keep them in a safe, useable condition. In addition, there are a multitude of widening schemes and smart motorway (hard shoulder as a running lane) schemes being introduced up and down the country, which inevitably bring with them a reduction in running lanes, cones, reduced speed limits, cones, reduced-width lanes, cones, contra-flow systems and of course, cones.

Motorway roadworks are definitely an embuggerance, but contrary to popular opinion, they aren't just thrown up randomly to cheese us all off. There is a considerable amount of thought and planning put into the design of roadwork systems. Don't believe me? Have a look at chapter 8 of the traffic signs manual. But make sure it's a very wet, boring weekend.

To start with, I'm going to go all "AA" and talk about planning your journey. If you're about to set off on a longish trip, there is a shed-load of information available to you via the internet which gives real-time information about roadworks and traffic problems. My daily commute is mostly motorway, so I always have a quick look at the Highways Agency website while I'm having my breakfast. I've also got a free app which gives access to a network of Highways Agency CCTV cameras, which can be very useful. 2 minutes of my morning can occasionally save me up to an hour in travelling time.

The "TA" or "TP" button on your radio is a useful addition if you're on a long journey. It will switch to local radio channels when traffic announcements are broadcast, overriding whatever channel, CD or track you're listening to.

Sat navs also have traffic information systems built in - they usually require a subscription, but I managed to get it free with my iPhone sat-nav app and it works pretty well.

If you've explored all other options, or if you've been caught out by some motorway roadworks, you should still get plenty of prior warning to stop you from ploughing in to the signs, cones and Highways Agency staff.

Chapter 8 dictates that on a motorway, the first warning sign for roadworks should be placed 2 miles before the start of the works, or 3 miles prior if congestion is expected. You'll then get a series of signs as you approach the works which will give you an idea which lanes are closed, what the speed limit will be, which vehicles are permitted in which lanes and an indication if speed enforcement cameras are present.

If there is a lane closure ahead, the best approach is to merge-in-turn, by which I mean that if you're in the closing lane, you should drive right up to the taper (the diagonal line of cones used to close the lane) and then merge in a "zip" fashion with the vehicles in the open lane.

There is a key advantage to merging in turn, in that all the vehicles approaching the roadworks will stay in lane right up to the lane closure.

This means that any tailback caused by the roadworks is kept to a minimum because the slow-moving and stationary vehicles are spread across all available lanes, right up to the roadworks.

There is, however, a major problem with merging in turn.

People don't like it.

By which I mean that there is a general misunderstanding about merging in turn which is held by the majority of drivers. It goes against our traditional British propensity for queuing. Those in the open lane feel like those in the closing lane are "pushing in". Some will shake their heads in a disapproving manner. Others will glue themselves to the bumper of the car in front to prevent you from merging in front of them whilst maintaining the "I haven't seen you" straight-ahead stare.

The worst ones (and this particularly includes HGV drivers, who as professional drivers, should know better) will deliberately block the closing lane well ahead of the taper, forcing vehicles to back up behind them and preventing merge-in-turn.

Its daft, to be honest - and dangerous too at times. Once we're all in to the roadworks, we should keep moving at a reduced speed, and within a few minutes, we'll be emerging from the other end and we're on our collective ways again. Why make it more difficult than it has to be? But that's the British attitude towards queuing and taking-your-turn, and I fear we're stuck with it.

So, taking this problem into account, I like to strike a compromise and aim to merge some distance before the cone taper. Look for a suitable gap nice and early and try to slide subtly in without braking (or with the minimum of braking). Additionally, I aim not to be "that" driver (or in this case, one of "those" drivers), and allow others to merge.

It's probably the right point to give a brief mention to contraflow systems. A contraflow system is a roadworks system designed to allow work to be carried out on some or all of an entire carriageway by diverting traffic onto the opposite carriageway **contra**ry to the normal **flow** of traffic. The danger is that, rather than being separated from opposing traffic by a central reservation and Armco barriers, traffic is generally only separated by a line of those skinny traffic cones, or, at best, a temporary concrete barrier.

An ex driving school colleague of mine had worked as a motorway patrol officer for many years, and he had seen one too many crossover accidents in contraflow systems. He wouldn't allow his students to use the right-hand lane in any contraflow system on the basis that, even in a reduced speed limit area, the risks of a head-on collision due to a simple lane change error were too great.

I take a slightly more flexible approach, whereby as long as there is some clear space to my left; I'm comfortable using the right-most lane. In other words, try not to linger alongside other vehicles. If the speed of traffic is similar in both lanes, then try to make sure you're alongside a gap rather than a vehicle. And of course, the leftmost lane *is* the safest option if you're not too bothered about progress, which is usually severely hampered by temporary speed limits anyway.

Stopping in an emergency

Vehicles are much more reliable these days. 30 years ago, it was quite common to see cars pulled up on the hard shoulder with the bonnet up and a plume of steam rising from within, but punctures aside, it's not as common these days to see a breakdown on the motorway.

The problem with this is that when things *do* go wrong, people are even less likely to know what to do other than pull on to the hard shoulder and reach for their mobile phone.

The first tip is to avoid stopping on the motorway altogether. I don't mean in a patronising "AA advice to drivers" kind of way as I'm sure this isn't being read by someone who is likely to run out of petrol on the motorway (is it?).

What I mean is that pretty much all vehicle faults do not result in the vehicle coming to an immediate, unexpected stop. If your engine were to cut out at, say, 60mph in lane 2, dipping the clutch or popping it into neutral should allow you enough momentum to coast for probably close to a mile or more. This may well be enough to get you on to the nearest exit slip, or to the next ETB (see below).

But to start with, let's look at one of the very small number of absolute "rules" that I believe it's important to abide with.

Unless it is absolutely, completely and utterly unavoidable, never ***ever*** stop in a "live" or "running" lane. If you absolutely have to stop on the motorway, do everything that you possibly can to get your vehicle on to the hard shoulder and out of the live lanes (lanes 1, 2 and 3 in the picture at the top of the page).

Most drivers are never expecting to come across stationary vehicles on an otherwise free-flowing motorway. Relatively minor incidents and accidents can very quickly become very serious, multiple vehicle accidents if vehicles are allowed to remain stationary in live lanes.

Even if you're involved in an accident and you *think* that your vehicle is immobile, you should at least try to move it on to the hard shoulder. Ignore all the scraping and crunching sounds - if the engine runs, put it in gear and shift it if you can. If the engine won't start, put the car in gear, leave the clutch out and try moving it on the starter motor - this can be more effective than you might imagine.

Make no bones about it - the motorway is an extremely dangerous, alien and fast-moving environment if you're stationary or on foot. Ask anyone who has ever had to stop and get out of their car on a hard shoulder. It is a frightening place to be and your plan should be to avoid stopping there if at all possible.

But, as we know, the devil does occasionally piddle in your kettle and you may have to stop on the hard shoulder. What to do? Well, first off, try to stop near an emergency telephone box (ETB). These are the orange boxes spaced at regular intervals (usually 1 mile apart, so that you're never more than 1/2 mile from one) along the left side of the hard shoulder.

They generally look like this...

This is where coasting to a stop can be useful. Every 100 metres along the left hand side of the motorway you'll see marker posts like this...

There are a couple of bits of information on these marker posts. The top number is the distance in kilometres from the start of the motorway, and the bottom number is the decimal place, so in this case, 85.0 km from the start of the motorway. More importantly, if you have to stop on the hard shoulder, is the little picture of a telephone on the side of the marker post. The arrow under the phone indicates the direction to the nearest ETB. If you're coasting to a stop, look at the nearest marker to decide if you should stop immediately or continue coasting to the next ETB.

But why should you stop near an ETB? Surely they're a largely redundant anachronism these days? Don't most people have a mobile phone?

Well, yes they do, but mobile phones can be as much of a hindrance on the motorway as a help. If you were to break down on the motorway, would you actually know **exactly** where you were? Believe it or not, most people don't. They usually know which motorway they're on, where they joined, and where they are heading for, but they don't generally know whether they're heading north or south, which junctions they are between or which town they are near.

I've spent quite a bit of time in police control rooms, and it's fascinating to see just how many calls come in when there is an incident or accident on the motorway. It's even more fascinating listening to the process the operators have to go through just to narrow down the motorway and carriageway where the incident has occurred.

Stopping and using an ETB removes this problem almost instantly. Pick up the telephone and the operator immediately knows exactly where you are. They will have all the recovery companies on speed-dial and will be able to give you detailed instructions on how to stay safe. They may even dispatch HATOs or police officers to make double-sure that you are safe.

The control room operators will call whoever you like to get you off the motorway as long as they can get your car removed from the hard shoulder in less than 2 hours. Years ago they called my dad for me and he turned up with a tow rope and a grumpy face and towed me home.

They will ring the AA, RAC, Green flag or any other recovery company on your behalf, but if you're not a member of a recovery service, your car will still have to be removed from the motorway within 2 hours, so they will call out a recovery firm - usually the next one on their rota of approved companies.

If a rota garage attends, you'll be paying the bill for recovery and it's up to you to negotiate where you want the car taking to. To be clear though, this service isn't free, apart from when there is a section of roadworks with cameras and "free recovery" signs. These are usually set up when the hard shoulder has been taken up with roadworks and any breakdown is in a live running lane. Even so, the limit of the free recovery will be off at the next junction into the first lay-by and then it's over to you to organise your further recovery.

The new sections of "managed motorways" (hard shoulder as a running lane), use a similar system to roadworks arrangements for free recovery.

My advice would be to get at least a basic level of breakdown recovery so that at least you can be sure that you'll get home in the event of a breakdown.

Should you attempt a repair yourself on the hard shoulder? Only if you're competent and it will take a few minutes. Changing a wheel, for instance, but I'd be less inclined to change an offside wheel than a nearside wheel unless I could get my car almost completely off the hard shoulder and onto the verge.

If you have to wait for recovery, you'll be advised to get out of your car, climb over the Armco and stand on the verge or embankment well away from the carriageway. This may seem daft, particularly when the weather is terrible and you've a nice, warm car to sit in, but there is a very good reason.

The vast majority of serious and fatal accidents occur on the hard shoulder and involve a stationary or broken-down vehicle.

"Target fixation" is a phenomenon in which people have a tendency to drive towards something they're looking at. It makes stationary vehicles on the motorway extremely vulnerable and is the reason you'll be advised to leave your vehicle. I always carry a nice, big umbrella just in case.

And what if - God forbid - you are stopped by the police? If an officer wants you to stop, they will almost always stop you from behind, by lighting their blue beacons, flashing their lights and possibly pointing to the left. In other words, they'll make it plainly obvious they are stopping you.

At this point, don't panic and slam on the brakes. Instead, move towards the nearside when it's safe, and stop gradually on the hard shoulder. Try to stop in the centre of the shoulder and then stay in the driver's seat.

The police officer should then approach your passenger side and speak to you either through the window or by opening the door. Follow their instructions - although they may want to speak to you about an offence or infringement, their first duty is to keep everyone safe, so they will give you very specific instructions and it's very much in your interest to follow them.

When your encounter with the officer is over and you're about to set off, please get up to speed on the hard shoulder before re-joining lane 1. In other words, treat the hard shoulder as an acceleration lane in much the same way as you would with a slip road, then look for a suitable gap and join lane 1.

32

Motorway driving
Part 4

YouTube link - **Motorway Driving:**

https://youtu.be/kWQzlWZG-lI

If you've managed to read this far without losing the will to live, you'll know that we've entered the motorway correctly, we've done some high-speed driving, dealt with roadworks and breakdowns and basically got on with our journey. There's only one thing left to do – leave the motorway.

That sounds simple enough doesn't it? Well, at low-to-moderate speeds, it really is – motorway exits are always signed well in advance – the first signs are usually at least a mile prior to the exit itself, so, even in heavy traffic there is plenty of time to plan and execute a nice, safe exit from the motorway.

If you're travelling at higher speeds, however, it becomes more difficult – you have less time to plan your exit and less time to execute it. The temptation is to bail out early and get into lane 1 as soon as possible, but we're trying to be advanced drivers aren't we? Advanced drivers should be looking for every opportunity to make a little more progress, and there are many opportunities to make a little more progress during your exit from the motorway.

So, in the following series of pictures, I'll look at the signage you'll find on the approach to a junction and the thought processes involved in making a nice, progressive exit from the motorway.

Why progressive though? Why not just aim to be in lane 1 by the mile board, slow right down and leave the motorway at a leisurely pace? Well, there's nothing inherently wrong with this approach, but if we're trying to be advanced drivers, we should be looking to make progress, which means that we should be looking to pass as many slower vehicles as possible. It's much easier to pass slower vehicles on the motorway than it is on an "A" or "B" road after you've left the motorway, so the more vehicles you can pass whilst you're still on the motorway, the less work you'll have to do when you leave.

There is one overriding rule, however, that you should bear in mind when leaving the motorway. Irrespective of whether you're bimbling along at moderate speed or flying along at high speed, you should always aim to be in lane 1 by the 300 yard countdown marker. If you stick to this rule, you'll never miss an exit and you'll never have to do a last minute lunging dive for the exit slip.

So, lane 1 by the 300 yard marker please.

The first indication that you're approaching a junction will normally be one mile prior to the junction. This can vary according to the junction and the first sign can be as far away as one and a half miles from the junction, or as close as two thirds of a mile, but helpfully, the sign tells you the distance in the bottom right-hand corner:

The sign – the one mile board - also tells us in the little black box that the next exit is number 37, that it leads directly to the A684 and that it's the correct exit to take if you're heading towards Kendle or Sedbergh. If we're making progress at this point, there should normally be no need to slow down yet – in light-to-medium traffic, I'd be perfectly happy to stay in lanes 2 or 3 at this point without losing any speed. In heavier traffic, I'd probably start the planning process at this point – particularly if I were out in lane 3 and pressing on, so I'd be looking to identify suitable gaps in the traffic to allow me to start moving across to lanes 2 and 1. But in this case, with this level of traffic, I'd keep my speed up and stay out in an overtaking lane, but I'd also be extending my observations into the far distance, towards and under the bridge in the distance, looking for the next sign:

The next sign is the half-mile board, which gives exactly the same information as the mile board. The distance given – ½ mile in this case – is the distance to the start of the deceleration lane. At this point, in light-to-medium traffic, I'd be looking to identify my route across to lane 1. This requires a careful examination of the traffic in lanes 1 and 2, the gaps between vehicles, their relative speeds and your speed. Ideally, you should "re-claim" each lane in turn, in the same way as you do when joining the motorway. Exits can be made much more difficult by drivers not leaving sufficient space between vehicles, and as the traffic gets heavier, your planning process needs to start further and further from the actual exit. In this case, however, I'd still be looking to make some progress whilst looking well ahead for the next sign and possibly a view of the junction itself:

And here it is – we can, of course, see the whole of the junction, the deceleration lane, the off-slip and the bridge, but to assist us in our planning, the highways authorities maintain consistent signage at every exit, most of which is visible in this picture, beginning with the 300 yard countdown marker which, believe it or not, tells us that we're now 300 yards from the exit – or more specifically – 300 yards from the start of the deceleration lane.

Remember my rule for motorway exits? *Lane 1 by the 300 yard marker.* Well, here it is – you should aim to be in lane 1 by this point. If your planning is good and there is a particularly slow moving vehicle in lane 1 at this point, then it may occasionally be fine to still be in lane 2 at this point, but your initial plan should always be to reach lane 1 by the 300 yard board.

If there is traffic around you, it's usually appropriate to indicate your intention to leave the motorway. If your speed is 70mph or over, then my preference is to put on a left indicator at the 300 yard board. If your speed is lower than 70mph, then it's ok to leave your signal a little later, but you shouldn't signal any later than the 200 yard board:

The 200 yard countdown marker – the latest point at which you should put on a left signal. Can you guess what comes next?

Yes, of course – the 100 yard countdown marker, which is followed shortly by:

The final exit board. The difference with this board is that it shows the destinations further along the motorway as well as the destinations available by leaving at this junction.

If you've planned your exit well, and executed your plan, you'll then easily roll off into the deceleration lane and start looking for the correct lane to allow you to continue your journey.

If you've planned your exit *extremely* well, and executed it *perfectly*, you'll have carried out all these actions using acceleration sense only, and you won't need to touch the brakes until you're squarely in the deceleration lane – this should be your ultimate aim for any motorway exit.

After leaving the motorway – particularly if you've been travelling at high speed – try to take a minute or two to re-acclimatise to driving on normal roads. Sustained driving at high speeds can give you the false impression that you're travelling slower than you actually are when you've left the motorway, so just keep a close eye on your speedo for the first couple of miles and use that time to get back into the rhythm of the road you've joined.

33

WE MAKE THE STANDARDS AND WE MAKE THE RULES...

YOUTUBE LINK - **BE WARY OF RULES!**:

https://youtu.be/qHFi26xB-OQ

...And if you don't abide by them you must be a fool.

Is it ever ok for an advanced driver to break the rules?

I was out on a local run recently which took me from my home on the outskirts of town, up onto a moorland NSL road for a few miles and then down into a more built-up area with associated speed limits & hazards.

The stretch of moorland road starts as a 30mph limit and for most of the 30mph section; the speed limit makes perfect sense. The road is bordered by residential properties, footpaths, minor road junctions and a few shops. In other words, it's a built-up area and the 30mph limit is quite correct.

The last 500 yards of the 30mph limit area are different though. There are no houses, entrances or other hazards, the road is open with a clear view ahead (albeit on a long, open right-hander), and the vast majority of drivers and riders completely ignore the 30 limit on this section and accelerate early up to and beyond the national speed limit.

Now, before you jump to conclusions, I'm not trying to justify these drivers' actions. It should be obvious to anyone that it is still a 30mph speed limit - it has street lamps at regular intervals and there is a pub situated just before the increase in speed limits, so potentially some hazards associated with the pub car park, customers etc.

If I'm driving along this road with no following traffic, I'll stick to the speed limit right up to the NSL signs before increasing my speed. I then like to drive the NSL section at a speed I consider to be spirited but safe. Inevitably this is generally higher than the majority of other road users.

The problem is that when I'm in that last section of the 30mph limit and I've got following traffic, I tend to be the slowest car on the road. It's not uncommon to have a buildup of quite a few vehicles behind me on the approach to the NSL signs, all bunching up, driving close and looking to overtake me.

Now, I have no problem whatsoever with being overtaken and I'm not a road captain, so I'm not out to spoil anyone else's progress. However, in a few seconds time I will be accelerating away up to a speed which will likely be in excess of that which the following vehicles will be accelerating up to. In other words, if they overtake me in the 30mph limit, I will almost immediately be behind them, looking to overtake them when the speed limit increases.

So what to do? The opportunity to overtake comes just as the right-hander opens up, immediately next to the pub, but probably 50 yards before the speed limit increases.

So, to ensure I'm not overtaken, if there is close following traffic, I wait until I have a clear view into the pub car park, and then start to accelerate early, before I reach the NSL signs. To clarify, I don't absolutely floor it - I just add around 10mph or so, which creates a gap between me and the following vehicle and discourages them from moving into the overtake. Once I reach the NSL sign I apply some firmer acceleration and I'm off.

To clarify even further, very occasionally, the following vehicles (and this will usually be a motorcycle), will "go with" me and then still go for the overtake. In these circumstances I will not accelerate when being overtaken, and the overtaking vehicle will be quickly past me. Mostly though, I'll quickly see the following traffic rapidly disappearing into a tiny dot in the mirror never to be seen again.

So, if we go by "the book" (whichever book you choose to abide by), I'm choosing to break the speed limit. The book will tell you that this is wrong, wrong, wrong and that I'm a bad, bad man. But am I? Really?

In my mind I am weighing up the difference between the risks involved in momentarily exceeding a speed limit in a relatively hazard-free area, with the risks involved in overtaking slower vehicles on an NSL road.

What would you choose to do?

Here's another one. On the same stretch of road, only a few hundred yards further past the pub, the road rises up and then drops into a small dip. The road remains straight, but this dip forms a zone of invisibility and so the white centre lines become solid double white lines for a short time. As I approached these lines, I could see a cyclist ahead travelling in the same direction as me & just approaching the double-whites.

The road is reasonably wide, but for their comfort, I prefer to straddle the centre lines when passing cyclists along that road. The Highway Code tells me that this is fine for double-whites, providing the cyclist is travelling at 10mph or less.

The trouble is, he's one of those cyclists who looks like he's dropped off the peloton on at the Giro d'Italia. Fully lycra'd up on an expensive looking carbon bike; it's highly unlikely that he's travelling less than 10. On that road, he's likely to be in the 25-30mph range.

What to do? If we're going by the book, we should slow right down, sit in a following position on the cyclist, wait until the solid lines break, and then move out to overtake him.

What I actually did is lift off the accelerator on the approach, wait until I had a view into the dip, and then move out to straddle the white lines to pass the cyclist without losing much speed. It was perfectly safe, there was no risk for either of us, and neither of us was inconvenienced.

Wrong? Well, strictly speaking I'd committed a moving traffic offence by contravening the double white lines.

Again, I had weighed up all the options and chosen one which presented the minimum of risks, but in the process I became an offender. I suppose I could argue that I *thought* he was going less than 10mph, and it would be difficult to prove he wasn't, but deep down I know he wasn't and I was committing an offence.

What would you do?

Does any of this mean I'm any less of an advanced driver? Well, if I was undertaking an advanced driving test, these actions would likely go against me. But out in the real world? I'm not so sure.

You be the judge.

34

CRITICAL SELF-ANALYSIS (OR HOW TO REBOOT YOUR OWN OPERATING SYSTEM)

When was the last time you tested yourself? By which, I mean when was the last time you looked critically at your own driving?

It's not as easy as it sounds. The first hurdle is our natural tendency to think we're better than we are. Ask your friends and family if they think they're good drivers and a huge majority (over 90% in a very short straw poll in my office) will assess themselves as above average drivers. Mathematics alone shows that they can't all be right. No-one will ever admit to having a weakness at driving. In much the same way that no-one will ever admit to having a poor sense of humour. Or to being bad in bed.

But as we all know, there are plenty of humourless people out there, and plenty of poor lovers.

Take a drive - any drive of any length and you'll see some poor, and some appalling driving. It's clear, then, that many of the 90% of people who assess themselves as above average must be way off the mark in judging their own skill levels.

So how do you accurately assess your own abilities? How do you address your faults? It's as much about the psychology of driving, and how to develop a critical thought process, as it is about the physical and mental skills of just driving, so let's start with some basic psychology and see how it applies to driving.

The Four Stages of Competence

Many of you may be familiar with the four stages of competence. I first encountered this theory when I was on a management course a couple of years ago and I immediately recognised its relevance to driving skills.

1. Unconscious incompetence

The individual does not understand or know how to do something and does not necessarily recognize the deficit. They may deny the usefulness of the skill. The individual must recognise their own incompetence, and the value of the new skill, before moving on to the next stage. The length of time an individual spends in this stage depends on the strength of the stimulus to learn.

2. Conscious incompetence

Though the individual does not understand or know how to do something, he or she does recognize the deficit, as well as the value of a new skill in addressing the deficit. The making of mistakes can be integral to the learning process at this stage.

3. Conscious competence

The individual understands or knows how to do something. However, demonstrating the skill or knowledge requires concentration. It may be broken down into steps, and there is heavy conscious involvement in executing the new skill.

4. Unconscious competence

The individual has had so much practice with a skill that it has become "second nature" and can be performed easily. As a result, the skill can be performed while executing another task. The individual may be able to teach it to others, depending upon how and when it was learned.

So, in other words, before you start to learn a new skill, you don't know how to do it and you don't know *why* you don't know how to do it. Then you start to learn, and you realise what you need to do, but you can't do it. Then your skills improve, but you still need to think about what you're doing. And then finally, you're able to easily carry out the task without giving it much thought.

Sound familiar? I think it's almost a perfect description of the development of a new driver, from their first lesson, through learning, passing their test and then the first year or so of independent driving.

The thing is, though, these four stages can be reapplied to any driver of any experience level. At 25 years old, with 8 years driving experience, a few years in panda cars, and a mk2 Golf GTI, I thought a was a good driver. In fact, I thought I was a great driver. Then I went to the police driving school for my advanced course and after the first day of lectures and a demonstration drive by my instructor - Dicko - the cold realisation hit me. I was rubbish. In fact, it was amazing that I'd actually survived the past 8 years with all 4 limbs intact.

Fast forward 4 years, I'd achieved a good first class pass on my advanced course, and been driving traffic cars, chasing stolen cars and generally rushing round for a few years. I was pretty handy in my opinion.

Then I went on my car instructor's course. First day, demonstration drive by my instructor - Ricky this time - with full instructional commentary, and I realised once again that I was rubbish and we were back to rung 1 - unconscious incompetence again and 6 weeks to get through all 4 stages of competence.

The point I'm trying to make with these examples is that the four stages of competence aren't restricted to just learning new skills. They are just as relevant to improving, correcting and polishing the skills you've already got. It doesn't matter how good you are - the first principle of assessing yourself correctly is to recognise that you can always, *always* be better. There is *always* room for improvement.

Here's another good point I've unapologetically nicked from a psychology textbook...

Overestimating Your Ability

Whilst almost everyone overestimates their skill level, knowledge and abilities, their degree of overestimation goes down as skill/training/education/practice goes up. So your assessment of yourself after studying something in a formal fashion with evaluation and comparison grows closer to your actual skill.

In other words, the more training and experience you get, the better you become at *realistically* assessing your own abilities.

Here's another one I've taken from the management course which I think relates very well to driving...

Justifying Bad Behaviour / Habits

This might ring true with some of you, so brace yourself for a dose of cold reality...

We have a very strong tendency to view other people's mistakes and misdemeanors in a very different way than we view our own. If someone cuts you up in traffic or pulls out on you at a roundabout, it's because they're an inconsiderate, incompetent pillock, and they deserve to die in a fiery ball of crumpled metal (or at least to suffer your wrath with a toot from the horn - the horror!).

But when the shoe is on the other foot and it's you who has made the mistake, it's not because you're a numpty - it's because you're in a rush, you've other things on your mind, you're late for a *very* important appointment and, well, nobody died and you're a good driver really - aren't you?

Emergency response drivers are notorious for this kind of thing. So much so that it's been given a label - "noble cause risk taking". It's much easier to justify making an error or taking an unnecessarily risk - even a life threateningly dangerous one - if you're on the way to a bank robbery, or a heart attack, or a kitten up a tree.

This leads me on to my next point quite nicely...

Learn From Your Mistakes

Try to develop a different attitude towards your mistakes. Instead of justifying them, or beating yourself up, or ignoring them, try to use them as a learning tool.

I strongly believe that driving students - at any experience level - need to be allowed to make mistakes. As an instructor, your job is to teach the correct methods, but rather than trying to talk students through every single situation (over instructing), you should, instead, let them make some mistakes so that they have a genuine memory of the consequences upon which they can then build their experiences.

Not very serious, dangerous mistakes of course, but enough to allow you to say to them "remember last time" on the approach to a similar situation.

You need to adopt this approach yourself with your own driving. Mistakes are an inevitable part of any journey - there is no such thing as a perfect drive - so try to mentally "bank" your mistakes, think about what went wrong and what you could have done differently, and then apply what you've learned in your future driving.

Can you see the four levels of competence running through that last paragraph?

Here's another good tip...

Work On Your Weaknesses, Not Your Strengths

We all know what we're good at, and we all know what we're not so good at. The trouble is that we have an inbuilt tendency to stick with the things we're good at because we like them, and avoid addressing the things we're not so good at, because they tend to be the things we don't enjoy.

So, if you're good at making progress on "A" roads, but you're nervous on motorways, you'll tend to stick with the "A" roads and avoid the motorways. Your "A" road skills will, of course, continue to improve, but avoiding the motorways means that you never improve your motorway driving skills.

So you should learn to push yourself - by which I mean that you should seek out the situations you don't enjoy and which concern you, because only by practicing and making mistakes, will you improve in those areas.

I used to hate giving presentations to groups of people. The very thought of giving a lecture or lesson filled me with dread and led to sleepless nights. I avoided anything which required these skills for years.

Then I found a job I wanted. It was a great job, but required me to give occasional presentations. I bit the bullet, underwent some training, and took every opportunity to carry out public speaking. Nowadays I'm perfectly happy to give public presentations to large groups - often with a minimum of notice without becoming stressed at all. Avoiding public speaking was the mistake & I learned from it.

You can pull together all the different aspects I've covered by regularly...

Testing Yourself

To start with, have an idea in your own mind what standard you're going to test yourself against. Those of you who have undertaken some form of advanced training may want to use the "test" standard on whatever course you took. Those who haven't had the benefit of training may want to consider a chapter from Roadcraft, an article on driving that they may have read, or (God forbid!!) something written in an advanced driving book by a self-proclaimed "expert".

Don't set out on a special drive just to test yourself. Instead, carry out your "self-test" on an ordinary journey. To or from work, for example, or any other journey you undertake on a regular basis.

Drive as you normally would, but at the same time, try to imagine what a critical third party would think of your driving. Would they be happy with that overtake? Would they think you were too close to the car in front? Would they approve of your position on the approach to this corner?

I also try to imagine an instructor sat next to me, talking me down the road. There were a couple of instructors I had for whom I have a huge amount of respect and I like to think "what would Ricky or AJ be saying to me now?"

You don't need to do it on every journey, but if you self-test every month or so, you will keep your skills up and recognise mistakes before they become long term, habitual faults.

It's a bit like rebooting and reinstalling your own operating system every few weeks.

35

FAMILIARITY BREEDS COMPLACENCY

There is a road I drive along regularly. It's not particularly long - a couple of miles at most - and it's not a particularly fast road. It's single carriageway NSL, but it twists and turns with a whole variety of different corners. It has varying degrees of negative and positive camber, uneven patches of tarmac, areas where it's less grippy than others and is interspersed with double white line systems.

Now, I've been driving along this road, on average, three or four times a week for at least the last ten years - possibly longer. I know the road intimately - I know where it stays wet after a rainstorm and where it dries more quickly. I know where patches of frost tend to linger into the afternoon, and where it thaws out. I know which farm entrances are likely to have mud near to them, and which ones a herd of cattle is prone to emerge from occasionally. I know which junctions are blind and difficult to emerge from, and which ones I've got a good, early view into. I know exactly where I can overtake (two areas in one direction and, helped by a downhill stretch if I'm behind something slow), three in the other direction.

With all this detailed local knowledge, you'd think that it would be one of the safest roads I could possibly drive along, wouldn't you?

Well, I've been giving this some thought and I've decided that it's actually quite the opposite - it's probably the *most* dangerous road that I use.

The problem with familiarity with a road is that there is an inevitable "autopilot" mode that kicks in, whether you want it to or not. Now, I'm not saying that I blindly drive along this road without thinking, but I monitored myself as I drove along it today, and I realised that, because I knew it so well, I was automatically looking in the same places for a view, I wasn't assessing bends, because I knew how tight they were, my attention was placed in well-rehearsed areas along the length of the road, and my thought patterns, generally, seemed to be pre-determined, rather than free-thinking.

If I drive an unfamiliar piece of road, I have to assess bends for their severity, look for areas of visibility and invisibility, spot actual and potential hazards, work out driving plans and *alternative* plans, etc. etc. On the familiar road, I've pretty much got one single driving plan for the whole road. Of course, circumstances change every time I drive the road, but it's very easy to think that you've seen everything before and you've already got a plan for it happening.

I know where the stables are, for instance and I've seen enough horses on that road to know exactly what I'm going to do if I come across one. I know where to deal with cyclists, and not just *where* to overtake other vehicles, but what gear I need to be in and how to carry out the overtakes.

The problem is - because I'm not approaching the road with a fresh, open mind, I could end up in deep trouble if something genuinely unexpected happened. We all know about the safe stopping rule, but

I know for a fact that I'll carry more speed into a corner if I know it well, than I will if it's unfamiliar. Would I *still* be able to stop on my own side of the road if something unexpected happened? I asked myself that very question whilst driving today. The answer was yes, I could, but it'd be a close thing. Closer than I'd like it to be, anyway.

You see, although I've encountered pretty much everything that I'm likely to on that road, there are still many situations that I haven't, and which are a real possibility. I've never encountered a fallen tree, for instance, or a cyclist who's had a fall, or a recent accident. The fact that I'm probably giving these possibilities less credence than I would if I *didn't* know the road is what's been bothering me.

On the way back home, I approached the road with a different mind-set. I pretended that I didn't know it. The difference was surprising. Although my lines through corners didn't change, the way in which I assessed them certainly did, and my entry speeds were slower as a result. I found myself looking in places that I haven't looked for ages - probably years - and assessing possibilities that hadn't really come up before.

I've decided that this is something that I'm going to do on all the routes I use regularly, starting with my route to work, as that's probably the route I drive most often, so it's almost certainly the route I've become most complacent with.

Have a go yourself - you'll probably be quite surprised at how many possibilities you haven't considered on roads that you know well.

36

Acceleration Nonsense

YOUTUBE LINK - **ACCELERATION SENSE:**

https://youtu.be/cn85aXnuhs8

My police driving career spanned two different versions of Roadcraft. My standard course took place in 1992 when the police were still teaching the seven phase system from the old blue Roadcraft, whereas I undertook my advanced training in 1995 in accordance with the (then) new five phase system.

For both courses, some commentary was required during the final test drives. On a standard course that was one drive with an instructor during which about 2 minutes of commentary was expected and on an advanced course you would have two final test drives (one auto, one manual) during which 10 minutes of commentary was required during each drive.

Commentary is not easy, especially for beginners, but one of the tips my instructors gave was to have some stuff in reserve for when there wasn't much to talk about. So when there was a lot going on, you'd talk about the hazards, grading them in importance, what your plans were etc. but when you were on a featureless road with nothing much presenting as hazards, the tip was to throw in a few Roadcraft definitions.

You would describe the four advantages of the following position, talk about scanning, and throw in some verbatim paragraphs from Roadcraft and the Highway Code (even learning a few paragraph numbers for extra anorak appeal).

Having done two courses under two books, my repertoire was a bit of a mixed bag. To this day I can still remember two full definitions without (I promise) any reference to the books. Firstly braking sense from the old blue book...

"The ability of a driver to appreciate a situation and apply the brakes in a gradual and timely manner to stop, or reduce the speed of the vehicle where this cannot be achieved by deceleration alone."

And the old definition of acceleration sense...

The ability of a driver to vary the speed of the vehicle, by accurate use of the accelerator, to meet changing road and traffic conditions."

When the new book came out, these definitions were altered slightly and weren't as clearly identifiable from the rest of the text as actual "definitions", but they were still relevant and I included them in my advanced test commentary (and in my instructor's tests a few years later) without any negative comments or marks.

In my view, acceleration sense is one of the abilities which really separates a skilled road driver from the rest of the motoring public. It's a skill that very few people will ever notice; it's a skill which can be extremely difficult to learn, a skill which can be very satisfying to practice, a subtle and unobtrusive skill which can be used to fine effect on any and every journey and a skill which I doubt anyone ever *truly* masters.

It's also a skill which is based on the most simple of principles...

The accelerator works both ways.

I know this seems a ridiculously simple principle, but honestly, correct use of the accelerator is an absolute key skill in advanced road driving, no matter what type of vehicle you're driving. To be clear though, I'm not just talking about increasing the speed of the vehicle by pressing the gas pedal. Acceleration sense is much more subtle and wide-reaching than that.

What I'm talking about is how you use the accelerator pedal whilst you're driving along, approaching and negotiating hazards, how you use the accelerator in reaction to changing road and traffic conditions, changing speed limits and changing gradients and how you use the accelerator to maintain a following position on other vehicles.

When I was teaching advanced police courses, I'd get my students to perform a number of exercises to improve their acceleration sense.

One exercise involved driving a road which included a series of different bends. Most drivers would accelerate between corners and then brake for the next corner (rinse and repeat etc.). Now, there's nothing inherently wrong with this approach, but I would ask my students to drive the road at a reasonably quick pace in a single gear (usually 4th) without braking. I would expect the corners to be negotiated correctly with a little acceleration for balance, and I'd expect some reasonable acceleration between corners, but the student's job was to assess the bends and pick the correct point at which they should lift off the accelerator to achieve the correct speed for the bend.

Another good exercise was to drive a section of NSL road leading to a reduced limit of 30 or 40 and get the student to practice bringing the car down to the correct speed before entering the reduced limit just by lifting off the accelerator.

I've heard a few people talk about how a good driver should never brake whilst driving on a motorway. This isn't quite correct, but the point they're trying to make is that if you extend your observations to the far distance, plan well and spot situations before they arise, then you should be able to deal with most speed changes on the motorway without having to touch the brakes.

There are a few things to bear in mind. Vehicles can vary dramatically in their response to a lift of the throttle. Diesels have a high compression ratio and tend to provide a little more retardation than petrol engines. Retardation is always more pronounced in lower gears than in higher gears. The vehicle's weight makes a difference - lighter cars will slow at a faster rate than heavier ones. It's particularly difficult to reduce the speed of a car with an automatic gearbox by lifting the throttle as they are much less responsive in this respect than manual cars.

You may have noticed that I've rambled on this long without mentioning "engine braking". This is deliberate.

If you need to brake, your car is fitted with a perfectly adequate braking system which has been kindly fitted by the manufacturer at no extra cost for this very purpose.

I'm actually writing about a much more subtle and unobtrusive use of the accelerator to *vary* the speed of the vehicle, rather than a quick change down and lift to dramatically reduce the vehicles speed. Using the gears to slow the car is a fairly basic approach and has some downsides. No brake lights are displayed by the slowing vehicle, for instance, and it can unsettle a car and lock wheels if done badly, which can be bad news in a RWD car.

Another very nice use of acceleration sense is during overtaking. When overtaking a car and slotting in to a gap behind the next car, it's very common for a driver to over-accelerate and then come in to the gap under brakes. Again, nothing inherently wrong with this, but here's a nicer method...

Once you've moved out and accelerated until you're alongside the subject vehicle, *lift off the accelerator*. You'll already have enough momentum to complete the overtake, but you should be able to slot nicely in behind the next vehicle without braking. It results in a less aggressive-looking overtake and is usually appreciated by passengers.

It can be very unnatural at first - lifting off when you think you should keep the throttle pinned, but once you've tried it a couple of times (in appropriately safe circumstances of course), you'll realise the benefits.

There are other benefits to improving your acceleration sense too. A 2 second following position is achievable through acceleration sense only, but any closer and you'll be dabbing the brakes regularly. It will also improve your extended observations as you'll need to spot evolving hazards earlier if you're going to negotiate them on acceleration sense alone.

You'll also be able to impress the ladies with your skills by pointing out the driver in front who has braked twenty seven times in the last mile whilst you haven't braked at all due to your superior skill.

Trust me - she'll love it. Mrs. Local almost woke up last time I showed her that one.

Anyway, I've rambled on long enough now. Go and play with your throttles!

37

BRAKING BAD

YOUTUBE LINK - **INTRODUCTION & BRAKING:**

https://youtu.be/PkE0q1s-lng

...Or how to brake good.

Braking is another one of those actions we take completely for granted. Press the middle pedal (or the left pedal depending on your choice of transmission) and the car will slow down and eventually stop. Press it harder and the car will stop more quickly. There can't be any more to it than that, can there?

Come on - you should know me better than that by now!

If there is one skill which immediately separates the good from the bad, the smooth from the rough and the delicately dainty ballet-footed from the clumpy clog-footed lead-diving-boot types, it's braking. Jump in with a rough driver and their poor braking skills will be the first thing you notice. Sit alongside a smooth driver and you'll never notice their braking at all.

For passengers who have no experience of advanced driving and even those with no interest in driving, smooth braking is something they will appreciate more than any other skill - especially if they are used to sitting next to a poor braker.

Good braking is a skill which should always be combined with good acceleration sense, so an understanding of the principles of correct accelerator use is important. If you're well practiced and your timing and planning are good, it's surprising how little you actually need to use the brakes, even in traffic. This may sound like an obvious statement, but not using the brakes is always smoother than using the brakes.

The Brakes

So, where do we start with braking? Let's have a look at what's happening mechanically when you press the brake pedal. Like all mechanical systems, brakes have developed considerably since the early years of motoring, but the principles have remained the same for many years.

The service brake, or foot brake, is connected to the brakes on all four wheels through a dual-circuit hydraulic system. Press the brake pedal, and with the mechanical assistance of a servo or vacuum pump, pressure is built up in the hydraulic fluid, through the brake lines, to the brakes themselves.

Once the hydraulic pressure reaches the brakes, it is used to force a pair of brake pads inwards against a rotating brake disk, or to force the brake shoes outwards against a rotating brake drum. The friction between the pads and disk, or the shoes and drum, cause the wheel to slow.

The next bit is really important, and is often forgotten when thinking about braking. The slowing wheel then slows the car due to friction between the tyre and the road surface. So the tyre, and the road surface itself, form an integral part of a cars braking mechanism.

If you think about it, the tyre and the road surface are by far the most variable and inconsistent components in the whole system. Disks, pads, shoes and drums are all subject to wear, of course, but their function usually only deteriorates over time, and rarely deteriorates suddenly without warning. Road surfaces, on the other hand, are almost universally inconsistent. They vary from street to street, road to road, and often from lamp-post to lamp-post.

So although you may be extremely diligent when it comes to maintaining your brakes, tyres and tyre pressures, the one aspect of your braking system which you have no control over - and which you therefore have to use your observation and planning skills to negotiate - is the road surface.

An inevitable consequence of braking is weight transfer and how it affects the balance of the car under braking. I explored balance previously in chapter 13 with a small section on braking.

One way in which vehicle manufacturers compensate for the forward weight transfer under braking is by generally fitting larger, more powerful brakes on the front of the vehicle than the rear. The braking system will be designed to apply more braking to the front wheels and less to the rear wheels to keep the car balanced under hard braking. Most cars used to be fitted with disk brakes on the front axle and drums on the rear, but this is becoming less common these days.

This is one reason why brakes are considered to be less effective when travelling in reverse - the weight transfer makes the less effective brakes at the rear do most of the work and the stronger brakes at the front are less effective.

The other reason brakes are traditionally considered to be less effective in reverse is due to the design of twin leading shoe drum brakes, but this will be a long enough chapter without going into detail about drum brake designs.

Brake Testing

We'll look at braking in detail shortly, but it's always good to know that your brakes are actually working. Isn't it?

We all, consciously or unconsciously, have our own little "starting drill" when we first get into the car. It might just be start-up and seatbelt on, or it might be a full advanced starting drill, or an old fashioned CID starting drill (we're in, we're off).

Whatever you prefer is fine by me, but it's good practice to include a quick "static brake test". Nothing complicated - just give the brake pedal a quick shove before you start the car. There should be plenty of resistance in the pedal - particularly with the engine off, due to the lack of servo assistance. If there isn't, and the pedal is soft, or "long", there is likely to be a serious fault with the brakes and probably a puddle of brake fluid under the car, so you'd be best advised not to continue with your journey.

I should add at this point, that in 28 years of driving, I have never once had a major brake failure, but for the sake of shoving your foot on the brake pedal for a second while you're putting your seatbelt on, the small amount of effort has got to be worthwhile, hasn't it? Try it for a couple of weeks and you'll soon be doing it without thinking.

Many police driving schools also advocate a "moving brake test". Just after setting off from stationary, students are required to accelerate up to around 20mph, before giving the brakes a short press and braking down to about 10mph. This allows them to check the brakes are operating correctly and evenly without pulling to either side.

A moving brake test is good practice, of course, but it's also a bit of a faff at times, and there is no reason you can't just incorporate a brief brake test into your ordinary driving, without it being obvious. Setting off from home? Just brake a little earlier than normal for the first hazard. Car park? Brake slightly earlier for the first corner or exit. Either way, make a quick mental note that the brakes are working fine, and if they're not, you're only travelling at a low speed and a combination of gears and handbrake should bring you to a halt. Even if this doesn't work, the low speed should allow you to find a suitable object to nudge into without causing too much damage.

Operating the Brakes

As with most of a car's major controls (apart from, of course, the switches), the brake pedal is *not* a switch. By which I mean, the brakes are never simply "on" or "off", but instead, they are almost infinitely variable in their effectiveness, depending on how softly or firmly you press the pedal.

For this section, we'll consider that the application of the brakes is part of a well-planned approach to a hazard, rather than an emergency braking situation (which we'll look at a bit later).

Three Phase Braking

Many advanced drivers and instructors make reference to "three phases of braking", by which they mean that the brakes are first applied smoothly and gently in the first phase, then more firmly and assertively in the second phase, and then tapering off smoothly in the third phase until the brakes are completely released or the car comes to a stop.

Although "three phase braking" is a simple enough concept, particularly when teaching a relatively inexperienced driver, I'm not so sure that it is an accurate description of the actions required to smoothly reduce the speed of a vehicle. Each of those three phases could easily be split into many more phases, from the very first initial touch of the pedal, through the first small application of pressure, right through to the delicate smooth release and then re-application once the car is stationary.

In other words, in my view, there is either one phase - braking, or there are an infinite number of phases from start to finish.

To avoid getting too complicated, and to keep this chapter relevant to the proponents of the three phase principle, I'll split braking into the three phases, but explain them all in detail. Just bear in mind, though, that each phase should blend seamlessly into the next; so it's not simply three separate braking actions, but one single action which contains separate elements throughout.

I hope this makes sense so far!

Phase 1 - First Application

Your right foot is almost always occupied when you're driving. It's either on the accelerator or on the brake and it's by far the most sensitive for most drivers. There are many advocates of left foot braking, and although I fully appreciate the benefits in competitive driving, I'm a strong believer that left foot braking is for the track or forest stage only and not for the road, even in cars with two pedal transmissions.

The nature of the brake pedal is that, unlike the accelerator and clutch, it has a resistance in its operation which requires a reasonably firm pressure from your right foot. For this reason, it's important that the ball of your foot is squarely on the pedal, rather than brushing the right hand edge of the pedal.

Think about it - if your foot slips off the accelerator, it is highly unlikely that you'll be put in danger (unless you're in the middle of a very tight overtake - which you shouldn't be!). If your foot slips off the brake, however, things can go very wrong, very quickly. So, roll on and off the accelerator by all means, but make sure you're squarely over the brake pedal when you're using it.

First application should be a very light touch - this will start to build up hydraulic pressure in the system and push the brake pads up to the face of the disk. Effectively, you're "taking up the slack" in the system, although the "slack" is actually tiny. Think of the first touch as priming the brakes ready for use. If it's raining or the roads are wet, it will also dry the disks and pads before you start to use them.

Then start to apply the brakes very gently. Bear in mind that the first actual pressure that you apply to the pedal will switch on your brake lights, letting following drivers know you're braking and slowing.

Phase 2 - Increasing the Pressure

Moving on to what is commonly referred to as the second phase, start to gradually and smoothly increase the pressure on the brake pedal.

How much by?

How long is a piece of string?

The correct answer is *"by however much is appropriate in the circumstances"*. How much speed do you need to lose? How much distance have you got? How effective are your brakes? What is the road surface like?

The middle phase may only involve a very light squeeze of the brake pedal to lose a few miles per hour. At the other end of the spectrum, it is possible to brake *extremely* hard in the middle phase if you're pressing on or if information changes, whilst still keeping the braking action smooth and controlled.

So *how* much is entirely up to you, but keep your inputs "tapered" rather than sudden and sharp, and your braking will be effective and competent.

Phase 3 - Coming Oooooooooooff the Brakes

As you come towards the end of your braking action, the speed of your car will be getting down close to the speed you require and you'll start to reduce the pressure you're applying to the brake pedal.

This is where many people - even very competent and qualified advanced drivers - can regularly get it wrong.

I'll split this section into two parts - braking to slow and braking to a stop.

When braking to slow - let's use braking to slow for a corner as an example - a driver will assess the corner on approach, concentrate on braking down to the appropriate speed, but then jump immediately off the brakes to get the appropriate gear for the corner. It's this "jumping off" the brakes which is the most common fault.

The idea, on entering the corner, is to smoothly balance the car under a little acceleration which will increase as the corner opens up. By jumping straight off the brakes, you're unsettling the car and moving the weight and balance around in a rough manner.

If you take just half a second longer to come off the brakes, the weight transfer is managed in a much smoother manner and the car will be better balanced when you move to the accelerator and start to steer.

Those instructors and observers amongst you may want to try my little instructional technique, which usually cures people of this habit. Just before the driver's speed is correct, tell them to come *ooooooooff* the brakes. Works a treat!

When braking to a stop, many people have a habit of keeping a little too much pressure on the brake pedal just as the car actually comes to a full stop. Keeping too much pressure on makes the brakes "grab" at the point the car stops, and results in driver and passengers nodding forward in their seat, and then back into their head restraints.

This is a very common fault, and part of the problem is that drivers notice it less than passengers, so most ordinary drivers never pick the fault up or learn how to correct it.

The solution is very simple - just before the car comes to a stop, reduce the pressure on the brake pedal and reduce the rate of retardation for the last couple of feet. Once the car is down to 1 or 2mph, it will need only the slightest touch on the brake pedal to actually bring the car to a stop and it should be possible to come to a stop with almost no physical reaction by the car's occupants.

One key aspect with this technique is that as soon as the car has actually stopped, you should then increase the pressure on the pedal until you have applied the handbrake or moved off. This is because the very light pressure required to roll the car to a stop is often not enough pressure to hold the car once it's stationary. So the very light touch down to a stop should be followed by a quick increase in pressure to hold the car stationary.

Trust me on this - you can brake as hard as you like when you're stationary and it'll be silky smooth!

Braking Distances

You've read the braking distances in the Highway Code, and no doubt you've memorised them for a test at some point or points in your life. But how realistic are they? Does it really take 45 feet to stop from 30mph? Or 245 feet to stop from 70mph?

The truth is that even an average driver in a modern, well maintained car can easily beat those distances, even on a wet road.

Think of the HC braking distances as a worst-case scenario. A dopy driver in a poorly maintained car with bald tyres and a slippery wet road surface will probably need the full 45 feet plus thinking distance to come to a stop. They may not be wholly relevant to you in 2014, but they may be relevant to the dopy driver in a poorly maintained car that is following you too close in the rain - something to bear in mind when setting your own following position. The more distance you give yourself to brake, the less chance there is of the car behind running into you.

Managing Heat

Slowing a ton and a half of metal down from high speeds through 6 square inches of brake pad rubbing against an iron or ceramic disk spinning at high revs inevitably generates an enormous amount of heat. If you're out on a spirited drive or a trackday and you're using the brakes hard and often, this heat can start to cause issues, so how do you recognise these issues? And how do you deal with them?

The first issue is glazing of the pads. Although brake pad material is extremely robust and designed to work at high temperatures, the particles on the surface of the brake pad can momentarily melt under constant heavy use, and then re-solidify as a glassy "glaze" which has much less friction and makes your brakes much less effective. At the same time, this melting can cause a release of gas from the pad material which can further reduce the effectiveness of the brakes.

Manufacturers have come up with a number of solutions to pad glazing and gas release, particularly on high-performance cars. "Slotted" brake disks are designed so that the edges of the slots constantly de-glaze the surface of the pads. Drilled or dimpled brake disks allow the gasses to disperse without causing a drop in braking performance.

How do you recognise glazing? You'll find that your brakes will require more and more effort in order to reach the same braking effect. I've also found that you can feel the smoothness of the pads against the disk through your foot on the pedal - you can feel that there is less friction in the system.

The solution, as with many aspects of driving, is to remove the cause. In this case, the cause is excessive heat build-up through hard braking, so if you're on the road, slow it down, try to use the brakes less, but keep driving for a few miles so that the air continues flowing over the brakes and cools them down. The temperature will drop quite quickly, after which you should de-glaze the pads by braking firmly in short busts about half-a-dozen times.

If you're on a trackday, pull off the track and let the brakes cool off. It'll take a bit longer if the car is stationary and you should leave the car in gear with the handbrake OFF, as a hot handbrake can stick itself to the disk as it cools.

The other potential issue is vapour-lock. Brake fluid is hygroscopic, which means that, over time, it can absorb tiny amounts of water from the atmosphere. If you've been braking particularly hard and your brake fluid is knocking on a bit, there is a danger that the absorbed water will boil and become a gas. Unlike brake fluid, gas is easily compressed, so the first you'll know is that the brake pedal will go to the floor.

The key to avoiding vapour lock is to make sure you change your brake fluid every three years or so.

Emergency Braking

If you're a good driver with sound observation skills and good planning, you should rarely - if ever - need to apply emergency braking. None of us are so conceited, however, to think that we'll never need it, so let's look at an emergency situation where, despite your best efforts, you need to stop urgently in as short a distance as possible.

Most modern cars are fitted with anti-lock braking systems. Much has been written about these systems and there is a big clue to their function in the name. Under very heavy braking, ABS recognises when a wheel is starting to lock up, and then momentarily releases that brake before re-applying it to the point of lock-up, releasing it again, rinse, and repeat.

But why do we not want our wheels to lock up? Surely if you've applied all the brakes to the point where the wheels lock and then skid along the road surface, you'll stop in the shortest distance, won't you?

Interestingly, no, you won't. Apart from on loose gravel or deep snow, in which case you *might*, but this chapter is getting long enough without me drifting off onto obscure details.

o on normal tarmac, the truth is that cars brakes are most effective at the point *just* before the wheels lock up. A very skilled driver can hold a car just at this point and stop the car effectively without locking up. It's called "threshold braking" and requires much practice, usually on a track or runway, before you become competent.

A rotating wheel will stop more quickly, and in less distance than a locked wheel. The other benefit of keeping the wheels turning is that there is still a little tyre grip left with which to steer the car. A car with locked wheels will simply continue in a straight line until it stops. A car with rotating wheels can still be steered around a hazard.

ABS effectively allows untrained drivers to apply threshold braking in an emergency situation.

The trouble is, that most people, even in an emergency, don't brake hard enough. Some manufacturers have recognised this and introduced "brake assist" systems which recognise the speed at which a driver has applied the brakes, and then add some extra brake effort to ensure the brakes are fully applied.

My advice in an emergency, if you're driving a car with ABS is simple.

Muller the brakes as hard as you possibly can, and steer around the hazard if possible.

I can't really make it any simpler, can I? Forget three phase braking and heat build-up and threshold braking and everything else. It's an emergency and all the niceties of smoothness and balance go out of the window. Stamp on that brake pedal as quickly and as hard as you possibly can and keep it pressed hard - try to push it out through the floor of the car until you come to a stop.

The car will work its ABS magic - you may feel a vibration through the pedal, which is the car releasing and reapplying the brakes in quick succession - and will stop as quickly as possible whilst allowing you to retain some steering control if you need it.

But what about the traditionalists who drive TVRs and Caterhams and old Porsches without ABS?

My advice - at least initially - is the same. *In an emergency, Muller those brakes as hard as you possibly can.*

The difference comes if your wheels lock up. If you realise that you've locked up, and you're travelling in a straight line with no steering, you must do something which is quite difficult in the circumstances.

Come off the brakes.

It's the last thing you want to do, but coming off the brakes for a fraction of a second will allow the wheels to rotate and give you some steering back. Then reapply the brakes till they lock, release, rinse and repeat.

It's called "cadence braking" and replicates - albeit at a much slower rate - the effects of ABS.

Cadence braking saved my life once. I was driving down a steep hill on a rural road in mid-winter at night. The road bent round to the right with a very long drop off a cliff to the left. I started to brake and... Nothing. The road was sheet ice and I was going over the edge - no question.

I pumped that brake pedal like I was trying to stamp a tarantula to death and steered right. It was quite odd, because my speed was already quite slow, but there was virtually no road grip, so unlike most accidents, I had time to take in what was happening.

I managed to get the car's speed right down and negotiate the bend without leaving the road. If I'd left the brakes fully on, without a doubt I'd have been over the cliff. So trust me - through personal experience, although it's an old fashioned technique, cadence braking does genuinely work. As long as you can keep your head and get off the brakes when every fibre of your body wants to keep the brake pedal mashed.

So that's it for braking. Sorry for rambling on, but as you can see, there is more to it than most people think.

38

It's Right For The Night...

YOUTUBE LINK - **NIGHT DRIVING**:

https://youtu.be/0wFfd5g13J4

...Thousands of lights show us the way.

Night driving is not an excessively complicated subject if I'm being honest, so once again, my apologies to anyone who finds this chapter patronising or simplistic in any way, but as per usual, it's aimed at all levels of driver, so feel free to take what you want and leave what you don't.

There's nothing inherently dangerous or excessively risky about driving at night. We're lucky to live in a highly developed country with a relatively high proportion of well-lit roads, particularly in urban and suburban areas.

Having said that, there are still many thousands of miles of unlit roads in between our towns and cities, but most modern cars have excellent lights and our annual MOT tests mean that most cars have defective bulbs replaced once a year at a minimum.

We also have many laws and regulations which govern what lights can or cannot be fitted to vehicles, how they must be maintained, and even when they must be switched on and off.

ADVANCED & PERFORMANCE DRIVING

I know this doesn't sound particularly advanced, but next time you're abroad - even in countries which are considered as advanced as ours - try driving at night and you'll immediately notice the difference - both in the quality and quantity of street lighting, and in the maintenance and use of headlights.

Go a little further afield and the differences are even more noticeable. I once had the misfortune of travelling in a taxi in Egypt at night. I don't think I saw more than three or four other cars with headlights on for the entire journey. Everyone simply drove at night with no lights whatsoever. Horns were a different story - they were used constantly, but headlights or sidelights? No. I tried asking the driver why no-one uses their lights, but he just shouted "baksheesh", which suggested he would have put them on if I'd have tipped him more.

Anyway, on to the driving tips. At the risk of sounding like I'm teaching you to suck eggs, there are two key things to remember when driving at night...

(1) It's more difficult to see.

(2) It's more difficult for others to see you.

Although having said that, there are a couple of advantages to visibility at night which we'll look at in a bit.

To help with both of these issues, car manufacturers fit a variety of different lights to their cars, so we'll start with a brief look at the legalities of driving at night.

Drivers **must** use **sidelights** between **sunset and sunrise.**

Additionally, drivers must use **(dipped) headlights** during the **hours of darkness (half-an-hour after sunset until half-an-hour before**

sunrise), *except* when using a road which has lit street lighting, in which case the only *legal* requirement is to use sidelights.

It's also a legal requirement to use **headlights** when visibility is seriously reduced (generally when, due to weather conditions or perhaps smoke, visibility is reduced to less than 100 metres).

Note that there is no legal requirement to use foglights when visibility is seriously reduced. The legislation outlines when you should *not* use foglights, but there is no law which states that you *have* to use them.

There is a lot more to the legislation, but for most car drivers, that's all you need to know.

On to the actual driving.

Although the legislation only requires sidelights at night in built-up areas, bearing in mind item (2) above, I can see no logical reason why you would not choose to use dipped beam headlights at all times when it's dark. Even on an older car with weaker headlights, dipped beam lights make your vehicle much more visible to other road users, so my advice is to use dipped beam headlights at all times when you're driving at night and save the sidelights for parking.

One thing to be careful of here - some car manufacturers, Vauxhall for instance, have an annoying habit of designing cars with instrument binnacles which light up night and day when the ignition is switched on, irrespective of whether the lights are switched on or not. It's very easy, particularly if you're in a well-lit area at night, to get in one of these cars, see the dashboard light up, assume the lights are on and drive off into the gloom, wondering why everyone is flashing at you. I did it myself a few times when the police panda fleet was updated about 10 years ago. You're less likely to do it if your own car has this feature, because we all tend to know our own cars well, but always look for the green symbol on the dash to confirm your lights are on.

So, built-up areas, street lights etc. - there's not a lot to say really. Leave your headlights on dipped beam, position yourself generally towards the centre of the road to allow vehicles approaching junctions to your left to get a slightly earlier view of you and try to go handbrake-neutral when you're stationary as modern brake lights can be very dazzling to drivers behind.

Many vehicles these days - my own included - are fitted with automatic headlights. Just flick the light switch to the "A" setting and the car monitors how light or dark it is and switches the lights on and off as appropriate. They are generally good systems and I use mine, but there are a couple of things to bear in mind.

Firstly, they will come on during the day if you enter a tunnel. This is generally a good thing, but can be misinterpreted by other drivers as a headlight flash, so keep a careful eye on the drivers around you and expect the occasional lane change.

Secondly, be careful if you lend your car to someone else, or if it goes in for service. It's easy to take automatic lights for granted (mine never move from the "A" position), and then be caught out if someone else uses your car and switches them off.

A note on courtesy. It seems to be a well-established tradition in this country that drivers acknowledge a courtesy by flashing their headlights. Personally, I can't think of a worse way to thank someone than by burning their retinas out and leaving them temporarily partially blinded. You wouldn't thank someone for buying you a pint by poking them in the eyes, would you?

I know a "thank you" wave isn't really visible at night, so my preference is to momentarily turn my lights from dipped-beam to sidelights and then back to dipped-beam again. It will acknowledge a courtesy from an oncoming driver without causing them to drive into the nearest bus shelter.

On unlit rural roads, there is much more to think about when it comes to lighting. The priority moves from being seen, to being able to see, and this is where you need to make use - by which I mean *intelligent* use - of your "main", "high" or "full" beam headlights.

If you are on an unlit road and there are no vehicles in front, use your main beam. It will illuminate the road much further ahead and allow a planned approach to hazards. It also simplifies a couple of Roadcraft principles. The overriding safety principle is that you should always be able to stop on your own side of the road in the distance you can see to be clear. At night, on an unlit road, this principle is easy to apply because the distance you can see to be clear is never any further than the distance illuminated by your headlights.

The second principle it simplifies is that of assessing the correct speed to take a corner using the limit point. The limit point is the furthest point in a corner in which you have an uninterrupted view of the road surface. At night, on an unlit road, this is the furthest point in a corner which is illuminated by your headlights.

If I ever had a student who struggled with limit points, I would try to take them out in the dark, after which they seemed to "get" it.

If you can see the headlights or tail lights of a car ahead, you should switch your lights to dipped beam. The principle is that if you can see their lights, they can see yours and you really don't want to dazzle the driver of a vehicle which is travelling towards you at speed.

There is usually no need to dip your lights *before* you see headlights or tail lights. Many people dip their lights when they see the "halo" of oncoming vehicles but this isn't usually necessary. Some people get quite nippy about it too. I often see the halos of oncoming cars furiously flashing their lights at me before their lights actually come into view. I always dip at the appropriate point, of course, but it's amusing to see how upset some people get before you've even done anything wrong.

The exception with this point is for large goods vehicles with a raised driving position. These vehicles have headlights fitted at normal height but the driver sits higher up, so it is possible to dazzle them even if you can't see their headlights, so dip early if you think it's an HGV approaching.

If I'm on an unlit road at night, using main beam, I don't generally dip my lights if I see a vehicle approaching a junction to the left or right. Over the years, I have found that dipping lights under these circumstances can be misunderstood by the vehicles in the junction as a signal to pull out. People are much less likely to pull out in front of a vehicle with high beam displayed than one which has just dipped its lights. You won't find this in a textbook anywhere - it's just based on my own observations. It might seem a little inconsiderate to dazzle a car in a junction, but they can look away and you can also usually pick out the driver and observe their actions better if your lights remain on high beam. If the vehicle pulls out regardless then, of course, dip your lights.

If you are dazzled by an oncoming vehicle, what's the best course of action? It's very tempting to give them a taste of their own medicine and burn out their retinas, but do you really want two partially-blinded drivers driving towards each other at speed?

The best advice is to look slightly away from the headlights. Shining a bright light into your eyes creates a "flash blindness" which is a sort of blob of blindness in one part of your eye, similar to when a camera flash goes off. This flash spot can remain for a few seconds or minutes, so it's best to look away slightly from the lights so that your flash blindness occurs in an area outside your main field of vision. Try to look to the left of the oncoming car - towards the nearside kerb.

If you want to indicate to the oncoming vehicle that they are a main beam numpty, try my courtesy signal of switching to sidelights a couple of times. This will flash your lights without causing excessive dazzle and might wake them up.

If the car behind is the problem, almost all cars are fitted with dipping rear-view mirrors which dim the appearance of following traffic. If you're a company director type, you may even have an automatic dipping mirror, but for most of us mere mortals, the mirror can be dipped by flicking the lever underneath the mirror, or in the case of BMWs, turning the red alarm light under the mirror.

When overtaking, keep your lights on dipped beam until the front of your car has passed the door mirrors of the overtaken car - or the front most overtaken car if you're overtaking multiple vehicles.

If you are being overtaken, or you think the car behind wants to overtake, help them out by keeping your main beam on until their door mirrors have passed the front of your car, and then dip your lights.

The "halo" I mentioned earlier is one of the biggest advantages of driving at night. During the day, your view is limited by hedges, trees, buildings etc. but at night, the halo of headlights can give you a very clear indication as to which direction the road is going and how severe the corners ahead are.

The only downside to using main beam on modern unlit roads is that road signs these days seem to be much more reflective than they used to be. So much so that I sometimes find that I have to dip my headlights as I get closer to some signs to avoid being blinded by the reflection of my own headlights.

There's progress for you.

Fog Lights (They're NOT Driving Lamps!)

There is a school of thought which suggests that a combination of front fog lights and sidelights is most effective in thick fog. Even the legislation allows for this, giving an exemption from dipped headlights on non-30mph limit roads if it's foggy & you're displaying a sidelight/fog light combination.

The problem with driving in fog is that any bright light you display to the front is reflected back at you by the fog itself (or by the tiny water droplets which make up fog if you want to be technical).

I used to spectate on a lot of stage rallies, and rally drivers will generally run with no lights at all in thick fog during the daytime because they find no lights gives them better visibility than any other combination of lights (and rally cars tend to have the most varied combinations of lights). On the road in fog, however, no lights aren't really an option because no-one can see you.

I've tried the sidelight/fog light combination in a number of cars and I've never really found it much better than just headlights, and I've often found it worse. The idea is that the low front fog lights project a beam across the road surface, whilst the sidelights prevent excessive light reflection from the fog. Sounds good in theory, but it's not great in reality.

A note on *intelligent* use of fog lights - many people see mist or fog and then just switch their fog lights on as a sort of pavlovian response & leave them on for the rest of the journey. In reality, the occasions you actually need to use fog lights are extremely limited. Visibility of less than 100 metres is *extremely* thick fog or *very* heavy snowfall (the only two weather conditions which would require high intensity fog light use) and those weather conditions are quite rare.

You don't need fog lights when it's a bit misty, or there's a bit of dampness in the air, and you definitely never need them when it's raining, no matter how torrentially, because the extra glare caused by fog lights reflecting off a wet road create more dangers rather than less.

If you *are* driving in <100M visibility, your rear fog lights are a priority to ensure traffic approaching from the rear can see you, but once you can see the headlights of following traffic in your mirror, it's usually best to switch off your fog lights, because if you can see their headlights, they'll be able to see your tail lights without fog light assistance. Don't forget that rear fog lights can mask your brake lights and make it more likely that a following vehicle will not see when you are slowing down.

Fog can be patchy too, so switch the fogs on just when they are needed and switch them off as soon as it's clear again.

And remember - they are *fog* lights - **NOT** driving lamps, posing lamps or fashion accessories. If you're not in thick fog or snow, leave them switched off!

39

I'VE BEEN FEELING HORNY LATELY

Let's reclaim the horn!

The horn has completely lost its way in the UK in my opinion. Every car has one, they're fitted for perfectly sound reasons, but for some reason, horn use has become a bit like one of those words which used to be used in normal day-to-day language, but for reasons of political correctness, are now deemed insulting, degrading or highly offensive.

"Consider use of the horn" used to be one of the individual phases of the old blue Roadcraft system, which meant that advanced drivers were encouraged to at least think about using the horn at every single hazard they encountered on the road.

The Highway Code has a very clear rule relating to the use of the horn – rule 112 in fact – which states:

The horn. Use only while your vehicle is moving and you need to warn other road users of your presence. You **MUST NOT** use your horn

- while stationary on the road
- when driving in a built up area between the hours of 11.30pm and 7.00am

except *when another road user poses a danger.*

That couldn't be any clearer could it? The horn is there solely to warn other road users of your presence. Makes perfect sense to me – an audible device which gives out a quick "honk" or "toot" whenever you're unsure whether another road user is aware of your presence. You gain the advantage of knowing you've made someone aware that you're there and they gain the advantage of knowing you're there. You'd think people would be grateful of the warning wouldn't you?

If you're approaching a badly-sighted junction and you see the front of a vehicle starting to emerge, but have no view of the driver, then it's entirely appropriate to give a short horn warning to the driver to alert them of your presence.

A bus stops in front of you and passengers start to disembark. There is always a real danger that, as you pass the bus, the passengers may cross from the front of the bus, into your path. A longer horn warning on approach will let them know you're coming and may deter them from stepping out in front of you.

You're alongside a large goods vehicle which starts to drift in its lane, squeezing you towards the central reservation. A short toot on the horn gets the driver's attention and creates you some essential space.

You're approaching a pedestrian walking in the same direction of you with their hood up and on the phone. They start to step into the road and a long honk on the horn gets their attention and they step back on to the pavement.

All good no?

Well, these days, seemingly – no…

For some reason, over an extended period of time (probably over the last 40 or 50 years), horn use and the *perception* of horn use has completely changed.

I would estimate that 99% of horn use in the UK these days contravenes rule 112 of the Highway Code. Horns are used as a rebuke, as an aggressive response to perceived poor driving, as an intolerant expression of dissatisfaction and often as a demand for another road user to make way.

Someone pulls out from a junction in front of you? **HOOONK!** *B$%#@~d!*

Someone cuts you up in traffic? **HOOONK!** *W$!@#r!*

Someone dares to give a quick **PARP** to let you know they're there? *F#@% YOU, YOU F#@%ING !£$%@#*$@£#!!*

Not very nice is it?

But how do we change things for the better? We've gone a long way down this road and it seems that horn use has changed permanently along with the perception of other people's use of the horn. How could we possibly stop this descent and go back to considering horn use.

Let's go back to my earlier reference to offensive derogatory terms. These days, minority groups who have previously suffered abuse through certain words and expressions have started to "reclaim" the insulting words and terms by using them themselves, often in a self-deprecating manner which has resulted in the terms becoming less and less insulting.

I have to be careful here, as I've no intention of offending anyone, so I've had to think long and hard about which of these terms I can use as an example. I've chosen the word "queer".

"Queer" was, for a long time, a word used predominantly as a derogatory term for gay men. It wasn't always the case though – "queer", as in "I'm feeling a bit queer" or "how queer" was a fairly normal word in everyday use many years ago, but over time, it became increasingly used as an insult or insulting nickname.

But then the gay community took the decision to "reclaim" the word by using it regularly within their social circles and as references to themselves to the extent that, over time, it became much less insulting and derogatory as a word. Queer has even become an academic term in reference to various aspects of LGBT studies, culture art and politics.

Many other words have gone through this "reclamation" process by various minority groups. If you think about it, reclaiming these words is a clever and inventive tactic to take the sting out of previously offensive language and put two fingers up at the bullies and bigots.

I'm sure you're wondering where I'm going with this, so I'll come back to the point.

It's time for drivers in the UK to reclaim the horn!

We need to change our opinions about horn use and we need to at least *try* to change other people's perception of horn use.

I've even come up with a tactic, which I've been using for a few months now and which seems to work quite nicely.

I'm using my horn much more regularly these days – always in appropriate circumstances where another road user may benefit – but much more often. The tactic, however, is to look for eye contact with the other road user – driver, cyclist, pedestrian – it doesn't matter who, but when I sound the horn I look to catch the other person's eye, and then I give them a cheery wave and a smile – as though I know them.

Nine and a half times out of ten, they'll smile and wave back as though I'm their best mate! Instead of getting an aggressive response, two fingers or a mouthful of abuse, I get a cheerful – if sometimes slightly puzzled – smile and a wave back. It's a much more positive response, and I'm then certain that I've got their attention and they are much less likely to do something careless or daft.

If we all start using this tactic, surely we can reclaim the horn for the purpose it is designed for?

40

A Classic debate

Do you take your car for granted? I do. It's not really anything special, but it accelerates reasonably briskly, has a top speed in excess of 130, its warm and dry inside and it brakes and steers how and when I want it to. It's also reliable and would (I believe) look after me to a certain degree in the event of an accident.

For anyone who drives a car made in the last 20 years or so, this is pretty much the case with any car, irrespective of the manufacturer, but it wasn't always so.

I started driving in the mid 1980's. It doesn't feel that long ago, but in those days, your first car or two would be at least 10 years old, if not older, so my mates and I started our driving career in cars which were new in the early to mid-1970s.

My first car was a white "K" reg (1972, not 1992!) Mini Clubman. In my uneducated 17-year-old eyes, it looked the part, with a ground-scraping front spoiler and one of those black slatted covers on the rear window. It also came with, at no extra cost, collapsed nearside hydrolastic suspension, brakes which needed several firm pumps before they would even begin to start the slowing process, and a manually-switched reversing light which I religiously forgot to switch off every single time I used it.

It also leaked in water. Badly.

Oh, and It also had a musical air horn which played "La Cucaracha". Barry.

It cost me £350 and probably about the same for my first years third party, fire and theft insurance.

It was unbelievably unreliable. Apart from having to bump-start it on almost every occasion I used it because I always left the reversing light on; it had a dynamo rather than an alternator, so even when it was running, the electric were weaker than my mum's tea. A previous owner had fitted a tiny air filter which sounded great, but iced up at the first hint of an open throttle on a cold day.

The floor was a patchwork quilt of welded patches-on-patches interspersed with holes through which you could clearly see the road. And did I mention the brakes? Drums all round and a very shonky set of brake lines meant that sometimes the brakes were "there" and sometimes they simply were not "there" at all.

First press would often push the pedal to the floor and I'd then have to frantically pump the pedal a few times to build up enough pressure in the system for the brakes to work.

Looking back, the combination of that car and a 17-year old Reg was potentially a very serious accident waiting to happen. The fact that the car had some egg-shaped bearings somewhere in the driveline which made such a racket above 50mph (WOWOWOWOWOWOW), that it created an unofficial speed limiter probably helped save me from a fiery ditch death.

But the thing to bear in mind was that this wasn't unusual in the 1980's. Most of us started our motoring careers in something similar.

My parent's cars, although a bit newer, were almost equally as shonky – a front nearside hub, complete with wheel and tyre, came off my Mum's Morris Marina on a roundabout, and my dad spent most weekends patching up his Triumph 1500 with body filler and gun gum.

Compare my experiences with those of my children, all of whom are now starting their driving adventures courtesy of the Reg Local free driving school. Since stepson number 1 got his first car – a non-turbo diesel Peugeot 106 – 8 years ago, none of my children have ever experienced a roadside breakdown. One of them had a flat battery at home, but then had no comprehension whatsoever as to how to bump-start or jump-start the car. There have been a couple of minor bumps, inevitably, but those were down to driver error rather than any kind of mechanical fault with their cars.

I was trying to imagine what it would be like for a new driver from 2014 if they had to drive my 1972 mini clubman. My kids laugh when I tell them what cars used to be like, as though I'm exaggerating & telling a tall dads tale. But in reality, I'm sure they would choose to walk rather than drive my old shed. Or go on Facebook – you know what kids are like.

The question though, is whether dealing with (and surviving) life with an old shed made me a better driver? The brakes certainly required extremely good forward observations and planning, and there was nothing like ABS, traction or stability control fitted to the car so I had to develop a level of car control. I was also acutely aware that the car would crumple like a crisp-packet if I hit anything more substantial than a small rabbit, so the concept of maintaining a zone of relative safety around the car became second nature.

Over the years, I've been lucky enough to drive a whole range of classic and vintage cars, and the more I've driven them, the more I've thought that everyone – particularly relatively new drivers – should run a classic car as a daily driver for a period of time. And not a nice, well restored classic – no – they should run a rusty, unreliable and borderline dangerous car, at least for a few months. In winter.

I ran a Morris 1000 as a second car in the mid-1990s. Now, this wasn't a show quality car, but it certainly wasn't as sheddy as my first Mini, and everything was in perfect mechanical order. I also had access to two vintage cars owned and operated by the police driving school which employed me. A 1922 Bentley 3-litre was the oldest, and the school also owned a 1936 Lagonda 4.5 litre drophead, which had been gifted to the Force when it was new by Lord Cottenham.

The Bentley really took some concentration to drive. Everything you've heard about Bentley gearboxes from that era is true, and combined with the centre-throttle and almost non-existent brakes, it was probably the most knackering car I've ever driven.

The Lagonda, by comparison, was a real old gent of a car. A smooth straight six engine, a part-synchro gearbox and brakes which almost worked. I had it up to 100mph once, and it felt like it still had some left in reserve.

Driving older cars requires much more effort, but the result is a much greater sense of satisfaction. Cars these days are great, don't get me wrong – they're far, far safer than they used to be and require much less effort and concentration to physically "drive", but I can't help feeling that, somewhere along the way, some of the actual skill of driving has been lost, together with the ability to carry out basic maintenance and repairs which used to be essential.

Older cars smell different when you first get in – they have a musty, lived in smell which can't really be described, but smells like the 1950's. They feel different to sit in – designed before ergonomics and soft-feel plastics had even been dreamed of, the surfaces are often hard and metallic, with any plastic usually being of the brittle Bakelite variety. Steering wheels are large. And very, very thin.

They feel substantially different to drive, too. The driving position will never be ideal in an older car for a start, so you'll have to compromise by scooching down or sitting on a cushion. Then when you drive them, there is no power assistance – certainly with the steering and often with the brakes. Every input requires a positive, substantial push or pull on the controls when compared with the effortless controls in modern cars.

On the move, the first press of the brakes will remind you how far brakes and tyres have come on in the last few decades, and you're forced, almost immediately, to re-assess your braking and following distances in traffic.

One of the other things you notice with an older car is the feedback though the wheel, pedals and backside. This is one area where modern cars have definitely not improved and most people who drive a classic for the first time will notice just how much detailed feedback you get from all the cars controls.

Despite the increased weight of the controls, driving a classic also requires far greater delicacy with the controls. Traction control and

ABS are generated by the driver's right foot only. Any loss of grip with the road surface can and must be recognised and controlled solely by the driver. Wipers and lights need to be switched on and off. With a switch.

Have modern cars generally reduced the overall skill levels of normal, everyday drivers? Does experience with a classic (shed or otherwise) make you a better driver? Were you ever subjected to "La Cucaracha" by a spotty 17 year old in a sheddy white mini clubman in Preston in 1986?

41

IN THE CITY THERE'S A THOUSAND THINGS I WANNA SAY TO YOU

About the young ideas...

City Driving - The Great Leveller

Urban driving - particularly in heavy traffic *is* the great leveller isn't it? It doesn't matter if you're driving a £300 shed or a £1.2 million LaFerrari, if you're in slow moving urban traffic, you're all in it together and no-one has any advantage. You'll get there when the traffic gets there and there is very little you can do to improve your situation.

Strange then, that urban driving can feel so much more competitive and aggressive than any other kind of driving, when there is so little to gain.

The pushing and shoving and lack of manners can often feel like...

ADVANCED & PERFORMANCE DRIVING

It doesn't need to though. As discussed in other chapters, a good driver should be able to reduce the negative emotions associated with driving to a minimum and avoid personalising situations. If you can achieve this rare mental state, as I've previously mentioned, you'll feel much more like Huggy Bear than Starsky or Hutch.

What to expect

You'll be cut up, chopped up, undertaken, pulled out on, gestured at, barged, sliced and twirled by cars, cyclists, mopeds, cyclists, taxis, cyclists, buses, cyclists, pedestrians, cyclists, mobility scooters and cyclists.

And, of course, there are the cyclists.

It really isn't the type of driving that any of us enjoy or look forward to.

But, it's still driving and it can still be done well or done badly, skilfully or ham-fistedly, cooperatively or un-cooperatively, assertively or aggressively, cleverly or cocknockerishly. Urban driving requires all the same mental agility, careful planning and accuracy that you would put into a spirited drive on your favourite roads. It just tends to be a bit more "mental" and a bit less "physical".

It's intimate too. You're far more aware that the other vehicles out there contain a living, breathing human being than you are on the open road. Look around you and you'll see all of life's rich tapestry around you. All with their own agendas and all making different decisions. The skill is much more about working out other people's intentions and planning yours. Hazards are multiple and constant - your plans are a constantly evolving, flexible and fluid process.

The traffic

Most of our cities weren't designed to handle the volume of traffic on the roads in 2014. In addition, the road network in city centres is knocking on a bit now and needs continuous ongoing maintenance just to keep it in the shoddy, pot-hole ridden state that we've come to know and love. It's not going to get better either. Traffic is going to keep on increasing and the roads are going to get worse.

So, on that cheerful note, let's see how you can make the most of a bad situation and at least try to make a decent hash of driving in city traffic.

Now, you should know by now that I'm not the preachy type and I don't promote absolutes - driving is a thousand shades of grey with very little black and white. However, I do have one absolute rule if you're driving a manual car in traffic.

Never.

Ever.

Ride the clutch.

When you're stationary, handbrake & neutral pleasethankyouverymuch. It doesn't just wear the clutch material prematurely. The vast majority of dual mass flywheel failures that are well documented across the various internet forums are primarily caused by excessive heat build-up from riding the clutch.

I'm not a clutch rider and in 28 years of car ownership and probably close to a million miles now I have never had to replace a clutch in any of my cars (and only one was an automatic, before you get clever!).

By comparison, Mrs Local was a clutch rider until I met her 10 years ago. In 10 years of motoring until that point, she'd had four cars and each of them had had a clutch replaced during her ownership. One had two. In the last 10 years, since I gently convinced her there was a better way, she's never needed a new clutch.

There is a safety issue too. You're a couple of feet from the car in front. One small slip and you're in their boot. Or they could be a motorcyclist. Or a cyclist if you're very lucky. So that's the first and last rule out of the way - what else?

These days, creeping along in traffic can mostly be done with no throttle. Again, the mechanical benefits are obvious and it doesn't require clutch slippage for more than about 1/2 a second. The less revs when moving away, the less clutch wear.

It's good practice not to stop too close to the car in front. This is an old police driving school tip which helps a police officer get moving in an emergency, but there is some benefit to the civilian driver if, for instance, the car in front breaks down or becomes otherwise immobile. Do you want to be reversing and faffing about in traffic? Or is it better to be able to just drive forward with full lock on?

A reasonable guideline is to stop far enough back so that you can see the bottom of the tyres of the car in front - just where they touch the road. A little bit further back for a larger vehicle or if you're in a car with poor steering lock (I had a go in a V6 Clio a few years ago and although it was fun, it had *appalling* steering lock!).

Giving yourself that little extra room will also allow you to maintain a better view of the road and traffic ahead. Whilst we're on that subject, you won't be able to achieve decent extended views in the city because of, well, the city, but there are plenty of nice clues to pick up on. Shop windows, for instance, can give a decent reflective view of the traffic ahead, and give you a few extra seconds notice that you're about to move off. If you're behind a bus, you can often pick up reflections of brake lights on the interior ceiling - when you see them go off, first-gear-ready-to-go-please.

I've mentioned this before, but we should all try to keep learning. When sat in traffic the other week behind yet another clown with their sat-nav mounted right in the centre of the windscreen, I suddenly realised I could see their route. It was giving him a right turn a couple of junctions ahead. I moved to the left lane. He turned right just as predicted (and with a predictably late signal) and I wasn't held up.

I now love the drivers who block their view with a sat-nav.

Cyclists

I think I might have briefly mentioned cyclists earlier. Perhaps now is the time for a brief discussion on the subject. Cycling is becoming more and more popular for a variety of different reasons. Some of you reading this will be cyclists. Heck, I've even been a bicyclist myself in the distant past.

The only trouble is, there is no requirement for cyclists to undertake any training whatsoever before heading out on the road. Sure, some of them will hold drivers licences, but can you tell which ones? Some of them may even be cycling because a court has taken their licence off them because they're not fit to drive on the roads. There's a thought.

On the whole, most cyclists act in a reasonable and safety-conscious way. Unfortunately there is a significant minority who do not. These are the balloons who spoil cycling's image and give the sensible majority a bad name.

As a car driver, my advice to you is probably very predictable. Give them plenty of room, check your blind spots with a shoulder check whenever you set off from stationary and don't get too intent on passing them, because they'll just be straight up your nearside at the next set of red traffic lights.

I should also add that there are a number of cyclists who consider red traffic lights to be optional. If you're approaching a green light at a junction or crossing and the way ahead seems perfectly clear, please have a good scan into the other roads for errant bicycles. Even if you're 100% in the right, having an accident with a cyclist is an unpleasant experience to be avoided at all costs. And they're not insured. And it's more inconvenience when you have to take a day off work to attend the inquest.

Pedestrians

Whilst we're on the subject of unpredictable road users, perhaps I should include a few lines on pedestrians.

Of all road users, I think pedestrians worry me the most. There is no less predictable group of people on the roads, and none that are more vulnerable. A pedestrian accident is always a horrible experience for all involved and having witnessed one first hand myself, they are another experience to be completely avoided.

Out of the large number of pedestrians you would encounter within a busy city, can you easily pick out and identify which of them is drunk? Or on drugs? Or deaf? Have a look at how many are staring intently at their phones as they negotiate busy traffic on foot. And at how many are wearing earphones.

Rain can be a particular problem when combined with pedestrians. Most would seemingly prefer to risk an impact with a moving vehicle than get slightly wet. Umbrellas also remove most of their field of vision and make them even more likely to leap out in front of you.

I know this all sounds like exaggeration and mostly it is. But if you think along these lines, and keep these considerations to the forefront of your mind, you're far more likely to spot the *one* deaf, drunk, phone reading, umbrella wielding pedestrian *before* they get the chance to leap on your bonnet. And remember - it only takes one.

Cooperation

Driving in city traffic requires a degree of cooperation on everyone's part. It may feel like a "not a chance" attitude when it comes to allowing some precedence at junctions is the most advantageous. In my experience though, this isn't the case. I find that a slightly more Christian (or Muslim, or Hindu, or Buddhist, or Scientologist - I'm not picky) approach to urban driving does not affect your progress at all. It also helps to keep your blood pressure down and keeps things much more friendly - you don't have to keep that false "straight ahead" stare either (you know what I'm talking about!).

So whenever possible, keep junctions clear and let a few drivers out - I tend to make it clear that I'm just letting the one out so I don't end up frustrating the drivers behind.

When affording a courtesy to another driver or otherwise allowing someone else precedence, I *never* signal, wave, flash, toot, or give any other indication that the other road user is free to go. I will leave the gap for them, and try to make it obvious from my positioning that I'm allowing them through, but the decision to go should always be theirs.

This was a point I used to teach to police officers. There are a number of incidents on record where a police officer has afforded a courtesy and waved another driver out of a junction, only for them to assume they can then emerge without any further checks and immediately have an accident. Some drivers have, in the past, successfully argued that they were following a police officer's directions at the time of the accident, and so the police officer must be to blame for their own myopic stupidity.

This situation is easily avoided by just leaving the gap and allowing the other road user to make their own decision.

If you're waiting at a junction and the traffic is busy, stop with your wheels at the line (I avoid creeping forwards) and try to get eye contact with the drivers on the main road. Winding your window down often helps. Look relaxed and friendly and very soon someone will let you out. Give them a smile and a thumbs up and set off briskly.

This is the social aspect of city driving. The part which involves genuine personal interaction with human beings. Give a little and take a little.

42

Roundabouts

YOUTUBE LINK - **AN INTRODUCTION TO THE SYSTEM OF CAR CONTROL:**

https://youtu.be/1u5ksf29ylI

Roundabouts are easy aren't they?

Give way to traffic approaching from the right.

There you go. Easy. Pass me another beer.

But hang on a minute. I've seen many threads on internet forums which demonstrate that qualified drivers of various levels of experience are regularly unsure as to whether their actions at various roundabouts are correct or not.

One involved a driver turning left at a roundabout from a right-hand lane approach, one involved the legality (or otherwise) of completing a full circuit of a roundabout to make progress, and the most recent one I read was a driver who had experienced an aggressive reaction from a following driver when she gave priority to a vehicle approaching from the left on a mini roundabout.

I know that to most drivers a roundabout is just a roundabout, but there is a lot more to it than that. Single lane roundabouts, multiple lane roundabouts, mini roundabouts, throughabouts, magic roundabouts, hamburger roundabouts, dogbone roundabouts and my current favourite (which surely must have at least been *named* by a petrolhead) - *turbo* roundabouts (yes, really!). There's a lot to consider, so I thought I'd go all traditional and start with a good, old fashioned systematic Roadcraft approach to a nice, straightforward four exit single-lane roundabout.

This chapter is based on a well-used lecture I used to give to standard and advanced police students on the first or second day of their course, before we'd actually been out on the road.

As I've mentioned in previous chapters, you may or may not agree with all or part of the Roadcraft system, but please feel free to take whatever you like and leave whatever you don't like. The usual disclaimer about this being appropriate for any level of experience applies, so please don't assume I'm being patronising.

Roadcraft system and a four exit roundabout

By way of an introduction, let's remind ourselves of the five phases of the Roadcraft system of car control - mainly to assist any readers who are not familiar with systematic driving.

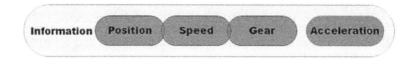

Information

Let's start at the beginning with the information phase. What do we mean by "information"? It's a bit vague when it's just reduced to the single word, so let's explore the information phase in more detail. Firstly, you'll notice that the information phase starts before all the others and runs throughout all the other four phases. It's depicted in the above diagram as a sort of pink "bubble" inside which the other phases appear in a definite order.

So, information - what do we do with it? Well, we give it a **TUG.**

By which, of course, I mean we **T**ake, **U**se and **G**ive information at all times, throughout the negotiation of the roundabout wherever appropriate.

Take information by continually scanning, from the horizon, back to the mid distance, the foreground, the sides and the rear.

Use the information you've taken in to formulate a plan as to how you're going to negotiate the roundabout.

Give information to other road users with a signal where appropriate.

So, we're driving along, tugging our information, and we start to pick up some visual clues that we're approaching a roundabout. If you're scanning correctly, you might pick up the movement of vehicles towards your road, in the distance - this is at least a clue that there is a junction of some sort ahead. You might see a clump of street lights too before you actually pick up any sight of the roundabout itself.

As you get closer to the roundabout, you'll see a direction sign with all the information you need to start forming your plan for the roundabout itself. Here's an example for the roundabout we're approaching (there is no significance of this particular roundabout - it was just the first hit on google images).

So, from this sign, we know we're on a secondary (B) road, because the sign is white. We know that there are three exits plus the road we're on. We know that the first exit, at 9 o'clock, will take us to Torbreck and Essich. We know that the second exit, at 12 o'clock, will take us to Holm and via an additional junction, to Dores. Finally, we know that the third exit, at 3 o'clock, will take us to Lochardil.

It took me a few minutes to write that, but in reality, it should only take you a second or so to look at the sign, identify your destination and pick your exit.

Position

Many roundabouts split to two lanes on approach. If the lanes are arrow-marked, then the choice of lane is made for you, but the majority are not lane marked, so what should your position be on approach to the roundabout?

Left is easy. Go in the left lane.

Right is also easy in this case. Go in the right lane. Piece of cake.

Straight on? Well, either lane is ok, depending on the circumstances. If traffic is light, approaching in the left lane will allow you to take the straightest line through the roundabout. If there is a line of traffic turning left, then straight on from the right lane is perfectly acceptable.

That's all nice and easy with a four exit roundabout, but what about something a bit more complicated? Like this:

I have a basic rule of thumb for lane selection on the approach to roundabouts. If my exit is between 6 o'clock and 12 o'clock, treat it as a left turn and use the left lane. If it's between 12 o'clock and 6 o'clock, treat is as a right turn and use the right lane.

Signals? Well, the information phase runs throughout the system, so you can stick a signal on at any appropriate time. For a first-exit-left, I'd give a left signal on approach, but in the above pic, if I were going second-exit-left to Tapton Lock, I'd approach in the left lane without signalling, and then stick on a left "breakaway" signal immediately after passing the Sheffield A61 exit. More on breakaway signals shortly.

For any exit past 12 o'clock, I would generally give a right signal on approach.

Straight on does not require a signal on approach. This seems to be a difficult concept for some people to grasp, but most cars are not fitted with a straight-on indicator, and left or right signals can be very confusing to other road users if you're going straight on, so please - no signal on approach if your intention is to go straight on.

Speed

The speed phase is next, but there isn't a definite separation between the position phase and the speed phase - they overlap in the diagram because they can overlap on the road. Position is *considered* before speed and any change in position generally comes before the speed is changed, but there is no problem in braking whilst altering your position on approach to the roundabout.

But how do you select the appropriate speed?

An old instructor colleague of mine came up with "**the three Vs**".

1. The **V**ehicles on and approaching the roundabout.

2. The **V**iew on the approach to the roundabout, and...

Any guesses?

The third "V"?

No? Ok then...

3. The cur**V**e of the roundabout.

Sorry - I did say it wasn't originally one of mine, but it's a nice little line to include in commentary if that's your thing.

So, your speed on approach is governed by the vehicles, the view and the curve, and the other overriding phrase to consider is...

Planning to stop, but looking to go.

In other words, your plan when approaching a roundabout should always include the option of stopping at the give way line if traffic is busy. But at the same time, you should be looking carefully at the traffic on the roundabout, and at the traffic approaching the roundabout (from *all* directions), in order to spot an appropriate gap in the traffic that you can pull in to without having to stop.

Looking right nice and early on approach should allow you to see what is or isn't approaching and whether you're likely to have to stop. A long line of traffic approaching from the right doesn't necessarily mean you'll have to stop though. Look straight ahead as well - look for traffic travelling straight towards you which will exit on to the road on which you are approaching. These vehicles will prevent the traffic approaching from the right from entering the roundabout and allow you to continue.

The term for these oncoming vehicles is ***a twelve o'clock block.***

So, to summarise on speed selection for the roundabout...

Your speed is dictated by the three Vs - the vehicles, the view and the curve, you should be planning to stop but looking to go and keeping an eye out for a twelve o'clock block.

Gear

Getting your speed correct will generally involve deceleration and / or braking, and you should aim to have your speed correct, and to have come off the brakes with enough time to select the appropriate gear for the roundabout.

There's no secret here. Just whatever gear is the most appropriate and flexible. Preferably - but not always necessarily - one which will get you on to, round and off the roundabout without taking another gear.

Aim to have your gear selected and the clutch re-engaged before you cross the give way line and enter the roundabout.

Acceleration

The last phase is acceleration - "the correct amount of safe, smooth acceleration to negotiate and leave the roundabout".

Not a particularly difficult one this. As much acceleration as is appropriate. Less when it's wet, more when it's dry, less when it's busy, more when it's quiet, less when you're drunk, more when you're sober.

I'm joking of course. More acceleration is better when you're drunk because you'll be home sooner and there will therefore be less risk to other road users. (A drunk driver did actually use this excuse with me once!).

Breakaway signals

I mentioned breakaway signals briefly earlier in the post. A breakaway signal is a left signal to confirm which exit you intend to use to leave the roundabout.

Give a breakaway signal just as you pass the exit immediately before the one you intend to use. It helps following traffic and it helps those approaching from other exits. I find that the "three flash" program built into many modern indicators is usually sufficient for a breakaway signal.

So there you go. System applied to a simple roundabout.

Roundabouts in Heavy Traffic

Normally I advise drivers to look to the right very early on the approach to a roundabout - *planning to stop but looking to go*. This isn't my advice when approaching a roundabout in a line of stop-start traffic.

A very common cause of rear-end shunt type accidents at roundabouts is the driver behind thinking that the driver in front is going, looking to the right and thinking that they can also go themselves, and then driving straight into the car in front because that driver has changed his or her mind and stopped.

To avoid this situation, watch the car in front carefully. When they become the front car at the give way line, keep watching them (albeit as part of your regular scanning routine) until they set off. Then keep watching them so that you are sure they are moving off before making your final decision to go. After a final look right, look ahead again before accelerating.

Also, try not to be hesitant when setting off. This will avoid the driver behind making the classic mistake if you change your mind. Be patient at the line if it's busy - when you go it should be a positive move.

43

DRIVE FOR FUN, FOR FREE!

Fuel economy.

I know, I know - motoring enthusiasts like to drive high performance cars *fast,* which isn't in any way compatible with economic driving. A few years ago, a friend of mine bought a large, high performance saloon, powered by a very substantial V8 engine. Someone asked him "what about fuel economy?" And he gave the best answer I've yet heard to such a pointless question.

"Well, when it looks like the fuel is getting low, I just stop and put some more in."

We all know that fuel economy has nothing to do with enthusiastic driving, but how much of your driving *is* actually enthusiastic? By which I mean how much of your driving is carried out on nice roads, in light traffic in circumstances which allow you to really stretch your cars legs?

I have a daily commute of 23 miles which takes in about a quarter of the M60 at peak hours, and so I reckon that only about 5% of my own driving is enjoyable these days. Add to that the fact that fuel is very expensive and despite some minor fluctuations, it's unlikely to ever be considered cheap again and the benefits of an economic driving style become clear.

My thinking is this. If I drive economically when the traffic is heavy and there is little or no opportunity to make progress or drive enthusiastically, then when the traffic *is* light and the road is nice, I can afford to stretch my car as much as I like and use up the fuel I've saved during the boring driving. In other words, my "fun" driving - when the opportunity arises - doesn't actually cost me anything. As the thread title suggests, when I drive for fun, it's free!

Of course, there are some people, like my friend with the V8, who are lucky enough to not have to worry about the cost of fuel, but even if you are one of those people, what if you're out on a run and you misjudge things and find yourself low on fuel and miles from the nearest garage? In these circumstances, an economic driving style could make the difference between continuing your journey or making that embarrassing phone call.

The first thing you should note is that I'm talking about a *driving* style and not about different types of vehicles. There are cars which are promoted on the basis of being very fuel efficient and there are a number of tips floating around the internet on how to ensure your car will use as little fuel as possible - high tyre pressures and weight reduction are two examples I can think of off the top of my head - but this thread is about how to get maximum MPG (or gas mileage if you're a Yankee Doodle) when driving *any* car, irrespective of whether it's a hyper-efficient supermini or a V12 supercar. The techniques are the same for any car, and the benefits (in percentage MPG terms) can be very similar for any car.

The other thing to remember is that economic driving on the road is like any other style of road driving - a compromise. In much the same way that you cannot safely drive a car to the limit of its performance on the road, it wouldn't be appropriate, most of the time, to drive a car to the limit of its fuel economy capability. You wouldn't, for instance, want to crawl along a motorway slip road with minimal acceleration and then attempt to join a fast-moving lane 1.

It's this difference between real-world driving and unrealistic test conditions which results in the often large differences between manufacturers claimed fuel economy figures and the MPG figures which are realistically attainable in everyday driving. I'll be examining a slightly more practical economic driving style which doesn't assume that you want to take all day to complete your journey.

So let's start with the basics. Firstly, remember that you're trying to achieve maximum **miles** per gallon. In other words, the distance travelled is just as important as the driving style, so there is no real need to crawl everywhere at a snail's-pace.

Secondly, the activities which use up most of your fuel are accelerating and driving uphill. Now, obviously, those activities cannot be avoided in day-to-day driving, but if you think ahead and plan your progress, you can easily improve your fuel economy.

Thirdly, air resistance is a problem, but again, it's an element of basic physics which you cannot avoid. Driving into a headwind can have a very dramatic effect on fuel economy and even without a headwind, when you're driving at higher speeds (70mph+), most of your fuel is being used to overcome the resistance of the air. If I'm driving in miser mode, I tend to stay within the posted speed limits.

The fourth and final principle to remember is that when travelling downhill, in gear, with your foot completely off the throttle, a car is using virtually no fuel whatsoever. Many reports (and my own car manual) state that a car is using no fuel at all when coasting in gear, but I find that difficult to accept - although I'm happy to be corrected by someone more knowledgeable. Whatever the truth on this question, coasting in gear (as opposed to coasting in neutral or with the clutch depressed - which allows the engine to drop to idle revs, which *does* require the use of some fuel) is the most fuel-efficient state to be travelling in and effectively gives you "free" mileage.

Coasting should always be carried out in gear anyway - irrespective of whether you're in miser mode or not. Coasting in neutral or with the clutch depressed is bad practice and removes an element of control from the driver. It is occasionally necessary to use some acceleration to avoid an emerging hazard, and coasting in neutral introduces an unnecessary delay which isn't present when you're coasting in gear.

I understand that some automatic and DSG gearboxes do allow some neutral coasting, but these systems instantly re-engage drive if the throttle is applied.

So, how do we string all these principles together into an economic driving style? Let's look at acceleration first - this is the real killer when it comes to fuel economy, so the less acceleration you have to carry out, the better.

Momentum is king when it comes to MPG, so a good advanced driver is already at an advantage in this regard. If you can plan ahead to avoid having to slow unnecessarily for hazards, get an early view at a roundabout so you can join it without having to come to a stop, and maintain reasonable speed through a series of bends using acceleration sense rather than having to brake and then accelerate again - all principles of good, advanced driving - then you're on your way to developing an economic driving style.

If, however, you stop at every hazard and roundabout before accelerating away, and use a "clog and anchor" style, using heavy braking and accelerating through corners, then you're likely to use much more fuel than is necessary.

Of course, some acceleration is necessary, and I find that using no more than the first quarter of the throttle pedal's travel is generally enough to make reasonable progress in most circumstances. Try to combine the quarter pedal technique with maximum revs of 2000rpm before changing up a gear and (in most cars at least) you'll be using as little fuel as possible.

Be flexible though - as mentioned previously, if you're joining a motorway, take a flexible gear and use as many revs as you need to match the speed of vehicles in lane 1, but once you've reached your desired speed, there is no need to go through every gear sequentially - just pop it into top gear, relax your pressure on the accelerator and sit at your desired speed with as little pressure on the pedal as required to maintain your speed.

I mentioned up-hills earlier and these require a little planning. Try to maintain, or even gain a little speed on the approach to an uphill stretch, and then aim to reach the top with as little throttle as possible. I'm not a big fan of losing speed for no apparent reason, but gradually losing a little speed on an uphill incline is usually fine and most other drivers generally do it without even realising.

A smooth driving style is a big advantage when you're in miser mode. If you're smooth and gentle - not just with the accelerator, but with the brakes also - then your MPG will improve. Treat the pedals as though there's an egg underneath them.

Many cars these days are fitted with stop-start systems. These systems recognise when the car is stationary and in neutral, and then switch off the engine whilst the car remains stationary. Dipping the clutch to take first gear causes the engine to re-start almost instantly and you're ready to go.

When I first tried a couple of cars with this system, I hated it - it felt very unnatural and I turned it off. I'm now on my second car with stop-start fitted and I leave it on all the time. I got used to it and I simply cannot argue with the fact that an idling, stationary car is using fuel when it really doesn't need to. I was originally concerned about battery life, but I've never had a problem in 30-odd thousand miles, so I'm now a proponent of stop-start systems.

Maintaining a *constant* speed once you're up and running is important. If your speed is inconsistent, it invariably will involve a constant pattern of unnecessary deceleration, followed by unnecessary acceleration - the MPG killer. So once you're up to your chosen speed, keep a regular check on your speedo and try to keep your speed constant.

And the final point I mentioned - coasting in gear - is the biggest fuel-saver of all. On any downhill gradient whatsoever, you should aim to reduce your throttle pressure to zero. Take your foot completely off the pedal if it helps. If you want to maintain or increase your speed, leave the car in a higher gear which will minimise engine braking. Alternatively, if you want the car to hold you or reduce your speed a little, take a lower gear - the revs may rise, but fuel use is still (virtually) zero, so don't worry about the raised engine speed.

Another point I should mention is "eco pro" and other switchable "eco", "sport" etc. systems.

These systems allow the driver to switch between different throttle maps to suit their intended driving style. Most cars these days employ "fly by wire" throttles, which mean that the accelerator pedal is no longer directly connected to the throttle mechanism by way of a cable. Instead, the pedal effectively sends an electronic signal to an actuator, which then operates the throttle.

This means that manufacturers can tune the throttle to respond in different ways. I have a new BMW, which has three settings - a default "comfort" setting, a "sport" setting and an "eco pro" setting.

The default comfort setting gives a straightforward, linear feeling throttle, by which I mean that the engine's output seems to be directly proportionate to the amount of pressure applied to the accelerator. Pretty much identical to how a more traditional, cable-operated accelerator feels.

The sport setting effectively "shortens" the virtual accelerator cable and makes the engine - in its lower rev range at least - feel much more responsive. I'm not sure if any other electric trickery is employed in this mode, but the impression to me is that the throttle mechanism is "geared up", and the accelerator pedal requires much less of a "prod" to get the car moving.

The third setting - eco pro - seems to do exactly the opposite to the sport setting. It seems to "lengthen" the virtual throttle cable, and in order to get the car to accelerate at anything approaching a brisk pace, it requires a very hefty shove on the accelerator pedal. The idea is that the car is doing what you should be doing and softening your inputs on the accelerator pedal to maximise fuel efficiency. The car manual also states that the air-con runs in a more fuel efficient way, heated mirrors are slower to work etc.

To the mechanically uneducated - Mrs Local for example - the car "feels" faster in sport and slower in eco pro. This isn't the case in reality, as all the cars performance is always available all the time, whatever mode you are in, it just requires different degrees of accelerator pressure to extract it.

If I'm on the daily grind, I tend to use eco pro to help with fuel economy, but the jury is out on how effective it is. I reckon I can match my fuel economy in all three modes, but I've not had the car long enough (or been anal enough yet) to try.

Incidentally, my daughter thinks "comfort" mode is ridiculous, because there isn't an "uncomfortable" mode.

This all may sound, to some of you, like very basic stuff. I've only scratched the surface to be honest and there are some far more extreme fuel saving methods discussed elsewhere on the internet, but I think this will do as a basic introduction.

And don't forget to use all that fuel that you save by going on a good blast every now and again!

44

DO YOU WALK THE DOG, OR DOES IT WALK YOU?

This is a short discussion on the merits of "driving" a car versus "guiding" it or in other words "letting it go a bit".

The first thing I would say on this subject is that it is, to a degree, car-dependant. Some cars are naturally predisposed to being gently guided down the road. "Wafting" is an oft-used PH term, and I think it's a good term for describing that feeling that a car is just carrying you along in comfort with nothing more than a little guidance from the driver. It's generally accepted that large Mercedes and Jaguar models, for instance, are "wafters".

Other cars, however, demand your full attention most of the time. It's nigh-on impossible to waft along in a Caterham, for instance, or any number of other ostensibly "sporting" cars where the priority of the manufacturer is to maximise driving enjoyment above all other considerations.

These are (in a purely road car context) the two extremes though, and there are elements of both mind-sets which can cross over all car types. For instance, I have had some *very* spirited drives in large Jaguar and Mercedes cars over the years, and their size and weight have required my full attention in order to maintain maximum progress. It's also true that some Caterham drivers use their cars as daily drivers and most commutes these days involve an element of stop-start and limited speed motorway driving. Are these drivers fully committed to controlling their cars under these circumstances? No, of course not - they will adapt to the daily use of their car and find a comfortable middle ground to allow them to feel at least a little relaxed on their mundane journeys.

Whenever I've taught someone high performance road driving, there is a tendency - even amongst drivers who have plenty of experience in high performance machinery - to try too hard and "overdrive" the car. It's sometimes nervousness and it's sometimes overconfidence and it's sometimes a determination to "show him what I can do".

To an experienced instructor, the signs are obvious. Although their seating position may be correct, they sit in a tense manner, shoulders tight and jaw set. They grip the steering wheel tightly and snatch for the gearstick as though it's a small mammal trying to escape. Head and eye movements are twitchy and quick and they never really look as though they are comfortable - always shuffling slightly in their seat, adjusting their position and fiddling with the mirrors. It's also common to see them constantly scratching an itch or rubbing an ear.

The result is that these inconsistencies - these tensions - have a subtle, but very real effect on their driving and the way the car moves down the road. A tight grip on the steering wheel results in rough steering inputs, particularly during the vital initial turn of the wheel. Snatched gear changes lead to jerky front-to-rear weight transfer. Tension and discomfort lead to pedals being pressed, rather than squeezed.

The thing is though, that these drivers often feel that they are getting the maximum out of their cars by putting the maximum effort into the driving, when the reality is that they are *overdriving* the car and probably not making the best or safest progress as a result.

My advice is that it's always better to relax a little and let the car do more of the work. It's inevitable that as you go outside your usual comfort zone, you'll feel tense and anxious at times, but bear a few basic principles in mind and your driving will improve no end.

Firstly, make sure you're completely comfortable with your driving position. I'll not patronise you with a full description of how to achieve a perfect driving position because we're all different shapes and sizes, but just make sure you can see out clearly, you can reach and operate all the controls fully and that your mirrors are set properly.

Secondly, try to *stay* relaxed. Monitor how you're feeling during a drive and take the occasional mental "step back". If you feel tension creeping in, take a little speed off, relax your shoulders, reassess where you are and how you are driving, and then carry on.

Thirdly - and this is probably the whole point I'm trying to make with this post - **let the car do most of the work.** Trust me on this - the car wants to go. Anyone who has driven a truly fast car will never forget that sense of urgency with which the car seems to want to get down the road, even at moderate speeds.

Even average cars these days have plenty of performance and want to get you down the road at a reasonable pace.

Your job isn't to force the car along the road. It is to guide the car in the direction you want to go, whilst allowing the car to go as much as it is safe to.

Does that mean that the driver's inputs are less important? No - if anything they are more important, because it's the driver's skills in gently moving the car away from its preferred straight and consistent path which make all the difference between safe, smooth progression and rough, jerky and potentially unsafe driving.

Think of driving in the same way as you might think about walking an untrained dog. You can walk the dog on a tight, restrictive lead and it will pull and stop and be awkward and generally hinder your progress. If you let the dog off its lead, it will run off, out of control and possibly cause mayhem.

If, however, you invest in one of those extending "reel" type dog leads, you can rein the dog in and control it when you need to, and you can also let it have a good old run-around whilst maintaining an element of control.

Driving.

Like having a naughty dog on an extending lead...

45

Driving is Awful These Days, Isn't it? Or is it?

Day to day driving is a bind these days isn't it?

Traffic, roadworks, "safety" cameras, congestion zones, traffic calming, civil enforcement, lowered speed limits and general day-to-day numptyism combine to make my daily commute, and most of my other driving pretty bloody awful these days.

Most of you probably feel the same. A quick scan of the PH forums certainly suggests that - even on a motoring forum - people aren't enjoying driving much these days. There are literally thousands of posts complaining about poor driving standards, poor road conditions, overzealous enforcement, restrictive legislation and a whole range of other general embuggerances.

However...

Occasionally - just occasionally - it's different. The traffic thins out, you're on an attractive and well maintained road, one which makes you work, but doesn't hold too many nasty surprises. Plenty of nice, easy to assess corners, well sighted, good extended views, helpful cambers and a nice overall rhythm.

The speed of your mental processes seem to increase, your observations switch to full scanning mode and, for the time being, all you're thinking about is driving - scanning, planning, reacting, *concentrating*. The car becomes an extension of your own body - you can feel the road surface through the wheel and the grip levels through the seat.

The physical interaction with the car brings its own little satisfactions too. Accelerating through a bend, timing your gear changes and rev matching to perfection, controlling the car, but also allowing it to flow with the road. You can feel and judge the grip levels on each corner, small inputs with throttle or wheel allow you to tighten the cars line and adjust its attitude. Precise management of the weight transfer, in both pitch and roll allow you to keep the car perfectly balanced.

Your body reacts in involuntary ways, which add to the moment. Your heart rate rises slightly, you feel a heightened sensitivity with the controls - particularly the steering - your pupils dilate and your consciousness instinctively focuses on the most important senses, so that you tend to feel like you're hearing less and seeing more.

Believe it or not, speed isn't that important when it comes to enjoying driving. It's far more about the feelings and emotions, the physical and mechanical connection with the car and the road. I've had some very enjoyable drives in relatively slow cars, and some pretty poor drives in considerably faster cars. It's far more about the time, the place, the road and your attitude than anything else.

You need to make more of an effort to experience driving enjoyment these days. An early start in a Sunday and a run out to more enjoyable roads, but believe me; it's still worth it every now and again.

I've been driving for 28 years so far and despite the day to day hassles, I still enjoy driving and I still occasionally make time to just go for a drive for pleasure. My Dad is 71, and he said something very similar to me the other day. He doesn't drive anything spectacular, but to this day, he still enjoys driving and still occasionally goes for a drive just for the sake of it.

So if you're fed up with the daily grind, sick to the back teeth with your daily commute and just generally disillusioned with driving, try setting you alarm clock for 7.00am on Sunday and head out for an hour or two on your own. It might just reignite your love of driving.

46

A Police Car and a Screamin' Siren...

...Pneumatic drill and ripped-up concrete.

Emergency response driving

"Emergency response" driving is the type of driving employed by the emergency services when they are required to attend an emergency incident. For the police, calls to the control room are graded by the operator into several different levels of response, and those graded as "grade 1" or "code 1" will receive an emergency response.

A grade 1 police response will be given to incidents which involve (or potentially involve) a threat to life, the use of violence, serious injury or serious damage to property. An emergency response will also be given to incidents where a (serious) crime is in progress, an offender has been recently disturbed or detained and for road traffic accidents where an injury has occurred or where the road is blocked.

Incident grading in the ambulance service is decided in each individual case, based on the immediate needs of the patients. It's one of the reasons that the operator asks a series of very detailed questions about the patient and their condition. As an aside, I've had cause to call an ambulance twice in the last year or so, and ambulance control room operators are some of the most professional people I've ever dealt with in an emergency situation.

The Fire Service are a little more old fashioned and tend to treat most calls as requiring an emergency response until they have arrived and assessed the incident.

Legal Exemptions

I'm not going to go into too much detail on legal exemptions, other than to say that police, fire and ambulance drivers (together with a small number of military, rescue and clandestine service drivers) are exempt from certain road traffic regulations, such as speed limits, red traffic lights, keep left/right signs and a few others.

The thing I will mention in relation to exemptions is the fact that they are absolute exemptions from specific regulations. In other words, they are not conditional on blue lights and sirens being used. Surveillance driving, for example, would be impossible if the surveillance officers were required to use blue lights to claim an exemption.

The other thing to bear in mind is that there is no exemption from careless or dangerous driving offences, so emergency drivers should remember that, despite their exemptions, they are still responsible for their actions should the wheel come off.

And a note on accidents. One key phrase in police driver training is "Drive to arrive". The ultimate aim isn't to get to an incident as quickly as possible – it's simply to *get* to the incident. If you crash on your way to the incident, you're out of the game, someone else will have to attend the incident, and someone *else* will have to come and deal with your accident. Getting it wrong can, very quickly, tie up a whole shift of officers unnecessarily.

Before I go any further, I'll add that the driving skills I'll be writing about relate solely to emergency response, and not pursuits, which require a completely different set of skills and a higher level of driver training.

These days, all standard level police drivers receive several days of emergency response instruction towards the end of their driving course. This was not always the case. Until around the early 2000s, (in my force at least) standard and advanced students received no emergency response instruction whatsoever. They would be taught how to drive systematically to a good standard, but the response driving was just something they had to work out for themselves.

As you can imagine, this wasn't ideal, and in the early years of my police career I was the passenger with numerous drivers who had – shall we say questionable skills - in making dynamic risk assessment.

Loonies, in other words.

Honestly – in the 1990's, there were some absolutely certifiable mentalists out there disguised as police officers. I try not to think about how many close calls, scrapes and "close your eyes and prey" moments I endured from the passenger seat. If I'm being honest, I was probably guilty of some lunacy myself in those early days, but I survived intact and subsequently saw the light.

The Equipment

The first panda car I drove was a 1986 two-door Rover Metro with a 1275 A series engine and a 4 speed gearbox. The only emergency equipment fitted was a single blue beacon, about the size and shape of an upturned plant pot on the roof and illuminated "police" signs on the front and rear. No Battenberg livery, no alternate flashing headlights, no rear flashing red lights, no light bar, no strobes and no sirens. It didn't even have an orange stripe along the sides.

These days, emergency vehicles are designed to be as visible and identifiable as possible, because above everything else, if you're driving to an emergency, the sooner other drivers see you, the longer they have to react, and as you'll see later, it's the reactions of other drivers that we're looking for.

A fairly standard emergency set-up these days is a flashing blue roof bar, alternate-flashing headlights and a whoop/wail siren. The blue lights can be operated with or without the flashing headlights, which you would usually want to leave off on unlit roads at night to avoid dazzling. The sirens are usually operated by the horn switch. When the blue lights are off, it just operates the horn as normal. When the blues are switched on, the first press of the horn will activate the "whooper" siren (the slower of the two sirens), the second press of the horn will switch to the "wailer" and the third press will switch the sirens off. We'll look at the advantages of switching from whoop to wail in a bit.

There are other combinations, depending on the service or area. There are numerous different types of flashing lights, strobes and sirens continually being developed – squawks, white noise etc., but for this chapter I'll stick with the standard set-up described above.

Protection

So, how much protection does the emergency equipment give you?

Some emergency drivers seem to think that the blue lights and sirens create an invisible protective force-field around their vehicle which will defend them from all possible threats.

They don't.

All the emergency equipment does is make you more visible. That's it. It does not mean that people will actually see you – it just means that they are more likely to see you. It does not give you any protection and it does not guarantee that you'll get the reactions you're looking for – or any reaction whatsoever – from other road users.

On to the actual driving

Believe it or not, emergency response driving, if performed correctly, can actually be quite a relaxing way to drive. This might sound implausible, considering the possible nature of the incident the driver is attending, but if you're able to separate that element out – compartmentalise it – and think only about the driving, it can, genuinely, be a relaxing way to drive.

Think about it – you don't have to sit in stationary traffic, you don't have to be held up by traffic lights or other junctions, you're not restricted by speed limits and almost every other road user will do their best to get out of your way and allow you precedence. If you can keep your concentration levels high and you employ good observation and planning, it's relatively easy, with a little experience, to stay quite relaxed on an emergency run.

Let's start with a single carriageway with traffic moving in both directions. You're looking for reactions from other road users which indicate that they have seen you and that they are giving you precedence. The traffic coming towards you is more likely to see you before the traffic travelling in your direction. You should position your vehicle in such a way as to make yourself as visible as possible and also in such a way as to indicate your intentions to others.

The key theme is to hold back, position yourself appropriately and wait for a reaction. Oncoming vehicles will move to their left to give you more room. Vehicles ahead will move to the left, sometimes with an indicator confirming that they're pulling over. The emergency driver should hold back, position to the offside – often straddling the white line – and wait for these reactions before passing and continuing.

There are some common bad reactions from other drivers which often catch out the novice, but can be predicted with a little experience. For example, if you're following two vehicles, it's quite common for the front vehicle to see you and react by pulling over to the nearside and slowing, only for the rear vehicles – the one which really *should* have seen you, to pull out and pass the front vehicle, oblivious to your existence, just as you are about to pass them yourself.

Drivers will often pull up adjacent to traffic islands and bollards, leaving you little or no room to pass. Be patient, either move to the offside of the bollard or sit and wait for them to wake up, which they usually do after a couple of seconds.

One bad reaction I've never understood comes from drivers sitting in junctions ahead. They're waiting to join your road, looking in your direction and they've definitely seen you approaching. Instead of waiting for you to pass, they will pull out and then immediately move over to the left to let you pass. Why not just wait? I've never been able to work that one out.

They key with all these situations is that the driver should hold back, keep a safe distance, and wait until it's safe to pass. Sounds familiar? Does it sound a bit like Roadcraft system? Stay on the brakes until it's safe to go, come off the brakes, take the appropriate gear and then accelerate. For many new police drivers, the emergency response training is the point in their driving course when system really "clicks" and they finally get the point of separating their actions into the five phases.

Traffic light junctions can be particularly hazardous. Emergency drivers should treat red traffic lights as a "give way" junction, so flying through red lights with a quick glance on approach is very bad practice. Instead, drivers should approach cautiously, at a speed which should allow them to stop if someone pulls across the junction.

If there is a build-up of traffic on the approach to a junction, there are generally two choices. An offside approach usually offers the least resistance, but can be risky, particularly at a poorly sighted junction. The other approach is to position yourself straddling the lanes, with lights and sirens switched on, and wait for the "parting of the waves". Once the other drivers have clocked you and realised your intentions, they will generally move to their left and right, and create an extra lane to allow you through.

There are times, however, when there simply isn't room for people to move, and it is occasionally good practice to switch off the sirens, leave your blue lights on, and just wait for the lights to change. When they do, switch your siren back on, and once the traffic is moving again, people will be able to give you room to pass.

When driving in urban areas, the high buildings and proximity of walls can make it difficult for others to work out what direction your sirens are coming from. This can be where the switch from whoop to wail (and back again) can help. Often the change in note or frequency of a siren helps people to recognise the direction it's coming from.

There is another problem in the cities – what I term "siren apathy". Sirens are so common in busy cities that people have started to either not notice them, or to actually ignore them. It's the reason that the motorcyclists in the Met's Special Escort Group don't use sirens, but instead use very loud whistles.

Whilst we're in the city, be very, *very* cautious of pedestrians. They may be sensible and alert to your movements. On the other hand, they may be deaf, or blind, or both, or drunk, or high, or listening to headphones or even mentally deranged. It's almost impossible to tell in the short time you've got to make an assessment, but look for reactions – people looking towards you or putting their hands over their ears. The ones to be really careful of are the people who *don't* react. They are the ones who are most likely to be unaware of your presence, and who may suddenly decide to cross the road…

On the motorway, at higher speeds, sirens tend to be fairly ineffective. The cars in front are travelling away from you at speed, so are very unlikely to hear a siren on a vehicle approaching from the rear. Position in the offside lane and wait for vehicles to move to their left. Keep a good following position and be ready for bad reactions –

sudden braking to a stop in lane 3 is not unheard of and it's occasionally necessary to pass drivers on the nearside.

In stationary motorway traffic the hard shoulder is your best option, but keep your speed down. Some drivers may react badly to your lights and move to the hard shoulder, so you need to be ready to stop. There is also a lot of debris on the hard shoulder, so you need to mitigate the risk of puncture by keeping your speed down. Also, don't forget what the hard shoulder is for – you may encounter stationary vehicles.

There are other risks associated with travelling in convoy with other emergency vehicles. Drivers usually see the first vehicle, move over, allow it to pass, and then fail to realise there is more than one vehicle. There are two approaches in these situations. The first is to close right up and keep a minimum distance between vehicles, effectively travelling as one large vehicle. This doesn't allow time for drivers to pull out in front of the second vehicle, but it does have associated risks and the second driver is very reliant on the decisions of the first driver, which isn't ideal.

The second approach is to increase the distance between emergency vehicles to a few hundred yards. This allows people to see and react to the second vehicle in plenty of time and is a safer option in my opinion.

And finally, some thoughts on the mental aspects.

There are two elements of emergency response driving which are entirely dependent on the driver's own mental state. They are red mist and noble cause risk taking.

We're all familiar with red mist - it's the situation when drivers emotions take over and their ability to make realistic dynamic risk assessments is seriously hampered by the amount of adrenaline being produced by their body. The adrenaline puts their body in "fight or flight" mode, which is a throwback to our animal days where the body is quickly prepared for running away or fighting by the effects of adrenaline - raised heart rate and blood pressure, and - worryingly for drivers - a tunnelling of their vision and reduction in awareness of their hearing. Fine motor skills become much more difficult and it dramatically changes a driver's thinking process.

Red mist shifts a driver's thinking on to the target or goal - the incident they are attending - rather than thinking about the job at hand - the driving.

The second element I mentioned - noble cause risk taking - allows drivers to justify their poor decisions by claiming that they are necessary because someone's life is at risk, or there is some other "noble cause" to justify their risky behaviour. Even for a driver who is fully in control of their emotions, noble cause risk taking can creep into their driving and create very real dangers.

Good quality driver training can help - if you're affected by red mist, for instance, a good grounding in systematic driving can at least give you a good "baseline" standard of driving to fall back on when the adrenaline is flowing.

But, ultimately, it's down to individual drivers and their ability to recognise when these issues are arising, and having the ability to overcome them and keep their attention fully on the driving.

47

Weather the Weather

YOUTUBE LINK - UK WINTER DRIVING:

https://youtu.be/sfxY8hT2BQs

We have a funny attitude to the weather in the UK. We always seem to be surprised by weather which, really, is only doing what it has always done during the appropriate seasons. We also always seem to delight in the extremes of British weather - it's always the wettest April since records began, or the coldest winter since records began, or the warmest year or the windiest third Tuesday in March in a year with a 5 in it since records began - you get the idea.

There is also a perceived inability for the UK to deal with any form of weather which falls slightly outside the norm. A light dusting of snow bring "**TRAVEL CHAOS**" headlines, a North Atlantic storm brings "**DISRUPTION TO THOUSANDS**", a particularly cold night brings "**DEADLY FROZEN HORROR ROADS OF FREEZING ICY DEATH**" - again, you get the idea.

Part of the problem is the ever decreasing quality of news reporting in this country. Instead of reporting the facts – you know – straightforward facts about what is actually happening, the press these days want to inflate every single incident into something terrible and terrifying. I've always been reasonably cynical about press reporting in general, but over the last 10 years or so, the main aim of the press seems to have been trying to keep the British population in a continual state of near panic and abject fear.

So let's start with some basic truths about the weather in the UK. We live in a temperate climate, on an island in North West Europe, susceptible to weather systems approaching from the North Atlantic. Compared with other parts of the world, none of our weather could accurately be described as "extreme". We sometimes get hot summers, but they're nothing like those experienced in the Sahara, for instance, or in the deserts of the South West USA. We sometimes get cold winters, but they're nothing like the winters in Siberia or parts of Northern Canada, where average temperatures are in the minus 30s. Our wet weather cannot compare with countries which are subject to monsoons and our windy weather is nothing like as extreme as the mid-west USA during tornado season.

Our weather is a bit like a Chinese buffet – we get a mild-to-medium taster of all the available weather conditions, without actually suffering anything which could be accurately described as "extreme".

But, having said all that, weather conditions can and do have an effect on our ability to travel and can be hazardous when driving if you don't know what you're doing. They sometimes need a different approach to normal everyday driving and some conditions need a carefully considered approach, so I thought I'd put together a post which includes all the weather conditions we're likely to experience in this country and give a few short tips for each. So let's start with:

Rain

Yes, I know – not a very extreme start, but I want to look at *all* the weather conditions we experience in this country, and, let's be honest, rain is, depressingly, the most common condition we're likely to come across in the UK.

Firstly, you need to be able to see, so keep your glass clean on the outside and the inside & replace your wipers when they start to streak.

Keep a little airflow over your windscreen at all times – my preference is to leave the A/C turned on all year round, as it dries the air inside the car and prevents windows from misting.

Don't be tempted to wipe mist from the inside of your windows with a leather, cloth or sleeve – it will streak badly and will affect your vision. Just wait a second or two and let your heater & A/C do the work.

The amount of rain hitting the windscreen increases with your speed. Use your windscreen wipers as a guide to whether your speed is appropriate. If it's raining *very* hard and you have your wipers on maximum speed, but you cannot properly see because the rain is so heavy, then slow down until your vision improves.

Use dipped headlights (but NOT fog lights) when it's raining to make yourself more visible to other road users.

A wet road surface has less grip – we all know that – but on the road, the difference isn't as much as you might think, as long as you're sensible and always drive within your, and the car's abilities.

Tyre condition is very important on a damp or wet road surface – it is the tread which removes water and allows the tyre to grip with the road surface, and as we all know, tyre grip is all important and can drastically affect your ability to accelerate, brake and corner – all the activities of driving, in fact. So make sure your tyres are good and pressures are correct.

Look out for standing water. If you keep an eye on the design of the road surface i.e. how it is designed to drain, you'll get a clue as to where the standing water will be.

On a traditional "crown camber" road, the centre of the road is higher than the nearside and offside kerbs, so the water will drain to both edges of the road and you can expect puddles to form from both sides of the road. If the road is crown camber and the water has spread across the entire width of the road, then your best position, if there is no oncoming traffic, is right in the centre of the road, straddling the white line, as this is will be where the water is shallowest.

On a more modern road which is built with "super elevation", the corners will be consistently banked with the corner apex at the lowest point and the outside of the bend being the highest point. In simple terms, this means that on super elevated roads, whichever direction you are travelling in, water will build up on the apex of left-hand corners. Be ready to adjust your position away from the apex and be ready to adjust your position to allow opposing drivers to do the same.

As for standing water, it can cause aquaplaning if driven through inappropriately. Aquaplaning, in simple terms, is when a "wedge" of water builds up between the front of the tyre and the road surface and the tyre tread can no longer effectively disperse all the water from under the tyre. In even simpler terms, the car effectively starts to "float" across the water and you can no longer steer, brake or accelerate. Not good.

To avoid the worst effects of aquaplaning, if you spot some standing water ahead, try to roll through it without making any driving inputs whatsoever. Lift off the throttle, don't brake, don't steer and roll through in a straight line. Grip will resume once you are out of the water.

Hitting standing water with the wheels on one side of the car only can cause a dramatic "pull" towards that side of the car. So if you hit a puddle on the nearside at speed, the car will pull hard to the left. Try to drive round puddles when you can, and keep your speed down & increase your grip on the steering wheel if you can't. Don't forget that puddles can hide potholes, so it's never a good idea to plough through them at unreduced speed if you value your expensive alloys.

If the road appears to be flooded, do not risk driving through unless you're absolutely sure of the depth of the water and the position of your car's air intake. If you spot a flood, trust Reg – turn around and go the other way. You really don't want to be one of those people in one of those pictures published by one of those newspapers. Even if it's a 30 mile detour, take it.

During autumn, wet roads are made more slippery by the helpful addition of wet leaves and leaf mulch. This can be very slippery – look out for it and adjust your speed accordingly.

Fog

Fog is tricky – it's effectively cloud which has dropped to ground level and it can be thick, thin, misty, patchy and usually any combination of all of these.

I've written some advice on the correct use of lights and fog lights elsewhere in the book, but it's worth repeating here. To start with – make sure you're at least displaying dipped headlights when it's foggy – that should be the absolute minimum and it's amazing how many people don't even bother with this basic requirement.

There is a school of thought which suggests that a combination of front fog lights and sidelights is most effective in thick fog. Even the legislation allows for this, giving an exemption from dipped headlights on non-30mph limit roads if it's foggy & you're displaying a sidelight/fog light combination.

The problem with driving in fog is that any bright light you display to the front is reflected back at you by the fog itself (or by the tiny water droplets which make up fog if you want to be technical).

I used to spectate on a lot of stage rallies, and rally drivers will generally run with no lights at all in thick fog during the daytime because they find no lights gives them better visibility than any other combination of lights (and rally cars tend to have the most varied combinations of lights). On the road in fog, however, no lights isn't really an option because no-one can see *you*.

I've tried the sidelight/fog light combination in a number of cars and I've never really found it much better than just headlights, and I've often found it worse. The idea is that the low front fog lights project a beam across the road surface, whilst the sidelights prevent excessive light reflection from the fog. Sounds good in theory, but it's not great in reality.

A note on intelligent use of fog lights - many people see mist or fog and then just switch their fog lights on as a sort of pavlovian response

& leave them on for the rest of the journey. In reality, the occasions you actually need to use fog lights are extremely limited. Visibility of less than 100 metres is extremely thick fog or very heavy snowfall (the only two weather conditions which would require high intensity fog light use) and those weather conditions are quite rare.

You don't need fog lights when it's a bit misty, or there's a bit of dampness in the air, and you definitely never need them when it's raining, no matter how torrentially, because the extra glare caused by fog lights reflecting off a wet road create more dangers rather than less.

If you are driving in <100M visibility, your rear fog lights are a priority to ensure traffic approaching from the rear can see you, but once you can see the headlights of following traffic in your mirror, it's usually best to switch off your fog lights, because if you can see their headlights, they'll be able to see your tail lights without fog light assistance. Don't forget that rear fog lights can mask your brake lights and make it more likely that a following vehicle will not see when you are slowing down.

Fog can be patchy too, so switch the fogs on just when they are needed and switch them off as soon as it's clear again.

And remember - they are *fog* lights – **NOT** driving lamps, posing lamps or fashion accessories. If you're not in thick fog or snow, leave them switched off!

Don't forget that fog is actually just tiny droplets of water and will settle on your windscreen. Use the wipers – front and rear – regularly to keep your screen as clear as possible.

And don't fall into the trap of just following the car in front. Your vision might be badly reduced by the fog, but try to keep scanning past the car in front, and as far into the distance as you can.

Freezing fog

Not much different from normal fog really, but freezing fog occurs when it is very cold and the tiny droplets which make up the fog are mad of ice, rather than water.

In freezing fog, the icy fog can settle on the road surface and make it slippery, so be aware of your grip levels.

You also need to set your heater on a high heat setting, blowing on your windscreen and keep your rear demister on. The freezing fog can settle on your glass and ice up very quickly, so it's important to keep your glass warm and free from ice.

Frost

If you get up in the morning and you have to scrape ice off your windscreen, then there is a very good chance there will be ice on the road. This might sound ridiculously obvious, but you would not believe how many people don't make this very simple observation link and after defrosting their car, go out and drive just as if it's a bright sunny day.

I've been informed by people with meteroeoloeoloeologiclogical (!) knowledge that the temperature gauges fitted to cars are not very accurate, but in my view they do at least give an indication when the temperature is getting close to freezing. Mine gives off an ominous "bong" when it drops below 3 degrees and flashes up a warning on the dashboard. This can be helpful when you're driving from day into night or from low to high altitude, as in those circumstances, it's not usually obvious to a driver in a nice warm car, that the temperature is dropping outside.

Frost forms a slightly grey-coloured coating on untreated roads, and it's not easy to spot, particularly at night. The good thing is that, actually, it isn't as slippery as you might think and it's quite possible to drive normally on a frosty road surface as long as you are aware that there is a little less grip, that you need a little more time to stop and a little less speed when cornering.

Keep all your inputs smooth and consistent. Be careful in how you transfer the car's weight around when operating the controls & try to "taper" your inputs. Avoid clumsy, clumpy and clonky inputs as these are more likely to result in a loss of control when Jack Frost is out.

Sheet / Black ice

This is significantly different to frost. Sheet or "black" ice is actually frozen puddles or frozen standing water on the road surface. It is as slippery as – well – as slippery as ice and can be absolutely treacherous if you're not careful.

Keep in mind all the awareness stuff I spoke about in the last section and the stuff I spoke about relating to standing water & where it forms in the first section. Black ice is frozen standing water - it looks just like standing water and it forms in exactly the same areas that standing water forms.

If you unexpectedly drive onto sheet ice, the first thing you'll notice is an almost complete lack of any tyre noise whatsoever – silence suddenly descends in the vehicle cabin.

There will be virtually no grip whatsoever between the tyres and the road surface, so avoid making any inputs whatsoever whilst driving over black ice. If you turn the wheel, the car will keep going in a straight line until you leave the ice – at which point you will regain grip, and the car will suddenly shoot off in the direction you have pointed the wheel, which can lead to a sudden loss of control.

So, if you're caught out by black ice, slide over it and then make any necessary corrections *after* regaining grip with the road surface. If you're on an ocean of sheet ice and heading for an accident, muller your brakes and keep them fully on. ABS will help you make the most of the tiny amount of grip available and if nothing else, will reduce the speed of the impact. If you're a traditionalist and you've no ABS, then read up on cadence braking and do the hokey-cokey on the brake pedal.

Strong winds

Strong winds are an invisible hazard, so you need to use your other senses to help you predict their likely effects.

In a car, high winds shouldn't normally stop you from driving, but it's a different matter if you're towing a caravan, riding anything with two wheels or anything larger than a Mercedes Sprinter van. Curtain-sided lorries – particularly when unladen – are probably the worst unless the driver has the nous to pull the curtains back and drive with them open. It still amazes me how many do not follow this simple procedure.

High winds are more of a problem on high and exposed roads and particularly on long, high over-bridges.

Don't grip the wheel tightly – rather, you should adopt a relaxed, reasonably loose grip on the wheel and try to feel how the wind is affecting the car, ready to apply pressure in the opposite direction to keep a straight course.

If there is a consistently high side wind, be careful when passing high-sided vehicles, as they will temporarily shelter you from the wind and it can feel like you're being "pulled" in towards them as you pass. If possible, try to pass high-sided vehicles with an extra lane between you and keep your time alongside at a minimum.

Snow

Snow is the weather condition which seems to create more problems than anything else in this country due to people's general inability to slightly alter their driving style to suit.

I'm not going into much detail about snow tyres & 4 wheel drive, other than to say that winter tyres can make a huge difference in any winter weather conditions and 4 wheel drive can improve your traction on a slippery road (although not as much as many people think), but gives no advantage in braking or steering.

If there is very heavy and consistent snow which is settling on the road surface, then snow chains, socks etc. will help with traction, but they must be fitted to the driven wheels.

In light snow, you should adopt a smooth, steady driving style in much the same way as I described earlier in relation to a frosty road surface.

One mistake many people make is to assume that you must drive very slowly in snow. In fact, it's important to maintain reasonable momentum, because traction is the issue – particularly on uphill stretches. If you crawl up a hill you're very likely to run out of traction and get stuck, whereas if you maintain some momentum and keep going, you're far more likely to make it up the hill.

In deep snow, there is an advantage in turning off your traction control to allow a little wheel-spin. I don't mean you should sit there with your wheels lit up, but a little slip can help to increase traction, particularly when moving off from stationary.

Tyre tracks form very quickly in snow, and at anything above 20-25 mph, moving out of these tracks onto the undisturbed snow can seriously unsettle the car. This is particularly noticeable on dual carriageways and motorways. Unless it's absolutely necessary, try to avoid changing lanes, and if you have to, do it very gradually with minimal, smooth inputs.

On exposed roads, snow can drift onto the road from adjacent fields. Look for gaps in hedges and fences, as this is where the snow will drift.

Hail

A hailstorm can be very unpredictable and can occur at any time of the year. It is most dangerous when it falls on a cold day on a dry road, and can be similar to driving on to millions of tiny ball bearings or marbles.

If you encounter sudden hail, just be aware of the immediate reduction in road grip and drive accordingly.

Hot weather

Yes, I know – we live in the UK, but humour me for a minute.

ADVANCED & PERFORMANCE DRIVING

Have you ever left your car on a hot sunny day and found it almost unbearable when you returned? A few years ago, Mrs L and I were on holiday in Las Vegas during an extreme heatwave – 45 degrees during the day. We left our car outside one day and on returning to it, it was impossible even to get in to the car due to the heat.

To cool a car as quickly as possible, get in, start it up and drop all the windows. Turn the air conditioning on and put the fan on full speed. Leave the windows down for a minute or so until you feel the air from the vents starting to blow cold. The fan will blow most of the hot air out of the car, then put the windows up, and switch the recirculate function on – this will keep the air inside the car cooling without drawing further warm air in from outside.

One other tip on a hot day – avoid parking on grassed areas during a prolonged hot period. Your hot exhaust can easily ignite the dry grass and this is a common cause of car fires in hot countries.

48

Left Foot Braking

Youtube link - **Left Foot Braking**:

https://youtu.be/0sZuKWKHnXY

If you spend any time at all on internet motoring forums, Youtube car channels or reading motoring magazines, it won't be long before the subject of left foot braking comes up. Now, as a lifelong motorsport fan, I've long known about the benefits of left foot braking in motor racing, rallying etc, but if you'd asked me even just 6 months ago, I'd have told you that there is no real need to use your left foot on the brake pedal when you're driving on the road (apart, of course, from some physical reason why you couldn't use your right foot).

To explain where I was (previously) coming from, let's start by have a look at the benefits of left foot braking in motorsport and then considering whether these benefits translate into genuine benefits on the road.

In motor racing, the first, and most obvious benefit is that left foot braking reduces - and even removes - any delay between lifting off the gas pedal and pressing the brakes. A good, quick drive will be able to instantly transition from full throttle to hard braking without that 0.2-0.3 second delay if he or she were using their right foot.

Let's be clear - a 0.2 second delay in going from gas to brakes for a single corner wouldn't translate into a 0.2 second reduction in lap time. For a single corner, the gain would be much less, but the technique has genuine benefits in that the driver can keep the car flat-out for fractionally longer, and get onto the brakes fractionally later than if they were right foot braking. Over a lap, this may translate into a gain of a few tenths of a second, but if you follow any kind of motorsport you'll know that teams are constantly chasing these types of marginal gains, and a few tenths, gained only by a change in driver technique, is hugely beneficial.

On the road, however, our priorities are very *very* different to our priorities on the track. We're never looking for maximum speed through a corner and we're definitely not looking to shave tenths of a second off our trip to Asda.

I've heard arguments that left foot braking, and the fact that it reduces gas-to-brake time, will fractionally reduce your stopping distance in an emergency, but, honestly, I don't see it. If you're applying all the principles of good observations & planning, you should reduce the times that you'll need emergency braking down to almost zero, and if you're in any doubt whatsoever, you should be covering the brake pedal anyway, so I don't see this as a valid argument for left foot braking on the road.

On the race track, left foot braking also allows the driver to brake hard, right up to the apex of the corner, whilst starting to re-introduce the gas at the appropriate point - effectively releasing the brakes against the drive of the car and allowing the throttle to be applied earlier whilst still controlling the cars speed with the brakes.

And in a turbocharged racing car, early application of the gas, whilst the brakes are still applied, allows some boost pressure to build up at an earlier point in the corner, which will give marginally better acceleration onto the next straight. Again, good for marginal gains in qualifying - not so much on your way to the butty van for a sausage barm.

In rallying, drivers use their left foot on the brake to effectively keep the rear of the car "loose". This ability is helped by the fact that competition cars have adjustable brake bias, where they can make choose how to distribute the braking effort between the front & rear axle. In a road car, the braking effort is heavily biased towards the front brakes (which you may have noticed are always bigger than the back brakes).

Having the ability to move more of the braking effect to the rear wheels means they are more likely to lock-up under heavy braking, which, if you're sliding a rally car around the forest, is definitely a good thing.

On the road, however, in a normal car without adjustable brake bias, I'm afraid you'll just have to stick to handbrake turns on McDonalds car park.

So you can see how, after 34 years of driving & many years of teaching advanced road driving, I'd come to the firm conclusion that left foot braking was a technique only suited to competitive or track driving, and that it had no place on the road. until…

I had an epiphany!

Maybe that's a bit of an exaggeration. There was no parting of the clouds & choir of angels. There was, however, a sudden realisation that I may have come to the wrong conclusion.

I received a reply to one of my YouTube videos from someone I'd been corresponding with for many years. This chap is a highly qualified chassis engineer and works on developing and calibrating suspension and stability control systems.

The video he was commenting on was one I'd made about the rear differential in my new BMW M2 Competition. Without getting too technical, the car has a variable-locking rear differential and I'd been highly impressed at the effect the diff had on the way the car steers and handles. My correspondent suggested that I'd get even more benefit from the diff & the car's chassis if I used left foot braking. "Your M2 *really* likes left foot braking" he told me.

But, unlike most Youtube commentators, he didn't just leave it there with a well timed but vague suggestion. No. He went on to give a very detailed explanation as to why left-foot braking has some benefits on the road, and this is what made me suddenly realise that I'd been judging the technique incorrectly all these years. I'll try to translate it from full-on engineer speak into something close to English, so you can understand…

Modern cars have what's called "anti-dive" designed into the suspension. This means that, if the diver brakes hard, some of the braking energy is transferred into the suspension in a way which prevents the front of the car "diving" too much. The front still dives, but it's much more controlled by the anti-dive geometry and the car stays more level (front-to-rear) than you may expect under braking.

Under *engine braking,* however (lifting off the gas in a lower gear to slow the car down), the car will dive towards the front in a much more dramatic way, because the brakes aren't being used, and the car does not get the opportunity to use the anti-dive geometry.

With me so far?

In addition, when you lift off the gas pedal, the engine takes some time - perhaps 3/4 of a second - to go from accelerating (positive torque) to braking (negative torque). As it does so, the engine needs to move on its mounts as the twisting motion of the engine is reversed and then transferred through the prop shaft to the rear wheels.

The effect of all this is that, lifting completely off the throttle on approach to a corner, rather than braking, means the car is more unstable as it is slowing - remember as well that engine braking only slows the driven axle, which in my case is the rear axle, and you can start to understand how the car isn't in it's most balanced state when slowing with only a lift from the gas - or even when continuing to slow after the brakes have been released.

And of course, as you get back on the gas in a corner, there is a slight delay as the engine goes back to positive torque and settles back on its engine mounts.

Back to school

Armed with this new information, I decided that I should eat some humble pie & teach myself to left foot brake. I honestly wasn't convinced by the argument & I still had a fixed view that it wasn't necessary on the road, but in the interests of fairness & honesty, I decided not to dismiss it out of hand, and to learn how to left foot brake.

Here's a valuable piece of advice. You need to train your left foot how to operate the brake pedal. This may sound daft - it's just a pedal after all, but think about it for a minute. Your left foot is trained - I.e. it has developed a muscle memory - for the clutch pedal only. And how do we operate the clutch pedal? We stomp it into the floor & then release it gradually. Fast in, slow out.

Trust me when I say this - that action does not work well on the brake pedal!

The first time you try braking with your left foot, I can almost guarantee that you'll stand the car on its nose in a full-on emergency stop & then sit there, wide eyed & sweaty, wondering what the hell just happened!

So, find a quiet piece of road and check your mirrors very carefully before you try it. For the first few goes, it'll feel impossible, but as with any other kind of driving skill, over time, you'll start to develop a good feel for the brake pedal with your left foot. I did this for around 3-4 months, just in ordinary every-day driving before I started to fully develop the technique. It is really important that you get to a point where you're fully comfortable using your left foot for ordinary driving before you start to use the technique at faster speeds.

It's also worth mentioning that the technique is much easier in a two-pedal car. Manual cars have the added complexity of needing your left foot for the clutch as well, so although you can use the technique in a three-pedal car, you're probably better off learning it in an auto or semi-auto first. The good news is that there are more and more really good two-pedal cars available these days.

There IS a benefit on the road!

And so to the point of my story. There actually is a small benefit from left foot braking on the road, but only under very specific circumstances, and those circumstances are when you're having a really fast drive on a road with plenty of corners & bends. Let's talk you through how I use the technique, and the benefits as I perceive them.

On approach to a corner, my more traditional technique is to use the system, assess the tightness of the corner, position my car correctly, brake (with my right foot, and so with the gas fully released), charge down to an appropriate gear and then introduce the gas at the start of the corner at the same time that I start to steer, so that the car remains balanced all the way through the corner. To be clear, this is still my preferred technique in most circumstances, even when I'm really pressing on.

But let's look at the alternative.

Instead of fully releasing the gas and going to the brake with my right foot, I'll keep my right foot partially on the gas pedal, so that the engine remains in positive torque, whilst pressing the brakes with my left foot & changing down if necessary.

I'll then keep the brakes and gas both applied as I turn into the corner, and once the car is settled, I'll slowly start to release the brakes & press the gas at the same time.

The result is that the car seems to come alive underneath me & fires out of the corner in a really satisfying & positive way.

What is really interesting is that left foot braking isn't really the secret to the technique - it's actually the fact that you can keep your right foot on the gas which makes the technique work properly. Just braking with your left foot without changing anything else does not make this technique work - it's that ability to balance the positive torque of the engine against the brakes, whilst the anti-dive geometry does its stuff which really makes it work on the road.

To be clear, however, it's not a magical technique which will transform your driving forever, and it should be avoided if you're doing an IAM or RoSPA course as the examiner is likely not to like it very much, but on the right road, in the right circumstances, it works very well indeed and results in a very nice, balanced & quick cornering technique if used properly.

Think of it as another tool in your toolbox of driving skills.

But remember - find somewhere quiet & check your mirrors before you try it for the first time!

Post Script
I went over to the dark side

Youtube link - **Motorcycling Videos**

https://www.youtube.com/playlist?list=PLTpqGstmcT4k_PVdqCfnaKRS6SjvVwG2A

After reading this book, you may have formed the view that I have a pretty low opinion of motorcycling. Please be assured that this genuinely isn't the case.

I do have a low opinion of a certain section of the motorcycling community, which I'll explain in a moment, but on the whole I genuinely have no issues with motorcycling. My dad rode a bike for many years and the majority of motorcyclists I've met have been genuinely enthusiastic & entertaining.

There is, however, a group of people within motorcycling who do their absolute utmost to spoil it for everyone else. You know the type. The bike is kept locked away most of the year, and occasionally wheeled out every third sunny Sunday in June for a "quick blast".

That quick blast usually consists of a couple of hours where they rag the nuts of their bike, knee down, overtaking from a 1" following position, frightening children with their loud exhausts & generally being two-wheeled hooligans. I exaggerate a little, but not much.

These are the motorcyclists who stand out from the rest, and as a result they're the ones by which the general public - myself included - tend to judge all other motorcyclists.

It's a bit like judging football supporters by the behaviour of football hooligans.

Over the years since the first edition of this book was published, I've had many comments from people who think I'm anti-motorcycling and I promise you that isn't the case. I did, however, state that I would never take up motorcycling myself, mostly for self-preservation reasons.

And so, dear reader, it is the for me to serve myself up a huge slice of humble pie, smothered in a thick layer of apology custard and a sprinkling of sorry sugar.

I am now a motorcyclist!

How on earth did this happen Reg? What ever possessed you?

Well, a couple of things really. Firstly, my mate daft Andy has been a motorcyclist for many years and has always been pecking away at me to give it a go. He regularly goes on long motorcycling tours which I've quietly always fancied joining him on, and he's also a very good, advanced rider. I like the idea of challenging yourself sometimes and I think it's good practice to learn new skills & test yourself. As an examiner for the IAM, it would do me good to learn a new skill 7 experience being a learner again.

The other thing that happened was something which happened most days to me. I was stuck in traffic. On the M60. On my way home from work. As bloody usual!

Thee lanes of almost stationary traffic had formed & turned my 23 mile commute into over an hour, as it did almost every day, and as I sat there in lane 2, two motorcycles filtered past between lanes 2 & 3. Not fast, not dangerously - very carefully in fact, but as I sat there in a puddle of frustration 7 despair, these two chaps sailed through at about 20mph, continuing their journey & probably getting home much quicker and in a much better mood than I was going to.

At that point, the light bulb stopped glimmering dimly & lit up very brightly. "There's definitely something in this" I thought to myself.

It's worth mentioning that it was probably a good thing that I'm a bit slow and it took me until my late 40's before having this revelation. If I'd have started motorcycling as a young man, I probably wouldn't be here now, or if I was, there would probably be less of me, so with my youthful, over-enthusiastic days (mostly!) Behind me, I took the plunge…

Back to school…

And so this is how, on 3 December 2017, I found myself wobbling round a small car park in Bolton, on a little 125cc motorbike, being shouted at by an instructor so I could pass my CBT (Compulsory Basic Training).

With my CBT under my belt, I returned in the new year to do a four-day direct access course, followed by my mod 1 and mod 2 tests. Yes, I passed first time, but not without some anxiety about doing a feet-up U-turn during my mod 1! In fact, the only time I ever successfully completed the U-turn was on the test!

With my freshly-updated driving licence, of course, I had to buy a bike & some kit. Being a bloke though, I'd already made the required purchases, so sitting at home, waiting for its first ride out was a 2003 Yamaha Fazer 1000.

And so started my second motoring career - that of a motorcyclist.

I was very conscious that I had a lot of catching-up to do, so I decided two things. Firstly that I would use the bike as much as possible, in all conditions, so that I could build my experience up in as short a time as possible.

Secondly, that I would check myself during the first couple of years by taking an advanced test.

In reality, I took things a little further than that.

After 8 months, I took my IAM advanced test. I passed, but did not receive top marks, which was actually a very good experience. I received some expert feedback from a very experienced examiner which I immediately put into practice on the road.

Another 12 months later, I took my IAM Masters test, which is promoted as the highest-level advanced riding test in the UK. This time I aced it & received a distinction and an invitation to start examining at advanced level for the IAM.

As an established car examiner, it was nice to get through the required quality assurance & start examining advanced bike candidates.

My thoughts on motorcycling

So what do I like about bikes? Well, there's a few things, so bear with me...

Bikes have a lovely, direct mechanical feel to them. If you've ever driven a good sports car, you'll know that they give you very direct feedback through the seat and steering wheel and that they respond instantly to your inputs. A bike is very much like that times 10!

You feel every imperfection & camber change in the road, and you can feel the front & rear tyres' grip levels as they change. Bikes - even quite ordinary bikes - have much greater acceleration than most cars and are extremely responsive to the throttle. And moving the bike along the road requires more than just operating its controls - you are physically involved in making it move - moving your body weight around & making the bike effectively an extension of your body.

You're out in the open air 7 sitting quite high, which gives you a new perspective and a really good view ahead. Not such a good view behind, which is why shoulder cracks are so important on the bike, but your view ahead is great & on a ride out, you feel much more like you're in the scenery, rather than just viewing it from inside a box.

They're quick!

Very quick, in fact, so if you like high performance cars, you'll love bikes! My current bike is a 2018 BMW S1000XR which weighs about 220kg and has 165bhp. Thats a power-to-weight ratio of 750bhp per tonne, and a quick google shows that's the same as a Ferrari LaFerrari.

It'll accelerate from 0-60mph in 2.8 seconds and 0-100 in 5.7 seconds. If you want acceleration without spending a (literal) fortune, then you should try a bike.

But there's more to them than outright acceleration. Riding them requires skill & finesse. Smoothness is vital and there is a genuine satisfaction in riding at a quick pace on a nice road, accurately and precisely linking corners together & leaning the bike into turns.

Filtering is a dream!

Really! For a lifelong car driver, being able to filter through lines of traffic & then fire off from the front of a queue is a dream! No more frustration from heavy traffic - just split the lanes, take your time and you will arrive home in a much better mood, according to Mrs Local!

Downsides?

Yes, of course there are downsides. You need to faff about putting all the kit on & taking it off to start with, and you're out in the open in all the elements, although this isn't really a problem if you buy good quality kit.

You are, of course, extremely vulnerable on the bike and a minor bump which may just cheese you off a bit in the car could have devastating consequences on the bike. On the flip side, though, reminding yourself of your vulnerability every time you put your leg over the bike focusses your mind & requires you, for instance, to leave all your work stresses firmly at work before setting off home. Keeping your attention fully on riding is an excellent way to get rid of work problems & arrive home in a better mood (again, thanks to Mrs Local for the insight!).

And the bike requires attention, much more than a car. These days it's easy just to use your car with just the occasional tyre pressure check and screen wash top-up. Bikes require more of a hands-on approach - chains need adjusting & lubricating, tyres need more regular checks (trust me!) And they generally need much more tinkering & TLC than a car. To be honest though, I quite like retiring to the garage once a week for a little bike-time!

Is that it then? What about cars?

Don't get me wrong - cars are still my first love & I'll never be quite as competent on a bike as I am in a car.

Although I've come to love motorcycling - commuting, days out, touring holidays etc. - I still love driving, and given the choice between a good fast car and a bike on a favourite stretch of road, I'd probably still take the car.

First.

And then probably go back & have a go on the bike as well!

About the Author

Reg Local joined the police in 1990. In 1995 he qualified as a class 1 advanced driver and worked as a traffic officer until 1999 when he qualified as a police advanced driving instructor.

He has taught everyone from learners to experts and has a passion for sharing his knowledge and experience.

He left the police in 2009 and now works in local government.

He is the author of two books & has a successful & rapidly growing YouTube channel.

Also by Reg Local

How Not To Crash

ISBN-10 : 1530991404

ISBN-13 : 978-1530991402

Made in the USA
Las Vegas, NV
12 February 2022